Detotalized Totalities

L. S. Dembo

Detotalized Totalities

Synthesis and Disintegration in Naturalist, Existential, and Socialist Fiction

The University of Wisconsin Press

The University of Wisconsin Press
114 North Murray Street
Madison, Wisconsin 53715

The University of Wisconsin Press, Ltd.
1 Gower Street
London WC1 6HA, England

Copyright © 1989
The Board of Regents of the University of Wisconsin System
All rights reserved

5 4 3 2 1

Printed in the United States of America

Library of Congress Cataloging-in-Publication Data
Dembo, L. S.
    Detotalized totalities: synthesis and disintegration in
naturalist, existential, and socialist fiction / L.S. Dembo.
    250 p.   cm.
    Bibliography: p.
    Includes index.
    1. Fiction—History and criticism. 2. Naturalism in literature.
3. Existentialism in literature. 4. Social realism in literature.
5. Nihilism in literature. I. Title.
PN3347.D46   1989
809.3—dc20   88-40429
ISBN 0-299-12020-1
ISBN 0-299-12024-4 (pbk.)

For Royce

It is to be learned—
This cleaving and this burning
But only by the one who
Spends out himself again.

Twice and twice . . .
                    and yet again.
Until the bright logic is won.
              (Hart Crane)

The modern Christian state is a soul-destroying force, for it is made up of fragments which have no organic whole, only a collective whole. . . . [It] is composed of myriad disunited fragments, each fragment assuming to itself a false individuality. Modern democracy is made up of millions of frictional parts all asserting their own wholeness.

D. H. Lawrence in *Apocalypse*

Contents

Preface xi

Introduction 3

PART ONE: DETOTALIZATION IN NATURALISM

1 The World as Will: Schopenhauer, Tocqueville, Zola 15
2 Zola I: The Detotalization of a Family 26
3 Zola II: Nihilism versus Socialism 39

PART TWO: THE TOTALITIES OF EXISTENTIALISM

4 Sartre I: The Scandal of Plurality 69
5 Sartre II: Perpetually Disintegrating Ensemble: France, 1938–40 91
6 Camus: Detotalizers and Monologists 117

PART THREE: SELF-DETOTALIZING HEROES

7 Orwell's Unrevolutionary Rebels 147
8 Sinclair's Socialite Socialists 169
9 Farrell and the Aesthetics of Nostalgia 191
10 Socialist Realism: The Undetotalizable Totality 202

Notes 215

Works Cited 223

Index 229

Preface

I'm not sure whether it is a quest for a gestalt vision of the modern social novel or simply a desire to investigate the often brilliant details of a number of loosely related texts that underlies this book. This ambivalence or contradiction is part of the price one pays for abandoning, as I have at least in part, the chronological or historical approach that lies so deeply in the scholarly psyche. It lies there for good reason, for it presents us with a rational, solid means of organization and a terminology that yields an apparently satisfactory knowledge and a familiar realm of discourse. Liberated from, or deprived of, chronological development as a principle governing discussion, we find ourselves adrift on existential seas of speculation and impression. On the other hand, starting as it did with the attack by an obscure instructor in the Ecole Pratique des Hautes Etudes upon conventional readings of Racine, the new literary theory was not without its own terrorists (see Hayden White) and terrors.

It is true that Roland Barthes did not seem like a terrorist at the time, especially since his argument appeared to be founded upon and reassert the values of the (American) New Criticism which, paradoxically, was itself to become, along with literary history, one of the major casualties of the coming revolution. In any event, it was certain that we could not return to a view of historical scholarship that had been so utterly deconstructed as was the traditional one—"deconstructed," I should say, not only by the deconstructionists in the Derrida and de Man line, but by a feminist criticism that has highlighted the neglected issue of gender as an essential component of literature and of criticism.

I hope I shall be forgiven for trying to present so sketchily the methodological state of affairs in which my book appears. This is not my last word on the subject, which will come up again in the introduction. It has been necessary to come to terms with the problem of method because in these days of high abstraction the old rules and criteria no longer seem pertinent. Lucidity has given way to density, idiom to technical vocabulary, and the horror of being identified with, or influenced by, an organized body of thought has been replaced by the desire to commit oneself to an ideology or at least to a discipline that in all ways attempted to give literary criticism the scientific foundation that humanistic studies by definition had avoided.

Actually, it is not in the structuralism of the early Foucault, semiotics, nor in deconstructionism that we discover the call for a human science at its most insistent. From the beginning, Marxism saw itself as *the* human science, a phenomenon all the more complicated by the emergence of a theory-laden "Western" Marxism that freely interacted with its structuralist counterparts. My own interest in Marxism has been limited chiefly (though not entirely) to the more traditional kind, where a holistic or "integrationist" view of social reality is very much in evidence. Still, I have made no effort to evaluate, in terms of an external, independent philosophy, theory, or ideology, the novels I discuss. My title, I confess, began in parody and ended in dead seriousness. It applies not only to the subject of this study (the perpetually disintegrating society in which a perpetually disintegrating hero struggles against his fate) but to this book as well, which, I think, may find its ultimate unifying principle in its negation both of affirmation and negation itself.

I am indebted to the American Council of Learned Societies for a senior fellowship and to the Graduate School Research Com-

Preface

mittee of the University of Wisconsin for its support of this project; and once again to my editor, Jack Kirshbaum, and assistants, Steve Luebke, Sarah Gomez, and Mary Morzinski. Special thanks to Barbara Hanrahan, Carol Olsen, and Betty Steinberg for their part in the publication of this book. Chapter Eight, "Sinclair's Socialite Socialists," originally appeared in *Toward a New Literary History: Essays in Honor of Arlin Turner,* ed. by Louis J. Budd, Edwin H. Cady, and Carl L. Anderson (Durham: Duke University Press, 1980) and is reprinted by permission.

Madison, Spring 1989   L.S.D.

DETOTALIZED TOTALITIES

Introduction

Even though this book is about neither "monologists" nor Jews, it resembles my earlier work, *The Monological Jew*, both in methodology and fundamental thesis.[1] As a matter of fact, it might well have been called *The Monological Socialist* if, besides being uneuphonious, that title didn't imply that the present work was just a sequel. It is not a sequel but a parallel study in which the subject is social fiction rather than Jewish American fiction and the perspective is that of Arthur Schopenhauer and Karl Marx rather than of Martin Buber; Jean-Paul Sartre remains a key figure in both, though not for exactly the same reasons.

My methodology is simple enough. Although the New Criticism has been replaced by the "New Theory" as the prevailing mode of inquiry into literature and the humanities are threatening to become the human sciences, I have assumed that there is still a place for interpretation and unmediated confrontation with the text. I am aware that the word "unmediated" is not as innocent as it looks and that the whole conception can be deconstructed by any rigorous idealist. At least let it be said that I am aware of the actual media that have shaped my views and further that I can recognize their limitations as well as their advantages in "understanding" the work under discussion. I also concede that the "use" of Schopenhauer and Marx, as of

Buber before them, scarcely can be called unmediated, though even here, since nihilism, socialism, and monotheism are finally irreconcilable, the media, not being monolithic, do not bias or distort the critic's perception in any consistent way. I count myself among the pragmatists, if such a category still exists, or let's just say that I am hopefully/hopelessly detotalized.

As to my thesis: in dealing with the conflict between nihilism and socialism in the naturalist, existential, and socialist novel, I came to realize that the heroes in these works reflected similar problems though on a different, broader plane of experience. Just as the monological Jew, as a creature of the Diaspora, is and is not a Jew, so the would-be socialist protagonist in the novel of a would-be socialist writer both is and is not an authentic socialist.

Having abandoned traditional Judaism, yet for social and psychological reasons unable to attain total assimilation, the monological Jew finds himself in an existential situation in which he has no authority but himself to judge and evaluate his conduct and therefore no justified system of either personal or social values. Correspondingly, the socially conscious hero is the creature of novelists who have flirted or have been deeply involved with socialism but have never been able to give themselves freely to it, at least not in their work. Thoroughly critical of bourgeois society, the protagonists of these writers are unable to challenge its values with a coherent and compelling ideology; still under the influence of the individualist ethic on which they were raised and educated, they might aspire to rebellion but never to total revolution, with its upheaval of all traditional values and its aim to establish a new society.

I am dealing here with the same phenomenon as that dealt with by the Marxist sociologist, Lucien Goldmann, who has argued that the novel, always reflecting the stage of historical and socioeconomic development through which the society is passing, has been "the literary form of the *absence* of supraindividual values, and of the insufficiency of the individualist universe where the self could not be founded on conscious acceptance of such values" (*Cultural Creation,* 86). What this signifies is that neither existential nor naturalist protagonists are capable of transcending the individualist values of capitalist society—and this is true, as I have said, even when the writers are inclined toward socialism.

In *Germinal,* for instance, one of Emile Zola's few works that Marxist critics could praise, the hero, Etienne Lantier, attains social consciousness and emerges as a spokesman for the exploited coal miners, all the while beset by bourgeois weaknesses that infect his motives. And even after all he learns about life in the coal pits, he is still faced with a confusing variety of socialisms, none of which he can accept definitively. Zola finally sends his bemused hero off to Paris with no clear idea of what positive action, aside from Parliamentary appeal, could be taken. Such an appeal, we know, has the form of a dire warning that if the lawmakers don't attend to the evils of capitalism, the oppressed will rise up as an avenging army to destroy the world. A rebel of sorts, Zola is no social revolutionary. The vision of germination, of the society renewing itself through violent upheaval, is a naturalist vision of cosmic forces, blind and irresistible, applied to a social situation.[2]

The neo-naturalist/socialist writers—those writers who posit a world dominated by natural, social, or psychological forces beyond human or rational control (what Schopenhauer would call the Will) and at the same time assert a "socialist" critique of capitalist society—have created heroes with the corresponding inner contradictions. Literature is filled with such protagonists as George Orwell's Gordon Comstock (*Keep the Aspidistra Flying*) and James Flory (*Burmese Days*); Upton Sinclair's Jurgis Rudkus (*The Jungle*), Hal Warner (*King Coal*), and Lanny Budd (of the series of a dozen volumes); and James Farrell's Bernard Clare (of the trilogy that bears his name)—all of whom are seeking either to escape from, or to change, the bourgeois society in which they find themselves but have internalized its values to such an extent that they cannot take the one path that might lead them out of the labyrinth of paradox and conflicting values.³

I have borrowed and taken some liberties with a neologism—or should I say solecism?—from Sartre to characterize the society with which these protagonists interact. "Detotalized totality" originally referred to an ontological state, though it does have wider applications.⁴ I mean by it any system, synthesis, or organization—whether metaphysical, social, or psychological—in a state of dissolution yet frequently taken to be a unity until it is too late and anarchy prevails. Social consciousness and socialism are totalizing forces; egocentricity and nihilism are detotalizing forces. (In that I write as a student of Marxism but not a Marxist, this statement is meant to be descriptive, not judgmental.) It is not the idea of disintegration itself, however, that is important here but the way in which that disintegration is regarded. What makes all the difference is whether we explain the phenomenon by invoking the law of entropy or by invoking the law of dialectics.

In the former, all living things tend to fall into dissolution. By analogy, all order falls into randomness, all unities into pluralities, and all totalities yield to the forces of detotalization. Thus atomism, individualism, and economic and political antagonism are characteristic of the kind of society that Sartre has described as a "perpetually disintegrating ensemble."

On the other hand, the law of dialectics emphasizes the ultimate unity or synthesis that is reached through the interaction of opposites and implies that inner contradictions, initially a detotalizing force, end in a new synthesis or whole by a process of "retotalization." For the Marxist, totalizing is an act governed by dialectics and as such is associated with creativity, the fundamental development of history, and progress. Ideally, it ends in the Marxist totality or synthesis that is the postsocialist society, in which, all major contradictions being resolved, all disruptive change disappears.

For Sartre, however, the emphasis is on detotalization; in fact, his very conception of what constitutes a totality is limited. As Wilfrid Desan explains it, the part, not the whole, is paramount, and the individual is prior to the group:

> What makes the group? The individual. What moves the inert? disturbs the sociological strata? starts the revolution? expels the king? The individual once more. Neither God nor devil, neither State nor society, only man is responsible for man, only the individual man makes and assembles the totality through his *praxis,* [acts]. There is nothing but the individual self and its . . . unexplainable power of synthesis. (*The Marxism of John-Paul Sartre,* 284)

"If for Sartre," Desan tells us, "individual totalization is supreme, it is because the Self is supreme. Totalization *is* the Self" (279). Thus, if Sartre can accept a "shaping of the present through the future" (the fundamental existential project of all humanity), it is only in the realm of individual existence. "He completely ignores the same influence of the actions of the collective upon its internal parts. The collective is denied any 'project.'" What makes this description particularly appropriate is that it pertains to the later Sartre, who is attempting to "purify" Marxist thought, and not just to the early Sartre of *Being and Nothingness.*

The ideal stability of the ultimate phase in historical materialism contrasts with the "false" stability of the bourgeois world, with its "spirit of seriousness" and misguided faith in the eternality of its conventions and traditions. For Marx, bourgeois man's delusion is the result of his ignorance of the dynamic, "totalizing" forces of history that, developing dialectically, lead beyond the increasing violence and apparent "detotalization" wrought by class struggle to the new "totality" of the classless society. For Sartre, however, bourgeois man's delusion is the result of his ignorance of the "detotalizing" forces that prevail in a gratuitous world and lead not to an ideal social totality but only to the kind that the individual man can "project" for himself—the totality that, emerging from a specific situation and subject to the contingencies of human living—or acting in endless situations—undergoes perpetual detotalization. Whereas both Marx and Sartre are in essence dynamists, proposing as they do a kinetic reality in which being is defined by action, a teleology exists in Marx that is absent in Sartre, for whom ultimate Purpose is but a vanished and irrecoverable God whom mankind endlessly and in vain seeks to replace with its own frailty.

In emphasizing the entropic or detotalizing aspect of the universe (as do Sartre and Camus when they proclaim the death of God and posit in his place the gratuitous and the Absurd), of the society (as do Zola, Sinclair, Orwell, and Farrell when they fail to extend their vision beyond the negations of bourgeois life) or finally of the individual person (as do say Robbe-Grillet, Duras, Butor, Sarraute, and Beckett when they reduce character to unconceptualized behavior, "tropisms," pure utterance, or blind ratiocination), these writers in fact move away from socialism and toward nihilism. I am speaking now not just of writers like Kafka or Mann, who for Georg Lukács represent the two kinds of bourgeois art, decadent modernism and critical realism, but of those who with varying degrees of commitment considered themselves to be socialists. By decadent modernism, Lukács was referring to the absurdist novel, with which he associated a nihilistic despair that, supposedly having metaphysical origins, could in fact be traced to capitalist social conditions.

Despite its social orientation, the naturalist novel, emphasizing as it did the primitive nature of mankind and the vulnerability of the world to forces far beyond human control, was no more realistic than its existential counterpart. In other words, from a Marxist perspective, the naturalist has no true grasp of the social totality—the totality in which men and forces interact and reality is viewed as the dialectical development of certain elements and relationships centering on class struggle. This limitation is manifest not only in the conditions of life described in the fiction but in the very style and technique of the author.

Thus we learn from Jan Varloot that naturalism is rooted in "factography," a concentration on details to the virtual exclusion of generalization. In short, the author's alleged inability to grasp the organizing principle of society in general is paralleled by his inability to get beyond the description of superficial detail or raw fact. Or to put it yet another way, the naturalist text is itself a totality perpetually undergoing detotalization. The vision of unity behind Zola's Rougon-Macquart novels, the working out of the fate of a family during the Second Empire in terms of the heredity and environment of the individual members, is to the Marxist both limited by a neglect or ignorance of actual social and economic forces and relations, and rendered invalid by its choice of atypical characters whose abnormalities strip them of social significance.

This failure is reflected in Zola's reliance on biology for both his metaphors and "factography." He conceives of society as an organism with diseased parts that can be treated locally, a view that justifies not revolution and violent qualitative change, but reform and evolution—a view that is, in essence, geared to a concern with the individual part as an isolated phenomenon.

I am aware that the notion of the failure of naturalism to achieve a genuinely holistic understanding of society and its development or to apprehend the actual realities of social life has become virtually a cliché of Marxist literary criticism. Georg Lukács criticizes Kafka for presenting a narrow and abnormal image of social life; he sees in Mann a fuller, more representative depiction of social reality and its dislocations but laments Mann's inherent inability to go beyond his own bourgeois limitations to envision a socialist society. Conscious that holding a correct view of history does not ensure the quality of one's art, Lukács can appreciate the limitations of socialist realism while continuing to recognize it as a potentially higher, more developed form.

A nearly definitive application of the standards of socialist realism to the whole span of European and American literature was done a few years ago by the Soviet critic, Boris Suchkov, and is now available in this country under the title *A History of Realism*. This is to say nothing of Granville Hicks's classic of the thirties, since repudiated, *The Great Tradition,* an interpretation of American literature since the Civil War that attempted to document the failure of such figures as Twain, Howells, James, and, for that matter, every significant poet or novelist of the late nineteenth and early twentieth centuries, to reflect the "actual conditions" of a society in the throes of industrial expansion and capitalist exploitation.

Since I am not a Marxist, I shall not pursue the historical or social and political significance of this phenomenon. I am more interested in its philosophic significance and in the specific ways in which nihilism and socialism interact in literature. This approach will not satisfy Marxists, who are uncompromising in their rejection of all nihilistic thought (especially biological determinism and naturalist primitivism in general) in favor of the kind of humanism expressed in the socialist novel, notably but not surprisingly that writing which appeared in the Soviet Union after the revolution. Optimism is the only attitude appropriate to fiction worthy of the name of socialist realism; the authentic hero, who performs acts of social amelioration and helps to usher in the new world, is both an ethical and aesthetic ideal. He stands in stark contrast to the "self-detotalized" existentialist hero, who has no transcendent or central values and therefore no self-confidence, just the anxiety of being wholly responsible for his acts. A creature not of solidarity but of solitude, his triumphs are those of his own psyche and are irrelevant to society at large.

The socialist hero also stands in contrast to the naturalist hero, whose dynamism and will power, unguided by stable values and directed only by obsession or instinct, make of him a *bête humaine.* Thus the socialist realist sees the world as a totality that, aided by its enlightened men and women, essentially of the proletariat, dialectically works itself free of the detotalizing elements that characterize the capitalist state from which the new society will emerge. Just as historical materialism asserts that all detotalization will be transcended during the epoch in which dialectic reaches its final stage, so socialist realism asserts complete confidence in its own totality. As the

Soviet critic A. Ovcharenko succinctly put it in his argument for a strict interpretation of the contents of socialist realism, "'it knows its potential and does not doubt its future" (*Socialist Realism*, 66). What he is implying here is that the West, consumed with self-doubt and negativism, has produced an art for which there can be no future.[5]

Having already said that I am not a Marxist, I justify my introduction into this study of some of the central ideas of Marxism and socialist realism not on polemical or ethical but simply on pragmatic grounds. For in its unwavering faith in itself as an undetotalizable totality socialist realism is a touchstone by which we can measure or better appreciate the significance of the detotalized totalities that are the fate of naturalist and existentialist writing or indeed of all literature that, unable to accept socialist answers to nihilist problems, can give only nihilist answers to social problems.

Part One
Detotalization in Naturalism

1 The World as Will
Schopenhauer, Tocqueville, Zola

Rest assured that I do not see in Alexis de Tocqueville or Emile Zola any signs of the direct influence of Arthur Schopenhauer. The epistemology and ontology that are central to Schopenhauer's argument are irrelevant both to *Democracy in America*, the work of an acute observer with a flair for social psychology, and to the Rougon-Macquart series, that literary reaction to Second Empire France by a novelist with a penchant for current scientific theories.

I say this in full awareness that Schopenhauer was a principal authority for an age of romantic pessimism in France as well as in Germany. Indeed, one French historian, Alexandre Baillot, has specified the effect of Schopenhauer on almost every major figure, novelist and philosopher alike, whose work appeared between 1860 and the turn of the century. More comprehensive than insightful, this study argues that, despite his protest that he was no Schopenhauerian, Zola in truth was so, more than he realized. Both in his pessimism and his notions about the Will, Zola "resembled" Schopenhauer, whether he had merely read through him (as he had claimed) or not. Since Huysmans has denied that Zola was ever a real pessimist, even that connection, vague though it is, is debatable.[1]

On the other hand, Schopenhauer's view of the world as Will —as endless struggle, and competition—does have something

1. Detotalization in Naturalism

of a counterpart in Tocqueville's description of American society, just as Tocqueville's description illuminates something fundamental in Zola and, indeed, in the whole movement known as naturalism. This being the case, Schopenhauer's metaphysical context may have more relevance to a study of Zola than meets the eye.

For Schopenhauer, it will be recalled, Will, "constantly striving without end and without rest," is the essence of life, "the inner being of unconscious nature." It is the equivalent of Kant's ding-an-sich, except for the crucial fact that it is expressed (manifested, objectified, mirrored) in the phenomenal (visible, physical, conscious) world. The phenomenal world is there, Schopenhauer asserts, "only as idea; i.e., only in relation to something else, the consciousness, which is [man] himself." "The world is my idea" in that all objects exist only in terms of a subject; that is, only insofar as they are "passed into perception."

Of the many implications of this view, that which concerns us most is the one that asserts the inevitability of pain or suffering, a motif not foreign to nihilistic thought. Since all life is Will, suffering can be understood as "hindrance":

> For all striving springs from want or deficiency, from dissatisfaction with one's own state or condition, and is therefore suffering so long as it is not satisfied. No satisfaction, however, is lasting; on the contrary, it is always merely the starting-point of a fresh striving. We see striving everywhere impeded in many ways, everywhere struggling and fighting, and hence always as suffering. Thus that there is no ultimate aim of striving means that there is no measure or end of suffering. (*World as Will and Representation,* 1:309)

Satisfaction of wants brings no release; "attainment quickly begets satiety" and either desires arise in a new form or else "dreariness, emptiness, and boredom follow, the struggle against which is just as painful as that against want" (1:313-14).

What Schopenhauer is implying here is that as soon as the Will objectifies itself in the phenomenal or conscious world—

the world as idea—pain and suffering arise. If "the world is my idea," so indeed are pain and suffering, which are not merely inevitable but an indispensable part of human nature. Accordingly, "The measure of our pain and our happiness is on the whole . . . subjectively determined for each point of time, and the motive for sadness is related to that" (1:317). That is, if we weren't being tormented by one thing we would be by another of equal magnitude or by many other smaller things that would make up the difference and thereby maintain the "suffering quotient" at which our psyche operates.

Although Schopenhauer is speaking here of personal vexations, he eventually surveys what he takes to be the real miseries of human life:

> If we were to conduct the most hardened and callous optimist through hospitals, infirmaries, operating theatres, through prisons, torture-chambers, and slave-hovels, over battlefields and to places of execution; if we were to open to him all the dark abodes of misery, where it shuns the gaze of cold curiosity . . . he too would certainly see in the end what kind of a world is this *meilleur des mondes possibles* (1:325).

What is ironic about Schopenhauer's irony is that its logic will lead to a theory that, if it does not affirm this world to be the best of all possible ones, does argue for its "eternal justice." This brings us to the crux of the matter.

All misery, all good and evil, we learn, "always confirms the one and the same inner being [the will-in-itself]," even though the phenomena in which it is expressed is made up of different individuals. Thus the difference between victimizer and victim is purely phenomenal (1:354). "Tormentor and tormented are one." The former "lives in everything that suffers pain in the whole wild world"; the latter embodies the same Will from which "all the wickedness that is or ever was perpetrated in the world proceeds. . . ." Thus,

> as the will is, so is the world. Only this world itself—no other—can bear the responsibility for its existence and its nature. . . .

1. Detotalization in Naturalism

> Eternal justice prevails; if [men] were not as a whole contemptible, their fate as a whole would not be so melancholy. . . . the world itself is the tribunal of the world. (1:351-52)

The logic of this argument requires that we accept the phenomenal world as it is. First, there is no appeal to external forces or deity for deliverance—they do not exist separate from the Will, if indeed they exist at all. For the same reason, "metaphysical rebellion" (in Camus's sense of rebellion against God) is equally impossible. Struggle, suffering, and individual extinction are men's fate, a fate that allows only one form of transcendence. It is possible for will to negate itself through the kind of knowledge that is not used for action; that is, the knowledge of contemplation through which—though very rarely—a man rises from "the common knowledge of particular things to the knowledge of the representation" to become "the pure willless subject of knowledge" that "rests in fixed contemplation of the object presented to it, out of its connexion with any others, and rises into this" (1:178). Such knowledge, says Schopenhauer, cannot come by design or intention (for that would be mere "willing") but only suddenly and spontaneously from "the innermost relation of knowing and willing in man" (1:404). Its reward is "that peace that is higher than all reason, that ocean-like calmness of the spirit, that deep tranquility, that unshakable confidence and serenity" that comes with the renunciation of the willing world (1:411).

I started out by saying that the metaphysical context of Schopenhauer's view of the world as will and representation was irrelevant to a study of Tocqueville's sociological description of American democracy as well as to Zola's recreation of French society under Napoleon III. The true significance of this statement can be best appreciated if we first look at its approximate converse: namely, that judging from its total absence, social criticism seems to be wholly irrelevant to Schopenhauer's metaphysics. Specifically, his theory of eternal justice is merely the logical deduction of an abstraction (the will-in-itself) asserted as an a priori reality, just as he sees human life not in social or historical terms but *sub specie aeternitatis*. And this is exactly as it should be! For according to the epistemology we've been discussing, empirical or "scientific" knowledge, which is rooted to observation, can deal only with phenomena and therefore comes under "the principle of sufficient reason," by which objects are known only in their relations, never in their essence; and to study men in terms of their social conditions or their historical development would be to see them only in their illusory multiplicity, where differences and distinctions take on a false importance. Thus the very concept of Eternal Justice is a Platonic Idea, a revelation of "the inner nature of things"—to which the average man is blind:

> For pleasure appears to him as one thing, and pain as quite another; one man as tormentor and murderer, another as martyr and victim; wickedness as one thing, evil as another. He sees one person living in pleasure, abundance, and delights, and at the same time another dying in agony of want and cold at the former's very door. He then asks where retribution is to be found. (1:352)

"Where is the retribution?" indeed. If this question—the fundamental question of the reformer, the revolutionary, the humanist in general—represents an illusory distinction, then it is equally illusory to distinguish between the best and worst of all possible worlds and between free and determined acts in the realm of social and historical experience.

If *Democracy in America,* with its short chapters that follow each other according to no visible plan, seems a diffuse thing next to the rigorously philosophic discourse of *The World As Will and Representation,* Tocqueville no less than Schopenhauer is concerned with a single causative force or idea, so much so that he was constrained, not as a metaphysician but as an objective reporter sensitive to particulars, to preface the work

1. Detotalization in Naturalism

with a caveat: "Because I attribute so many different effects to the principle of equality," he writes, "it might be inferred that I consider this principle as the only cause of everything that takes place in our day. This would be to attribute to me a very narrow view of things." Be that as it may, the thesis that egalitarianism is responsible for the conditions described—and particularly that condition that Schopenhauer took to be an absolute in all human affairs—makes Tocqueville the interesting figure he is for the purposes of this discussion.

Nowhere in his study does Tocqueville presuppose a definitive human nature governed by a universal, transcendent principle such as the Will. What is metaphysical in Schopenhauer here becomes social and relative. Thus in the chapter entitled "Why the Americans are more Addicted to Practical than to Theoretical Science" this version of the world as will and representation emerges:

> Nothing is. . . . less suited to meditation than the structure of democratic society. We do not find there, as among an aristocratic people, one class that keeps quiet because it is well off; and another that does not venture to stir because it despairs of improving its condition. Everyone is in motion, some in quest of power, others of gain. In the midst of this universal tumult, this incessant conflict of jarring interests, this continual striving of men after fortune, where is that calm to be found which is necessary for the deeper combinations of the intellect? How can the mind dwell upon any single point when everything whirls around it, and man himself is swept and beaten onwards by the heady current that rolls all things in its course? (43)

It is true that "meditation" here refers to the method of "theoretical" (as opposed to practical) science and not to Schopenhauer's "aesthetic contemplation," but requiring as it does calm amid incessant conflict, it is a secularized equivalent.

As we have just seen, Schopenhauer defines suffering as an inevitable result of struggle, a hindrance that all who desire must in some way endure ("all suffering really results from the want of proportion between what we demand and expect and what comes to us" [1:88]). Here again is Tocqueville's sociological equivalent:

> The same quality that allows every citizen to conceive . . . lofty hopes renders all citizens less able to realize them; it circumscribes their powers on every side, while it gives freer scope to their desires. Not only are they themselves powerless, but they are met at every step by immense obstacles, which they did not at first perceive. . . . they have opened the door to universal competition. . . . This constant strife between the inclination springing from the equality of condition and the means it supplies to satisfy them harasses and wearies the mind. (146)

This situation often leads to melancholy and disgust with life. Tocqueville concludes:

> In democratic times enjoyments are more intense than in the ages of aristocracy, and the number of those who partake in them is vastly larger: but, on the other hand, it must be admitted that man's hopes and desires are oftener blasted, the soul is more stricken and perturbed, and care itself more keen. (147)

The rounded rhetoric of the translation, which captures the spirit of the original French, reflects the balance of the author, a balance that, as a French aristocrat writing as a "friend of democracy," he felt incumbent upon him to maintain. The point is not an idle one. Tocqueville does not see in American society the hell that Schopenhauer saw in the phenomenal world; there are in his work no overwhelming lists of miseries that accompany the "incessant striving" and "universal competition" endemic to an egalitarian society. Such miseries in Schopenhauer, taken to be of metaphysical origin and therefore irremediable, have no sociopolitical significance. Although they may "detotalize" the individual man, they do not necessarily affect the state. Their appearance in Tocqueville's context, however, would be another matter entirely—precisely because their only significance would be sociopolitical.

Since Tocqueville was a devout Catholic, we are not surprised to find him favoring religious vitality in a democratic society. In at least one important instance, however, his reasoning curiously recalls Schopenhauer's, though, characteristically, it is translated wholly to the world of action. Hence, the very practical title to the chapter on this subject: "How, When Conditions Are Equal and Skepticism Is Rife, It is Important to Direct Human Actions to Distant Objects." "Religions," argues Tocqueville, "give men a general habit of conducting themselves with a view to eternity." Therefore, in ages of faith, far from becoming unworldly, they "set up some general and certain aim and end to their actions here below, towards which all their efforts are directed; they do not turn from day to day to chase some novel object of desire, but they have settled designs which they are never weary of pursuing" (158). It is when they lose their faith and become skeptical that they no longer look to the future but "seek to gratify without delay their smallest desires; and no sooner do they despair of living forever, than they are disposed to act as if they were to exist but for a single day" (158–59). When skepticism appears in an egalitarian society, the social instability engendered by universal competition reinforces "the natural instability of men's desires." Nothing "great, permanent, and calm" can be established, and men know only the "thousand petty selfish passions of the hour." To repeat, this condition is roughly equivalent to that in Schopenhauer's phenomenal world. It can, however, be corrected with much greater ease. Philosophers, moralists, and those in power, we are told, "ought to be always striving to place the objects of human actions far beyond man's immediate range," to persuade men "to conceive and to execute protracted undertakings" "even in the midst of . . . perpetual commotion" (159). No doubt Schopenhauer would find this solution naïve.

Tocqueville is the liberal aristocrat, a believer in reason and the possibility of virtue. Born after the revolution, he is also a believer in the virtue of possibility—hence the voyage with Beaumont to the New World, where he is fascinated equally by the American wilderness, the American character, and American institutions and mores—open to possibility, but as a child of the Enlightenment. If the world he sees resembles in one of its aspects that of Schopenhauer, Tocqueville is neither overwhelmed nor disillusioned but in his appraisal remains calmly utilitarian. He is celebrated for his unbiased political analysis —and it is not hard to understand why. Rational man, says Hegel, sees a rational world, and for all its crudeness and unfamiliarity the world that presented itself to Tocqueville was such that he could see it as a peaceable and orderly land. Egalitarianism bred universal competition and strife, but competition and strife did not breed, as Schopenhauer indicated, any suffering or injustice that was so pervasive and profound as to elicit the observer's moral outrage. Defects of human nature were correctable by moralists and philosophers; the defects of democracy in Jacksonian America—those that were visible to an observant, open-minded, sympathetic, and studious traveller during a period of nine months—were also correctable or endurable or cancelled out by counterforces and compensations in the social system. Europe could learn from the American experience.

Schopenhauer, seventeen years the senior of Tocqueville, is temperamentally more romantic and politically more reactionary. Indeed in his renunciation of the world and his total denial of the validity of "temporal" ideas of justice and morality he is the very negation of all social and political thought associated with Western humanism.

Schopenhauer saw the Will as a universal, the essence of life and being; Tocqueville saw it chiefly as an effect of egalitarian society. Zola came to see it as both—sometimes in stereoptic resolution, sometimes in unresolved double vision. Since Zola was reaching maturity in the 1860s, Schopenhauer's metaphysical legacy came to him in the guise of biology and ideas of human nature inspired by the writings of Darwin. Thus Hippolyte Taine, an early influence on Zola, had argued that men were dominated by "physical temperament, bodily needs, animal instinct, hereditary prejudice, imagination, ruling passion in general, specifically personal interest, cast, or party." "We badly deceive ourselves,'' he had added "if we think that men are good by nature, generous, sympathetic or at least gentle, tractable, prompt to subordinate themselves to social interests or those of others.'' The only really logical conclusion one can draw from this conception is exactly the one that Schopenhauer did draw: if man is "bestial,'' all notions of personal morality are vain, all discussions of the good society are meaningless. This must be so because the final significance of the expression "la bête humaine'' is that *all* men are fundamentally animals and therefore, morally, on a level. The philosophers, moralists, and wise governors called upon by Tocqueville to guide men out of the morass of the "thousand petty passions of the hour'' —the men who are the leaders, heroes, and educators of society —can be nothing more than hypocrites or the mere phantasms of sentimental humanism. Any of the Rougon-Macquart novels will attest to the appeal this view had for Zola, a view he unwaveringly maintained in the face of outraged critics and readers not because he enjoyed shocking the public but because he believed himself a "scientist'' whose duty it was to report the truth, just as Schopenhauer envisioned himself a cold, passionless philosopher pursuing reason to its unbearable conclusions.

But Zola did not have the kind of temperament that would allow him fully to embrace a Schopenhauerian vision of the world. In his personal life he counted himself a Republican and a humanist—a believer in Reason, Virtue, and Justice as ideals that could and ought to be maintained. When it was put to the test (anticipating, toward the end of his career, elevation to the French Academy and perhaps a less frenetic life, he suddenly became involved in the cause célèbre of the century), his commitment to these values proved to be stronger and deeper than anyone, including Zola himself, could have imagined. Moreover, even though the Rougon-Macquart novels do justice to Schopenhauer's conception of the phenomenal world, "naturalism'' did not necessarily mean pure nihilism or unqualified pessimism, as its Marxist critics always assumed. In the final pages of *Germinal* (1885), Zola turned to the myth of death and rebirth to express an ambiguous optimism about the future despite the unrelieved agony and strife that had occupied him throughout the novel. This principle, which clearly had more than a superficial importance to Zola, will reemerge in two of his greatest novels, *La Terre* and *La Débâcle*. Not content, however, with the mere prophecy of social salvation, he was to go on in *Les Quatre Evangiles (The Four Gospels)* (three of which were completed before his death in 1903) to detail the social, cultural, and moral conditions that could be brought about by secular saints. Secular saints: not Schopenhauer's contemplatives but men of virtue, heroes who triumphed in the phenomenal world. Zola brought to this work all the socialist and utopian idealism to which he had been exposed over a lifetime but that as far as his novels were concerned had remained largely unexpressed. Unfortunately, whatever their merit as gospels, sermons, morality plays, propaganda, or even hymns—all of which at one time or another they show evidence of being—the "évangiles" add nothing to Zola's stature as a writer and not much more to his stature as a social thinker.

Until now I have been dealing in generalities; the time has come to look at Zola's particular interpretations of the world as a "detotalized totality," a society in the throes of moral disintegration and governed only by ambition and greed. The half a dozen or so novels that I shall discuss represent only a small portion of the Rougon-Macquart series. Still they provide the basic coordinates necessary for mapping virtually the whole region, a task which I shall leave to those whose passion for thoroughness and tolerance for self-repetition are greater than my own.

2 Zola I
The Detotalization of a Family

Setting out to write "the natural and social history of a family under the Second Empire" and convinced that the novelist could emulate the scientist in detachment and precision, Emile Zola asserted that he was going to study his characters in terms of heredity and environment. As he described it in his plans for the Rougon-Macquart novels, he was seeking in the laws of heredity the cause of "similar or contrasting temperaments"; "I explain," he said, "the apparent confusion of characters; I show how a little group of beings, a family, behaves in spreading out to give birth to ten, twenty individuals who seem at first sight to be deeply different, but whom scientific analysis shows to be intimately connected." By environment, Zola meant specifically the kind of society ushered in by the "bourgeois emperor," Napoleon III, with its

> crowded shoving of all ambitions, the democratic impetus, the coming together of all classes (whence a familiarity between fathers and sons, the mixing and placing side by side of all people). My novel would have been impossible before 1789. I base it then on a truth of the time: the rush of appetites and ambitions. (*Oeuvres complètes*, 6:357)

With all his aspirations to discover the biological-psychological principles that bind his characters into a family, Zola still wanted to portray family disintegration, a disintegration that reflected the social atomization caused by "the democratic impetus" of the age. We have already seen that Tocqueville had observed the same phenomenon in America: "Aristocracy had made a chain of all the members of a community, from the peasant to the king; democracy breaks that chain and severs every link of it" (*Democracy*, 105). Thus, he continued, "not only does [it] make every man forget his ancestors, but it hides his descendants and separates his contemporaries from him; it throws him back forever upon himself alone and threatens in the end to confine him entirely within the solitude of his own heart" (106).

Elsewhere Tocqueville observes that democracy has removed the formal barriers between family members and created much more intimacy. Significantly, Zola will avoid this contradiction; the familiarity between fathers and sons, for instance, that is mentioned in the quotation above, is by no means a wholesome one, as *La Curée* (*The Kill*) will make abundantly clear. For Zola, then, in the "orgy of appetites and ambitions" released by the egalitarianism of the Second Empire, all authentic fraternal or communal values were lost and individualism reduced itself to the singleminded pursuit of material self-interest. This was half the real story of the Rougon-Macquarts.

The other half dwelt on the naturalist idea (derived in part from Hippolyte Taine) that civilized man, no less than his ancestors, had a beast within him or primitive instincts that were not simply ill-concealed behind his customs, rituals, manners, and institutions but actually succeeded in corrupting them. While environmental determinism decrees that egalitarian France evoked men's most selfish qualities, biological determinism states that men are by nature self-seeking and require only the proper environment to express their basest instincts. In this case the France of Louis Napoleon, with all its evils, is taken to be a natural phenomenon, a part of the *comédie humaine* that can be described or satirized but not altered.

It is fitting, then, that Adelaide Fouque, progenetrix of the

1. Detotalization in Naturalism

family, is mentally disordered if not mad—fitting not just because Zola's genetic theories require a "primary lesion" to which madness in the descendants may be traced, but for thematically more meaningful reasons. After the premature death of her husband (Rougon), with whom she has had a son, Pierre, she takes as her lover a drifter (Macquart) with whom she has a boy (Antoine) and a girl (Ursule). No matriarch, no authority or transmitter of values, she allows her children to grow up in a state of anarchy:

> Never was nature allowed such complete sway, never did such mischievous creatures grow up more freely under the sole influence of instinct. . . . They stole provisions from the house and pillaged the few fruit-trees in the enclosure; they were the plundering, squalling, familiar demons of this strange abode of lucid insanity. (*Fortune of the Rougons*, 44)

In her insanity, a biological determinant, she has created an anarchic household so that disorder is transmitted whether from the point of view of heredity or environment. And this condition foreshadows the relations among not only the members of the family when they mature but the citizens in general who will make the Second Empire what it is.

It is true that Zola tries to account for differences in temperament or personality in terms of inherited traits; yet these differences are, at bottom, simply a matter of the form that one's appetites and ambitions take. Of Pierre we are told,

> in his plump person of medium height, in his long pale face, in which the features derived from his father had acquired some of the maternal refinement, one could already detect signs of sly and crafty ambition and insatiable desire, with the hardness of heart and envious hatred of a peasant's son whom his mother's means and nervous temperament had turned into a member of the middle classes. (47)

Calculating and predatory, wholly devoid of fraternal or filial feelings, using intimidation and deceit to obtain all the family property at the expense of Antoine and Ursule, he is both a victim of his heredity and environment and a villain who is a part of the system. To the Marxist he would be considered "atypical"—not because he inadequately represents the middle class but because his behavior is partly ascribed to a pathological condition in his family. When not seen as the result of a historical situation, a given phase in the class struggle—when it is asserted to be an absolute in itself—pathology ceases to have any value as an explanation of social life.

Thus the Marxist; but to the naturalist what matters is not class struggle but the struggle of personalities. That is why the world he presents, and the story he tells, is always a totality in the process of detotalization, an imagined unity that becomes stable only on the level of the interaction of particles; that is to say, the competition of ambition-driven persons in a free market economy and egalitarian polity. Unlike the Marxist world, which advances according to the logic of dialectic and historical necessity, the naturalist world proceeds according to machination, deception, accident; behind its progress is the exercise of a Schopenhauerian Will that has neither purpose nor meaning beyond the fact of its own existence. (Indeed it is Schopenhauer who is frequently singled out by Marxist criticism as the very image of nihilism and pessimism.)

The title of the novel, *Fortune of the Rougons,* even though blandly conventional, tells us a great deal about its theme and structure. For one thing, it reflects the fatalism which Zola and the naturalists in general see in the flux of human events. For another, it confirms that the novel will be no deeper than the plot: a world in which events occur by reason of deception, machination, and the clash of individual wills is naturally expressed in a novel in which plot and personality are everything. We know that, to the Marxist, history is neither the effect nor record of great men, ideas, or atypical events; it is the expression of production forces and relations in necessary stages of development. For Zola, history is the epoch and the epoch is the result of remarkable personalities (or characters remarkable for their lack of remarkability) and their effect upon each other in bedroom, office, and other battlefield. It is in their very untypicality that they become typical.

The totality of the Rougon and Macquart families is the sum of its individual members, and its story is nothing more or less than the detotalization wrought by the innate desires and ambitions of these individual members. In the long run the distinctions between what is inherited and what is the effect of environment becomes lost in the overwhelming proliferation of episodes and situations that is life in a morally crumbling society.

There isn't a single character of importance in the whole range of the Rougon-Macquart who does not act out in terms of his specific situation a destiny that he has in common with all men. Tracing the lives and careers of these characters, we discover just how much Pierre (the rising peasant), Saccard (the financier), and Eugene (the politician) are brothers under the skin no less than in the flesh. Each of them in his efforts to realize his ambitions loses his ability to enter into human relations without self-interest guiding his every act. There are many kinds of beasts in the world, but men are the only ones who create their jungle around them—and they are the most monstrous.

Typically, Pierre Rougon, the second eldest son of Adelaide Fouque and Rougon, to better his position, marries Félicité Puech, an oil merchant's daughter, who turns out to be more than his match in calculation and ambition. An archetype of the domineering petty bourgeois woman—single-minded, obsessive, opportunistic, and megalomaniacal—Félicité, in her own struggle for position, chooses Rougon for a husband "as one would choose an accomplice" (56). Subsequently, after years of failure, she has placed all her hopes in her three sons, whom she has "nursed" with a "fervour in which maternal severity was blended with an user's solicitude"; she fattened them "as though they constituted a capital which, later on, would return a large interest" (60). As both wife and mother, then, she is fully and exclusively the exploiter.

The great event in the lives of Pierre and Félicité is their successful plot to appear as heroes during the coup d'état of Louis Napoleon (December 2, 1851) by steadfastly turning back a Republican insurrectionist assault on the town, Plassans, an enclave of conservativism. The motley political group over which they preside, including as it does Orleanists, Legitimists, and Bonapartists as well as clergymen, aristocrats, and merchants, reflects the influence of the new egalitarianism and the old biology. Here, once more, commitment follows self-interest, not principle. The group is a collection of political speculators, not a party of men unified by a cause; accordingly, human relations at this level recapitulate those on the level of family life.

Eugene, eldest of the sons, has gone to Paris and become a Bonapartist agent (he is destined to be prime minister under the Empire). He notifies his father that it will be to his advantage to support discreetly Louis Napoleon and he subsequently keeps him informed, by mail, of the developing situation in Paris. Promised the office of tax collector, Pierre tantalizes Félicité but will give her none of the details. Although she appears to accept the situation, she bides her time and eventually gets her hands on Eugene's letters. Saying nothing to Pierre, she formulates a strategem, ultimately successful, that will give her full revenge upon her husband and make her undisputed master of the household.

The Rougon plot centers upon the belief that if Pierre can contrive to act decisively and courageously in support of Napoleon, he will appear to be a hero. In the climax, having committed himself, he is desperate and on the point of collapse: no word has been received from Eugene, and the town, out of fear of the insurrectionists, has closed its gates. (Ironically, it is a false fear encouraged by Rougon himself.) Meanwhile, Félicité has gone to the post office and discovered a letter from Eugene announcing the total success of the coup. She tells Pierre nothing but, acting with all the assurance that the information has given her, she persuades her terrified husband to accept her leadership. A sham is concocted in which Antoine Macquart, who has long nursed a hatred for his half-brother for having cheated him of his inheritance, is bribed to lead a handful of insurrectionists into an ambush at the city hall where Rougon appears to be the only man willing to accept authority. The plot is an unqualified success: because of the total confusion and panic in Plassans, the phony raid is accepted as a full-scale invasion and Pierre emerges as the man of the hour. The fortune of the Rougons is made in a *coup de théâtre* that ushers in an age.

Zola never made Louis Napoleon the subject of a novel (we are given only fragmentary impressions of him in *La Curée, Son Excellence, Eugene Rougon,* and *La Débâcle*). Had he followed the view of the Republican historians, a view which in all essentials he shared, Zola might have portrayed him as a sophisticated Pierre, the ascent to empire in an egalitarian age requiring tactics that may have been more complex than those required for social mobility in a provincial town but were similar in inspiration. Marx called Louis Napoleon an "old crafty *roué,*" who conceived "the historical life of nations and their performances of state as comedy in the most vulgar sense, as a masquerade where the grand costumes, words and postures merely serve to mask the pettiest knavery" (*Selected Works,* 138). This could have been an epigraph to any number of the Rougon-Macquart novels.

Eugene Rougon and his younger brother Aristide (who will change his name to Saccard to avoid any possible embarrassment to Eugene) are perfectly equipped for life under Napoleon's Second Empire. Ambition (a product of deprivation and opportunity), calculation, and a willingness to engage in all-or-nothing speculation combine to bring one political power and the other riches. In a world in which all social relations are governed by manipulation or exploitation, genuine human attachments, including those of family, are either nonexistent or considered a threat to the fundamental business of life. Saccard cannot get his start in Paris until his first wife dies and for a large settlement he agrees to save the honor of a wealthy young woman (*La Curée*). Made possible by his sister, Sidonie, who will claim her fee, his marriage to Renée Bereaud quickly becomes a business arrangement in every sense:

> The family idea was replaced with them by a sort of partnership whose profits are divided in equal shares; each one drew his part of the pleasure to himself, and it was tacitly agreed that each should dispose of that part as best seemed to him. (*The Kill*, 119-20)

The deal will come to include Maxime, Saccard's son by his first wife, with obvious consequences in this novel that Zola called his new *Phèdre*.

Renée's affair with her stepson is presented as an example of the debauchery characteristic of Second Empire Paris. In an age of rapidly acquired fortunes and easily satisfied appetites, Zola tells us in the ébauche (a preliminary sketch that he made for each novel), restlessness and boredom give rise to the unending pursuit of new pleasures and sensations. Specifically, temperament (heredity) and environment have conspired to make the characters what they are. Of an epicene nature to begin with, Maxime is redeemed neither by the kind of family life nor education to which he is exposed. Having attended a school at which he suffered "an effemination of his whole being" that "was destined to remain in him, and to strike a lasting blow at his virility" (100), he completes his education under the tutelage of Renée and her coterie, treated like a girl and made party to all the gossip and intrigue of fashionable women. His relations with his father are hardly more promising. Tocqueville, as we have seen, had argued that democracy strengthened natural family ties in that it led to greater frankness and intimacy; in Zola's world, frankness and intimacy degenerate into the grotesque. Thus the ébauche:

> Aristide and Maxime live in a shameful promiscuity. Son has no respect for father. They visit women together, share a mistress. This can become a model for Maxime at the end, saying to his father, "we have had the same mistress, we might as well

have the same wife. I behave as I have been brought up by you." (*Oeuvres complètes*, 1:329)

For all their promiscuity, however, neither Saccard nor Maxime is a true lover or even a philanderer. Saccard's women are either part of his business dealings or diversions, nothing more; Maxime's, given his "temperament," are merely amusements or adventures. His response to his first act of sexual intercourse with Renée indicates all the emotion he is capable of experiencing:

> He was angry at the adventure. He laid the blame on the black satin domino. Whoever saw a woman rig herself out like that! You couldn't even see her neck. He had taken her for a boy and romped with her, and it was not his fault that the game had become serious. . . . So much the worse, after all! he would try and not do it again. It was a piece of nonsense. (*The Kill*, 156-57)

An almost identical logic underlies Renée's development. Generally neglected by her bourgeois family, she is raised in a convent, where, far from being controlled or reconciled with her naturally sober character, her instincts take free rein and there "sprouted and grew her prodigious fantasies, her every reviving curiosity, her unspeakable longings:

> Among the ladies of the Visitation, free, her mind roaming amid the mystic voluptuousness of the chapel and the carnal attachments of her little friends, she had framed for herself a fantastic education, learning vice, throwing the frankness of her nature into it, and disordering her brain. . . . (114)

The deleterious effects on women of a convent education will be one of the chief themes of Zola's third "évangile," *Verité* (1903). Renée's "milieu" has provided her neither the cultural nor moral education that might have saved her as a social being. To the contrary, it has nourished the wrong side of her nature and has therefore perpetuated her restlessness and confusion:

> Thrown into the world of the Second Empire, abandoned to her imagination, kept in money, encouraged in her loudest eccentricities, she gave herself, then regretted it, and finally succeeded in killing her expiring good principles, for ever lashed, for ever pushed onwards by her insatiable desire for knowledge and sensation. (115)

True knowledge, the social awareness that would allow Renée to transcend the torments of her narcissism and meaningless freedom, is beyond her grasp, as indeed it is beyond that of nearly all the Rougon-Macquart characters.

It is in Eugene Rougon, however, that Zola depicts the ultimate individualist, "the great man, the eagle of the family, disdainful, immune from any vulgar interest in profits" (*Dr. Pascal,* 94). Governed not by avarice but pride, "shockingly ignorant and terribly mediocre in all but the management of other men," he believes "exclusively in himself . . . he subordinated everything to the incessant aggrandisement of his own ego" (*His Excellency, Eugene Rougon,* 130). As one of the chief actors in a world of political intrigue from which all social values have been excluded, Rougon is committed neither to principle nor to person—indeed his opportunism is the secret of his ability to regain repeatedly power that he has lost. Recalled as Minister of the Interior after the Orsini assassination attempt on the royal couple, he is given carte blanche to carry out whatever repressive measures he thinks are necessary for the security of the state. This mission fully appeals to his desire for power for its own sake, "whatever the conditions under which it came to him." "To rule, to plant his heel on the neck of the mob, there you had his immediate ambition; all the rest amounted to various advantages which were quite secondary" (221). Accused of being a tyrant, he replies, "If someday I turn liberal, they will say I have let them down" (222). That day does come and, in his Republican speech to the Chamber of

Deputies, on yet another return to office, he in one hour gives "the lie to his whole political life . . . ready now, under the device of parliamentarism, to satisfy his furious thirst for authority" (376).

Again, in Eugene's world as in that of his father, association exists only for mutual material advantage. If Eugene has any "family" at all, it is the small band of intimates that surrounds him. But, as one might expect, his paternalistic feelings toward the group are tinged with megalomania and narcissism:

> They were like so many faithful dogs. It was not he alone who was the minister, they were all the minister together, as if those men were all subordinate parts of him. There was a hidden work going on in that triumph, bonds were being tightened, he had begun to love them with a jealous love, putting all his strength into not being alone, feeling his chest expand by reasons of their ambitions. (222)

In this strange relationship, Rougon is as much at the mercy of these "faithful dogs" as they are at his. Indeed, they are the chinks in his armor or, as Zola put in the ébauche, "la félûre dans ce crâne solide":

> He works for these people; he fights for them. If he acquires power, it is to give them places. . . . This man, contemptuous of all, works in reality only for these few. And at the denouement I will show him perhaps—he who is so strong—so superior—nibbled to death by his coterie, crushed by his responsibilities, emptied, finished off, annihilated. (*Oeuvres complètes,* 2:412)

All this is important for more than what it reveals about Rougon's character or that of the Autonomous Man it typifies. Zola also sees it as "the story of governments." "A government is not a king," he argues, "but the creatures who surround the king and to whose interest it is that he keep the throne—from them the maintenance of the party, from them the heroism and the stupidity" (2:412). Thus the egalitarian monarchy and its court is an analogue to the egalitarian family; the competition and struggle that characterize bourgeois society at large have determined their shape. Traditional ideas upon which social relations depended for their stability and harmony were supplanted, as were those upon which depended the cohesion of social groups. Loosening of ties between ruler and ruled, as between father and children, the emergence of self-interest as the only reason for association, made for the incessant motion and change of the egalitarian state, which in its extreme forms, as Zola has depicted it in his vision of the Second Empire, tends toward tyranny or anarchy or an unholy combination of both.

This is not to say that Rougon was modelled exactly on Louis Napoleon. The ébauche is explicit about the difference between the strong-willed absolutist, who would have preferred to have been a Napoleon I or a Louis XIV, and the emperor with his social and democratic dreams. Yet Zola also makes clear that whatever his temperamental differences, Rougon, who holds Louis Napoleon in contempt for "allowing himself to be led around by a coterie," is obviously part of the same system: "My minister [Rougon], however, will also have his coterie, his Morny, his Billault, his Persigny, his Saint-Arnaud; and it will be his coterie that drowns him" (2:415).

Rougon's true antagonist is not Morny, as the ébauche planned, but Clorinde de Balbi, a young adventuress who is a creature of the times no less than he is. Although fundamentally a puritan, Rougon develops a passion for this woman but refuses to marry her. Deeply offended she takes her revenge by rejecting, often violently, all his advances even though she freely sleeps with others. She taunts him by arguing that she has used herself only with those who can benefit him politically and need to be converted to his cause. Since he himself needs no conversion, there is no reason for her to sleep with him. "Very intelligent when acting in her own interests, stupid in everything else, in all that is not woman or intrigue," says the ébauche (2:419). A sure sign, in Zola's world, of her superficial

38   1. Detotalization in Naturalism

education is her apparent fervor for the Church. Her "devotion," however, is not above suspicion:

> Dévote. Elle est amie du pape "ma petite amie." Elle brûle des cierges, pour les entreprises délicates. Elle devient stupide quand on touche au pape et compromet ses interests. (419)

Her response to Rougon's triumphant speech in the Chamber of Deputies, at the conclusion of the novel, indicates the true object of her feelings:

> Clorinda was on the watch for him. They had not spoken a single word to each other for three years. When he did appear, a rejuvenated man . . . she was compelled to yield to her natural impulse [à un extraînement]. Her hand outstretched, she went up to him, her eyes moist and so deeply moved that her mere glance was a caress, and cried: "Oh, you! After all, how beautifully strong [d'une jolie force] you are!" (*His Excellency, Eugene Rougon*, 376)

Whatever aspect of social life Zola investigated during the quarter of a century it took him to complete the Rougon-Macquart novels, his conception of the Second Empire and the men and women who created or were created by it remained basically the same. Sometimes explicitly, sometimes by implication, he portrays an atomized world in which the struggle for wealth or position has warped all social relations and made constructive social action all but impossible. The bourgeois egalitarianism of the Second Empire (the environment), unable to provide positive social values, gave men the opportunity to follow their lowest (material) instincts and appetites.

3 Zola II
Nihilism versus Socialism

Whatever the attractions for Zola of socialist thought in the 1880s and 1890s—when in the full maturation of his talent he produced *La Terre, Germinal,* and *La Débâcle* among others—he never really conceived of social conflict in terms of class struggle. That is, classes, like all other kinds of social organization, were subject to the detotalizing effects of the egalitarian environment. Even when they are clearly defined and almost homogeneous, the communities and groups that appear in the Rougon-Macquart novels (food sellers, Parisian clerks and salesmen, peasants, railroad workers, et al.) are invariably dominated by rivalry and intrigue among individual members. When class struggle appeared, as in *Germinal,* it did so not as the central phenomenon in social history and development but as one form of social detotalization among many.

La Terre (Earth), Zola's great novel of peasant life, is a testament to the vitality of his earlier views. Georg Lukács has praised, implicitly at Zola's expense, Balzac's work on the same subject, *Les Paysans.*[1] Balzac's royalist and proclerical politics and his hostile portrayal of the peasants is overshadowed, Lukács believes, by his "realism," his ability to provide a "perfectly balanced picture of the forces locked in struggle" (aristocrats, bourgeoisie, and peasants). It is precisely Balzac's ability to depict what amounts to class struggle through character types—types that "bring into play every economic, political, ideological and other weapon in support of their cause" that Lukács so admires. (Whether a writer's politics can be so readily divorced from his characterization need not concern us here.)

As I have suggested, there is indeed no class conflict in *La Terre* except perhaps by implication. Zola is interested chiefly in the peasants' relation to the land conceived of as an omnipotent natural force and rendered in mythic terms. However, this does not mean that the novel is devoid of social significance.

La Terre deals with the relations of the members of a single family, the Fouans, after the father (Old Fouan), increasingly incapacitated with age, decides to divide his land among his three children. A victim of his own as well as his children's avarice, he suffers a fate similar to that of King Lear but with little of the latter's tragic elevation. The peasants' obsessive urge to possess the land, manifest in Old Fouan and even more intensely, if that were possible, in his youngest son, Buteau, is comparable to the "ambitions and appetites" that motivate the Rougons and Macquarts, and it has the same devastating results.

In his decision to divide the land, for example, Old Fouan reasons that age has prevented him from tilling much of his acreage and that rather than allowing it to lie fallow, he will distribute it to his children in return for an allowance. He is made aware that he runs a risk: "Many good people," the notary tells him, "disapprove of property being made over and regard it as a great danger to family bonds . . . indeed, many deplorable examples could be cited where children have behaved very badly after their parents had given up all they possessed . . ." (*Earth*, 24).

This matter-of-fact statement will, of course, turn out to be an accurate prophecy, but that is not my point. More important is that it only begins to make clear the extent to which the ownership of property has defined family relationships. All that Old Fouan is as a father, as an authority, indeed as a person, is a consequence not of his own family position but rather of land holdings, and to lose the latter is to lose everything. The inevitable day comes when his once cowering son confronts him with the naked realities by which they live their lives:

> "Do you think you can scare me! That sort of thing was all right when you were the master."
> "I'm still the master. I'm your father."
> "Go on with you, you old joker, you're nothing at all. . . . Have we got to have a hell of a row before it enters your thick skull that nobody cares a damn for you now! What are you good for? You cost money to keep, that's all. When you've had your day and passed your land over, your job's to swallow your soup and leave other people in peace." (257)

Buteau, we learn, had originally refused his share of the property not out of altruism, but because he feared being tricked. Having once accepted, "he could not console himself for failing to gain the whole inheritance." Still, Zola adds, "he felt his passionate longing assuaged in the brutal joy of possession—a joy that was doubled by the thought that his sister and brother had been swindled, his land being so much more valuable now that the new road ran alongside" (161).

I should make clear at this point that Zola does seem to distinguish between a "natural" love of the land, taken as a source of nourishment, and the obsessive lust for possession that characterizes Buteau and the other peasants of the Beauce. The former is a naturalist or vitalist ideal, a part of the order of nature; the latter is its perversion. Thus in the ébauche for the novel Zola explains,

> I want first of all to depict from the depths the peasant's love of land, an immediate love, the possession of as much land as possible, a great desire to have a lot because it is in his eyes the form of wealth. Then, moving upward, the love of the nourishing land, the land from which we get everything, our being, our substance, our life, and to which we end up by returning. Suddenly the peasant appears rapacious. A man of narrow passions on the wide land. (*Oeuvres complètes*)

1. Detotalization in Naturalism

Zola's mature vision of the ideal, in which human and natural fertility are integrated in the harmonious family, will not appear until *Fecondité*, first of the "évangiles."[2] In *La Terre* Zola is concerned mainly with the debasement of love into passion, need for nourishment into gluttony, legitimate ambition and desire for sufficiency into an orgy of greed. Thus Buteau's lust for his sister-in-law (Françoise), marked by repeated assaults upon her that end in rape and murder, is portrayed as a mere extension of his lust for the land. The association goes beyond simple metaphor; for if Buteau's passion for the land is partly "sexual" (and explicitly so described) his passion for Françoise is partly economic. Buteau wants to be sure that Françoise will remain part of the ménage-à-trois to which she contributes both land and labor, and to this end he seeks to marry her in all but name. "His two passions were fused, his resolute determination not to let go anything he'd got hold of, his tenacious possession of the land, his rabid lust sharpened by resistance" (*Earth*, 245).

"Lust sharpened by resistance" and avarice intensified by past and present deprivation: this principle is the basis of Zola's understanding of both the psychology and the historical situation of his characters. First, it is fitting that the family matriarch (Marianne Fouan, "La Grande"), like Adélaide Fouque, is no true matriarch at all but, as the elder sister of Old Fouan, merely the oldest and wealthiest surviving member. Having disowned her one child, a daughter, for "wanting to marry a poor man," this hard-bitten woman has, as progeny, only a granddaughter and grandson whom she "refused forgiveness, and was letting . . . die of starvation, allowing no one to remind her of their existence" (33). In referring to her in the ébauche as "the incarnation of the land," Zola was no doubt thinking of the land in all its harsher aspects:

> Too much rain rotted the seeds, hailstorms cut down the growing green wheat, a fierce wind beat down the stalks, two months of draught shrivelled up the corn ears. And then there were devouring insects, killing frosts, cattle diseases, leprosies of

poisonous weeds spoiling the soil . . . the battle had to be fought out every day, with mistakes liable to wreck your hopes and never a moment's relaxation. (70-71)

As the depriving, barren "Anti-Mother," she is the symbol of all the depriving mothers in the Fouan family whose own deprivation have resulted in a love-destroying avarice or "frigid parsimony," as with Rose, Old Fouan's wife, that in turn warps their children. This description seems to cry out for a psychoanalytic interpretation of Buteau's whole pattern of behavior, from his physical attack upon his father to his sexual brutality, but Zola provides another account that is more to the point.

Unlike Balzac's explanation of why the peasant behaves as he does, Zola's is not founded in scorn. True, we are given the history of the peasant through what is described as a "little greasy book, one of the Bonapartist propaganda works with which the Empire had flooded the countryside" (*The Misfortunes and the Triumph of Jacques Bonhomme*), but there is little doubt that we are meant to take seriously its account of the oppression of the peasant under feudalism and the ancient regime: "When the nobles were out for plunder, he was hunted, tracked down, treated as part of the loot. Every private war between lord and lord ruined him when it did not kill him off; his cottage was burned down, his fields ravaged" (67). Old Fouan knows the story well: "the earth so long cultivated for the lord of the manor by the lashed and stripped slave, a slave who owned nothing, not even his own skin" (70). After serfdom, when they had acquired "an acre or two" "paid for ten times over with their blood and sweat," the Fouans began a long struggle that

> had gone on four hundred years with a desperate passion that was passed on from father to son to hold and enlarge the property. Strips were lost, then bought back, the ridiculously small holding had its ownership continually in dispute and was passed under such heavy inheritance taxes that it seemed almost to

melt away; and yet pasture and arable [land] expanded bit by bit through a property-lust which conquered by sheer tenacity. (31)

Because the avarice of the peasant is at least partly a result of the great privation he suffered as both a serf and freeholder in the tenacious struggle against a hostile Nature and a predatory political and economic system, Zola finds in him a kind of grandeur.

Still, even though he recognizes that the peasant has been a victim of social forces, Zola makes no attempt to present this condition in terms of class conflict. Far from being set off against the Fouans, Hourdequin, for instance, the owner of the largest farm in the district, is caught up in the same obsessions over the land and suffers the same anxieties as the peasant, the only difference being that his are more sophisticated. Once again, the economic is fused with the sexual in a myth of the land as the fertile but depriving mistress. Loving her first as a mother and then as a wife, Hourdequin gives himself completely, forgiving "all her caprices and even her infidelities"; then, in increasing frustration over her refusal to bear, he accuses himself of "impotence" and seeks "new methods." But scientific cultivation proves to be no solution: "How many futile attempts lay behind him—experiments that went wrong, machines wrecked by his labourers, chemical fertilizers adulterated by dealers" (88). The land thus remains unmastered and Hourdequin sees himself on the verge of financial disaster. This struggle is acted out on both the sexual and political levels. Emotionally enslaved by an unfaithful mistress who frequently denies him, he is lured to his death by one of her lovers. His understanding of what constitutes their best interest in current economic and political issues goes for naught when the peasants, in stubborn ignorance, support the opposition and Hourdequin loses his mayoral post. He will eventually applaud, out of desperation, the call of an embittered anarchist schoolteacher (Lequeu) for the total destruction of society as the only hope for human salvation and thus add his voice to the ambiguous warning that concludes *Germinal*.

For Zola, then, class struggle is not the real problem; it is instead the self-detotalization of the individual man through greed, ignorance, and passion, all intensified by the elemental struggle for survival and the rising expectations (or, better, the "orgy of ambitions and appetites") associated with the Second Empire. Now, does Zola in fact see this problem as fundamentally of social origin and therefore remediable or does he see it as being of metaphysical origin and therefore eternal? *La Terre*, we note, ends with a meditation by the peace-loving ex-soldier, Jean Macquart, who came to La Beauce seeking tranquillity and found only strife and moral desolation. (He will reappear as a soldier in *La Débâcle*.) "The earth," he reasons, "takes no part in our maddened insect-struggles; she is the eternal worker, ceaselessly toiling and taking no more notice of us than a nest of ants." And he adds, in what seems to be a plea for resignation:

> Just as the frost that sears the crops, the hail that slashes them to shreds, the lightning that smashes them down, are all, maybe, necessary things, so it might be that blood and tears were needed to make the world move on. What does our happiness count in the great system of the stars and the sun? God cares precious little about us! We only gain our bread through a terrible struggle renewed day after day. Only the earth remains immortal. . . . She uses even our crimes and our miseries to make life and more life for her hidden ends. (429)

This may not be exactly the reasoning of Schopenhauer, but its implications are the same: men are reduced to struggling ciphers born to suffering and misery. We resign ourselves to the world or renounce it, but we will never succeed in changing it. It is precisely this "eternalizing" of social and moral conditions that Marxists like Lukács have deemed a fallacy of bourgeois philosophy in general.

1. Detotalization in Naturalism

The one novel that redeemed Zola in the eyes of the Marxists was *Germinal*—such is the opinion of Jean Fréville, one of Zola's most astute Marxist critics. Conceding that the socialism of *Germinal* was not "inspired by revolutionary Marxism" but remained "impregnated with petit-bourgeois sentimentality," Fréville asserts that Zola has accurately described the class struggle and that "realism" has triumphed in the novel. He sees *Germinal* as a great advance over *L'Assommoir*, written a decade earlier (1875), in which "the downfall of the workers had individual and moral causes." Those who were ruined were so by their own passions and vices, whereas in *Germinal* "the most zealous and serious workers, like all the others, are subject to hunger, destitution, and disease." Perhaps, when compared to *L'Assommoir*, *Germinal* is in fact a "socialist" novel; still, had Fréville chosen to emphasize its non-socialist qualities, he could have made an equally strong case for its being a naturalist one.

Thus, if for Fréville "realism" meant portrayal of the class struggle—a portrayal that by its very existence indicated Zola's sympathy for the working class—for the non-Marxist F. W. J. Hemmings it meant, as Zola himself had insisted, moral neutrality: *Germinal*, said Hemmings, was "neither revolutionary nor a reactionary work"; its emphasis was on "the graphic portrayal of social injustice." As Fréville implies, it is illogical to suppose that Zola or anyone else could present what he took to be socially unjust and remain neutral at the same time. Nevertheless, there are in fact no pure heroes or villains in the novel that are class determined. Men of either class can be "decent" or "scoundrels" or both alternately. This objectivity is more than a matter of scientific method; it springs from the naturalist's concentration on individual appetites and passions as the motivating forces of behavior. In *Germinal*, as later in *La Débâcle*, historical events and social crises demonstrate the fact of human impotence, frustration, and victimization by destructive passion.

If the story of Etienne Lantier is that of the growing revolutionary consciousness of the working man, it is not the story of a revolutionary hero in the Marxist sense. Socialist education in the naturalist world does not guarantee personal liberation from one's own egoism nor does it move society any closer to a successful proletarian revolution. Lantier's development is hindered at every step by his innate weaknesses as a human being (ascribed in part to heredity) and by the conflicting socialist viewpoints to which he has been exposed. His ferocity when he is drunk may or may not be relevant to his stature as a revolutionary, but his vanity certainly is:

> He treated himself to a pair of fine boots, and this immediately qualified him for a position of leadership; the whole village looked up to him. His ego delighted in it, and these first experiences with popularity intoxicated him . . . filled him with pride and bolstered his dream of a coming revolution in which he would play an important part. His very face changed, and he became serious, impressed with the sound of his own voice; his newborn ambition fired his theories and led him to more militant ideas of battle. (*Germinal,* 139)

Far from disappearing after his experiences as a strike leader, Lantier's vanity takes on a more complex and sophisticated form; the education that would free him also separates him from the workers:

> Slowly his vanity at being their leader, his feeling that he constantly had to think for them, was setting him apart and creating within him the soul of one of those bourgeois whom he so despised. (305) A feeling of repugnance, due to the uneasiness of his more polished tastes and the slow growth of his whole being toward a superior class, had gradually detached him from them. (363)

For all its seemingly revolutionary character, Lantier's rise in the world has something in common with those of his Rougon-Macquart relatives.

1. Detotalization in Naturalism

Lantier's failure, as I suggested, is also a matter of the specific kind of education he has been receiving. Competing socialist theories, all of equal weight to Zola, leave Lantier wholly confused:[3]

> Crowning everything were the ideas of Karl Marx: capital was the result of theft, and labor had the duty and the right to reconquer this stolen wealth. To put the theory into practice, he had at first let himself be won over by Proudhon's foolish dream of mutual credit . . . then he had become wildly enthusiastic about Lasalle's cooperative societies . . . but it was all still very vague; he did not know how to realize this newest dream, for he was still inhibited by scruples arising from sensitivity and reason, and he couldn't bring himself to the absolute affirmations of the dogmatists. (193)

"Scruples arising from sensitivity and reason": this is Zola's indictment of the socialist theoreticians in general; it is little wonder that Lantier has no guideposts. For Zola, the alternative to confusion is worse. Pursuing a synthesis, Lantier reaches a state of exaltation:

> At this pitch of intellectual strain, reason crumbled and only the singlemindedness of the fanatic remained. The scruples of his sensibility and common sense were swept away, and nothing seemed easier than the realization of this new world. (230)

It is not that the Marxist hero would not have bourgeois temptations and habits of mind to overcome; the difference is that he would have a stable set of values and ideas to guide him and there would be a reasonable chance for his success.[4] For all his good qualities, Lantier can become little more than a demagogue, who has his moment of adulation, only to lose favor when the miners' strike fails, as fail it must.

For all his exposure to the many doctrines of revolutionary thought and the personalities of those advocating them, Lantier never learns the "secret" of collective action. Even in his final speculations, which seem to affirm a basic Marxist principle, he is tentative and sentimental:

> Next time they would do it right: they would organize calmly, learn to know one another, band together in unions whenever the law allowed; then one day, when they felt themselves shoulder to shoulder, when they knew themselves to be millions of workers against a few thousand idlers, they would seize power and become the masters. (427)

There will be no next time for Lantier, who, as we learn in *Le Docteur Pascal*, will eventually be deported.

Too weak in knowledge, experience, and temperament to lead, Lantier finds himself losing control of the strikers; conversely, the strikers degenerate into the howling mob that is but one face of *la bête humaine*. This is virtually the essence of naturalist psychology and sociology. The sufferings of the miners can unquestionably be ascribed to a system created and perpetuated by the bourgeoisie, but the latter are no more in control of their destinies, their lives, even their own persons than the former. Thus Hennebeau, the mine manager, fails to act against the strikers because he is upset by his wife's adulterous relations with his nephew. Hemmings attributes this episode to Zola's "usual instinct for dramatic suspense," but surely there is more to it. All men—miners, capitalists, and revolutionaries—are vulnerable to the workings of temperament, society, and cosmos, however varying the proportions. Hennebeau, we learn, "dissimulated behind his mask of the cold and correct administrator a ravaging desire for this creature [his wife who has totally rejected him], one of those violent, late developing desires that increase with age." Sexual starvation leads him to this *cri-de-coeur:*

> He felt that he too wanted to be [literally] starving, to have an empty churning stomach that would make him faint and dizzy with pain; maybe that would have deadened his everlasting grief. Oh, to live like an animal, to have nothing of one's own,

1. Detotalization in Naturalism

> to be able to roll in the wheat with the ugliest and filthiest of the haulage girls and find contentment! . . .
> Those empty-headed revolutionaries could tear down this society and build up another, but giving everyone his slice of bread and butter would not add a single joy to humanity, nor spare it a single pain. . . . they would someday make the very dogs howl with despair by raising them from their simple satisfaction of their instincts to the unassuageable torment of their passions. (286)

The feelings are genuine even if the reasoning is dubious. Does Zola want us to find a grain of truth here? The agony of the deprived lover is one of his recurrent motifs—even Dr. Pascal, Zola's spokesman and hero of the final novel in the series, endures it. In any context but the present one, we might accept the argument as a typical product of naturalist logic.[5]

It has not been my intention to show that *Germinal* is wholly devoid of the sense of class and class struggle but rather that Zola even in this, his most "socialistic" of the Rougon-Macquart novels, tended to see individual passions as the fundamental force in social behavior and, at least until he wrote the utopian *Quatre Evangiles,* he could not get beyond this position. The optimism, suggested by the title, reflects a personal and abstract faith in "life" itself. And even here, there is ambivalence and ambiguity, if not outright contradiction:

> Now the April sun was high in the sky, blazing gloriously, warming the teeming earth. Life was springing from her nourishing flank. . . . On all sides seeds were swelling and stretching, thrusting through the plain in search of warmth and light. . . . Again, again, more and more distinctly, as if they too were rising to the surface, the comrades were continuing to hammer. . . . Men were springing up—a black, avenging army was slowly germinating in the furrows, sprouting for the harvests of the coming century. And soon this germination would sunder the earth. (428)

Is this a prophecy filled with hope or a vision of apocalypse? A cry of triumph or a dire warning? The anarchist Souverine

Zola II

would have welcomed the destruction of the world in preparation for the new society; but Zola has neither the ideology nor the temperament to herald this event. His sympathies are with the miners but he fears the mob, riot, upheaval. He is, in effect, rendered "neutral" by the very illogic of his position. His association of a working-class revolution with the processes of nature is little more than an attempt to find in myth what he could not find in social philosophy.

As it turned out, this kind of problem was not unique to *Germinal; La Débâcle*, undoubtedly one of the most powerful war novels of the last two centuries, contains the same attempt to mythify the evils that the naturalist is bound to expose but for which he has no social or political solution. Even though he did not participate in the war with Prussia—or in any other war—Zola appears to have been fully aware of its horrors. Here, for instance, is his description of the ambulance station hastily set up in a Sedan warehouse and manned by a single doctor and a few volunteers:

> Feet were sticking out with boots still on, but crushed and bleeding. Limbs were dangling loose from knees that looked as if they were broken with a hammer. . . . But the most upsetting wounds were gaping stomachs, chests or heads. Some men's trunks were bleeding through dreadful gashes, and knots of twisted entrails pushed up the skin, vital organs that had been pierced or hacked, twisted men into grotesque attitudes and paroxysms. . . . unseen internal hemorrhages struck men down all of a sudden in raving delirium and turned them black. Heads had suffered even worse things, smashed jaws with tongue and teeth a bleeding mess, eyesockets driven in and eyes half out, skulls split open with brains visible. (*Débâcle*, 278–79)

Certainly this description taken by itself would lead one to conclude that *La Débâcle* is a protest against all war, an impression seemingly supported by the story of Maurice Levasseur and his friend, Jean Macquart, who as soldiers in the doomed Army of Chalons endure the limits of hunger, fatigue, anxiety, and frustration for no apparent purpose. But toward the end of the novel, this exchange takes place between Maurice (now a communard, dying of a wound unwittingly inflicted by Jean, who is fighting with the Army of Versailles against the Commune), his sister, Henriette, and Jean, himself:

"Oh war, vile war!" whispered Henriette, looking at this city of ruin, destruction and death.

Wasn't this in fact the final, inevitable act, the bloodlust that had come into being in the disastrous fields of Sedan and Metz, the epidemic of destruction born in the siege of Paris, the final paroxysm amidst all this slaughter and wreckage?

But Maurice, still gazing at the areas burning out there, said haltingly and with difficulty:

"No, no don't curse the war. . . . War is a good thing, it is doing its work. . . ."

Jean cut him short with a cry of hatred and remorse.

"Oh my God, when I see you there, and it is all my fault. . . . Don't defend war, it's a vile thing."

The sick man vaguely waved his hand.

"Oh, what do I matter? There are plenty of others. . . . Perhaps the blood-letting is necessary. War is life, and it cannot exist without death . . . "

Henriette signalled to Jean not to argue. In her anger against human suffering she herself felt a wave of protest taking possession of her. . . . (500)

From the beginning Maurice has been described as a romantic and volatile bourgeois intellectual, a child of the Second Empire—not a likely spokesman for Zola's own views; Henriette has emerged as one of Zola's rare unblemished heroines; Jean Macquart has been characterized as a solid man of the earth. Yet in the end, it seems to be Maurice's view, or a modified version of it, that Zola wants his reader to accept. Indeed, visiting Sedan, in preparation for the novel, Zola noted that he experienced beneath a "terrible bitterness" a sensation of "salutary suffering, of virile healing." "I believe that I found at that moment in every breast," he writes, "that regeneration by sorrow, born in the very excess of our defeat; and I wanted, at that black date, to speak of all the light that spilled out of it, of all the germination in the field of our ruins." He goes on to mention the "necessary bloodbath" and its terrible but "profitable" lesson. Thus at the end of the novel, even while recognizing that Maurice's apocalyptic vision was "grandiose and monstrous," Jean has a vision of his own in which the sunset is taken to be an analogy of Paris burning, with a "new dawn . . . already breaking." "It was the sure renewal of eternal nature, eternal humanity, the renewal promised to all who hope and toil, the tree throwing up a strong new shoot after the dead branch, whose poisonous sap had yellowed the leaves, had been cut away" (508).

Thus in *La Débâcle* national history is absorbed into naturalist myth; a shattered, detotalized France is "retotalized," though not through any dialectical advance. The war is an expression of the powerful universal forces that have made the struggle for existence a central fact of human—of all—life; it is, as we have seen, part of the cycle of growth, decay, destruction, and rebirth, the *lutte vitale,* that characterizes all "natural" things. Accordingly, Zola's view of the significance of the defeat of 1870, culminating in the Paris Commune of 1871 and its collapse after a week-long civil war, was based not on analysis, Marxist or otherwise, of the social, political, and economic conditions of the Second Empire, but on a vision of apocalypse.

As he never tired of telling us, Zola was intent on describing and dramatizing the events or the facts of the conflict; this does not mean, however, that the broad panorama cannot be reduced to sharper focus in which a few key motifs become visible. Take, for example, the problem of epistemology and its implications. The logistical and tactical chaos brought on by a command that has no knowledge or understanding of the true situation that confronts it—an extension of a corrupt government that has been wholly ignorant of its lack of readiness for war—leaves the French forces atomized and helpless even before they have engaged the enemy. (Maps of France had not been issued to the French officers because the government had expected all the fighting to take place in Germany.) Out of touch with their senior officers, led by junior officers whose

1. Detotalization in Naturalism

patriotic pride is founded on ignorance or who seem otherwise distracted, the troops themselves, subsisting only on rumor, are prey to irrational hope, anxiety, and despair. Both literally and symbolically, General Bourgoin-Desfeulles, the division commander, has (Zola writes in his notes on the characters) an "ignorance insondable en geographie" (628). The chauvinistic Lieutenant Rochas suffers from the same blindness. Both are veterans of the African campaign, a triumph of the Second Empire in its earlier days; both exemplify the pride—now, during the decadence of the Empire, based solely on emotion—that has led the nation into a disastrous war. We find, therefore, that just as the "geographical" perspective of the French is fragmentary and haphazard, so that of the Prussians is complete and consistent. Positioned on favorable terrain, King Wilhelm has both a view of the entire battlefield and total freedom of action:

> The battlefield stretch[ed] out before him on all sides. The immense relief map went from one end of the sky to the other, and he, standing on the hill, looked on as though from a throne reserved for him in this gigantic box of a gala performance. . . .
> The hundred thousand men and five hundred cannon of the French army were packed together and hounded into this triangle. . . . In all directions the land belonged to him, he could move at will the two hundred and fifty thousand men and the eight hundred guns of his armies, he could take in with one sweeping look their invading march. (197-98)

The Germans do not emerge unscathed from the conflict but in comparison to the French they are virtually omniscient and invincible. In a sense they represent an inexorable force or the embodiment of a mathematical precision against which the weakness of the French plays itself out.[6]

In the detotalized world of *La Débâcle*—and this is the point to which I have been leading—effective cooperative action is limited to a small scale at best. The army, like a mass of striking coal miners in *Germinal*, basically leaderless, falls under the sway of anarchy. In a socialist view of the army (I am thinking of Henri Barbusse's *Le Feu* or even Dos Passos's *Three Soldiers*) class conflict works itself out in terms of officers and enlisted men, with the latter seen as victims or else as having a strength lent them by their solidarity. In *La Débâcle,* as in Zola's other novels, since class consciousness is not the real issue, no solidarity is apparent among the men. The enlisted men are portrayed no more sympathetically than the officers. Lapoulle, Zola tells us, is stupid, a "beast led to slaughter"; Pache is a religious fanatic, Loubet is venal, and Chouteau "knows nothing and speaks just the same."

For the naturalist, then, divisiveness leads to division, and not ultimately, as it does for the socialist, to a compensating solidarity. The basis of unselfish action or even self-sacrifice is personal attachment. Zola gives us not only the friendship between Maurice and Jean, in which both prove themselves capable of loyalty at the risk of their own lives, but the devotion of Henriette, who, braving death, sets out to find her missing husband, and the faithfulness of Silvine, who goes in search of the corpse of her lover. And even in these instances there is a suggestion of the obsessiveness that appears in most naturalist heroes or heroines. Thus Zola can at once applaud and draw back from a patriotism that in its very authenticity leads to suicidal heroics: the doomed cavalry charge, the artillery barrage with shells known to be of too short a range, the hopeless rearguard action in defense of one's property.

The unlikely friendship of Maurice and Jean has behind it an even more unlikely symbolism. Jean, says the ébauche, represents the balanced, courageous, rational side of France; Maurice, the proud, vain, cerebral, and volatile. Destined to rebuild France after the debacle, Jean must suppress or cut out Maurice, the aspect of France that, distracted by the empire, has been enervated and demoralized to the point of losing its reason. This explanation doesn't take us very far. A less mythical view is that this relationship between intellectual and peasant is another example of the "mixing of classes" that characterized the egalitarianism of the Second Empire. The war has brought its own kind of levelling to the army, as it has to the

1. Detotalization in Naturalism

civilian population in Sedan. On the other hand, Zola is clearly presenting this "fraternal compassion" as an ideal (it will reappear in *Le Docteur Pascal*):

> Was this not the brotherhood of the earliest days of the world, friendship before there was any culture or class, the friendship of two men united and become one in their common need of help in the face of the threat of hostile nature? (136)

Is this the first, infinitesimal step of the naturalist toward socialism or the reaffirmation of his belief that the world is hopelessly individualistic?

Zola's view of the Siege of Paris and the insurrection that established the short-lived Commune is wholly consistent with his view of the war in general: the irrationality of the populace on the eve of the war is matched by an even greater madness at its conclusion. The crushing of French pride after decades of military supremacy on the continent has brought a disillusion, coupled with a blind optimism, that turns the beleaguered Parisians wholly into creatures of emotion. Their solidarity in suffering is no more than "a sort of epidemic fever, magnifying fear just as much as confidence and letting loose the human herd to rush off unbridled at the slightest stimulus" (458). The prevailing influence, which has caught up Maurice and all of Paris, is radical chauvinism:

> Anything, destruction, even extermination, rather than yield up one sou of the wealth or one inch of the territory of France! . . . He had even already left behind theoretical moderate republicanism and was tending towards revolutionary violence, believing in the necessity of terror to sweep away the incompetent and the traitors who were busy murdering the fatherland. (459)

Herein lies Zola's explanation of the rebellion:

> . . . the insurrection sprang up quite naturally and organized itself in broad daylight among people thrown off balance by

months of anguish and famine, fallen into a hag-ridden idleness and haunted by suspicions of their own making. It was one of those crises of morale observed after all great sieges, when unsurpassable patriotism has been cheated and, after inspiring people's souls to no purpose, changes into a blind lust for vengeance and destruction. (467)

Accordingly, to Maurice, "the Commune now seemed to him to be the avenger of all the shameful things they had endured, a kind of liberator bringing the knife to amputate and the fire to purify" (472). Significantly enough, he is baffled by the "jumble of moderates, militant revolutionaries, and socialists of all colours, to whom this great task was entrusted," and he eventually becomes disenchanted by the "inept" leadership, with its internal conflicts and failure to bring about any social reforms. Nonetheless, he maintains the revolutionary fervor to which his increased awareness has led him and, as we have seen, speaks on his deathbed of the necessity of bloodletting for purifying the nation and bringing about a rebirth.

The Marxist view of the Commune is, of course, utterly different. Without denying the impetus of conditions exacerbated by the siege, it sees the movement as having a class origin and being essentially proletarian in substance, a movement wholly in the French revolutionary tradition and directly related to the Commune of 1848. Marx called it "the bold champion of the emancipation of labor, emphatically international," and ascribing its failures to lack of time and the pressures of war, he went on to list its achievements:

> The great social measure of the Commune was its own working existence. Its special measures could but betoken the tendency of a government of the people by the people. Such were the abolition of nightwork by journeyman bakers; the prohibition under penalty, of the employers' practice to reduce wages by levying upon their workpeople fines under manifold pretexts. . . . surrender, to associations of workmen, under reserve of compensation, of all closed workshops and factories. (*The Paris Commune, 1871,* 101)

1. Detotalization in Naturalism

Had the events of March 18 to May 28, 1871, been presented from the point of view of a class-conscious worker, rather than a middle-class intellectual or a peasant-soldier who was primarily apolitical, a different picture might have emerged, but it would have been alien to the conception of life Zola had been developing in his portrayal of the battle of Sedan. Again, Zola was interested in social upheaval for what it indicated about individual (or mass) psychology and about the nature of the universe. The Commune itself was as much a part of the debacle as its destruction; it was created not by an exploited "proletariat" whose grievances predated the war but by men driven by frustration and rage at their own impotence in the face of antagonistic forces hopelessly beyond their mastery. And other forces—nature, "the undying tree of life"— not the will of men would decree the time for reconstruction.

We remember that for Schopenhauer human misery and suffering were part of the essence of life (Will) and therefore irremediable and ultimately self-justifying. In Zola's version of this notion they are justified by a rebirth myth or a kind of tragic optimism. Half a century later, a "metaphysical rebel" named Albert Camus was to protest any justification of human suffering, especially in the name of a superior being or higher force. We can be sure that Zola was no less sensitive than Camus to the misery of others, yet the whole ponderous logic of *La Débâcle*, with all its weight of characters and events, moved toward reconciliation with history, with nature, with the future. As a result, Zola does not dwell upon the massacre of the Communards by the Versailles government.

Presented through the eyes of Jean, this episode occupies no more than a paragraph, and Zola's simple conclusion is that "Of the twelve thousand poor creatures who had lost their lives through the Commune, how many harmless people were there for each rogue!" (505-6). ("Combien de brave gens pour un gredin, parmi les douze mille malheureux à qui la Commune avait coûté la vie!"). Zola's indignation seems pale next to that of the Marxist historian, Lissagaray, who gives this account:

Twenty-five thousand men, women, and children killed during the battle or after; three thousand at least dead in the prisons, the pontoons, the forts, or in consequence of maladies contracted during their captivity; thirteen thousand seven hundred condemned, most of them for life; seventy thousand women, children, and old men thrown out of France: *one hundred and eleven thousand* victims at least. That is the balance sheet of the bourgeois vengeance for the solitary insurrection of the eighteenth of March. (Lissagary, 31)

Here, terms like "harmless" (*brave*) and "scoundrel" (*gredin*) seem wholly without meaning, whereas in an outlook that concerns itself with individual conduct in a basically deterministic world they are all that matters.

A year before he published *La Débâcle* (1892), Zola completed the story of Saccard in *L'Argent (Money)*, a novel about financial speculation. I did not discuss it with the earlier works in which this character plays a major role because the point of view it develops—that is, the one we have been talking about—is the product of Zola's maturity. *L'Argent* is important for our purposes precisely because it deals with a world that is at the opposite end of the socioeconomic spectrum from the world of *Germinal* and does so in terms of the same mythology, one whose weaknesses stand out more sharply in this novel than in *Germinal* or, indeed, *La Terre* or *La Débâcle*. Specifically, the rise and fall of a financial tycoon, like all other social phenomena in the naturalist world, is taken to be *sub specie aeternitatis*.[7]

L'Argent ends, characteristically, on a note of hope. Mme Caroline, a woman of scruples involved in Saccard's schemes, along with her brother (Hamelin), an engineer who envisions a vast transportation and utilities network in the Middle East, financed by Saccard's new Universal Bank, surveys the ruins of the whole enterprise and of her life:

[Saccard] was right: money has hitherto been the dung-heap in which the humanity of the morrow has grown; money albeit the poisoner and destroyer, becomes the ferment of all social

1. Detotalization in Naturalism

> vegetation, the compost necessary for the great works which make life easier. . . . Did her invincible hope come from her belief in the usefulness of effort? Above all the mud stirred up, above all the victims crushed to death, above all the abominable suffering which each forward step costs humanity, is there not an obscure, far-off goal, something superior, good, just, and final, whither we are going without knowing it, and which ever inflates our hearts with a stubborn need of life and hope?
>
> (*Money*, 427-28)

The naturalistic sentimentality not only dispenses with the suffering caused by a social buccaneer altogether too easily—that is, by rendering it as an abstraction in a larger scheme of things—it also reinforces the notion of the hopelessness of men's efforts to control their own destiny. A goal "whither we are going without knowing it": the universe is ultimately benevolent, but men are not responsible for its being so.

Mme Caroline's reflections on money merely repeat those she held when the enterprise was in full swing; she speaks for Zola in regarding it not simply as the instrument of a given economic and social system but as a universal force:

> She had cursed money, and now she fell in awe-stricken admiration before it; for was not money the sole force that can level a mountain, fill up an arm of the sea—briefly, render the earth inhabitable by men, who, once relieved of labour, would become but the conductors of machines. From this force, which was the root of all evil, there also sprang everything that was good. (233)

It made possible "the execution of the great works which would draw the nations nearer together and pacify the earth."

What makes this argument dangerous is its identification of the capitalist system with nature and its assumption that evil (actually injustice) is the inevitable source of all good. In his defense of financial speculation, one of the defining institutions of capitalism, Saccard supplies as evidence a cynical view of human nature that, as can be expected, stresses antisocial motivations:

Speculation—why, it is the one inducement that we have to live; it is the eternal desire that compels us to live and struggle. Without speculation . . . there would be no business of any kind. Why on earth would you have me loosen my purse strings and risk my fortune, if you do not promise me some extraordinary enjoyment, some sudden happiness which will open heaven to me. . . . just make some dream flare up on the horizon, promise men that with one sou they shall gain a hundred, propose to all these sleepers that they shall join you in a chase after the impossible, and gain millions in a couple of hours, amidst the most fearful hazards—why then the race at once begins, all energies are increased tenfold, and amidst the scramble of people toiling and sweating for their own gratification, birth is given to great and beautiful living things. (140)

Whereas Saccard is using these observations as a justification, Zola perhaps is merely recording a phenomenon, but it is a phenomenon that is fully consistent with life in the naturalist universe, in which men are always at the mercy of their passions.

In the total configuration of things, events are always superior to human will and frustration or destruction follows creation, ruin follows gain, just as surely as good turns into evil and evil returns to good. After decades of French military supremacy comes the debacle of the Franco-Prussian War and the beginnings of reconstruction; after the repression of the miners, a new army lies germinating; after the successful launching of its enterprises in the Middle East, the overextended Universal Bank collapses under attacks in the Bourse, but its survivors take hope. Similarly, Saccard is not simply the creature of a social institution; he is a type of Natural Man:

> For him there were neither bonds nor barriers; he rushed on to the satisfaction of his appetites with the unbridled instincts of a man who knows no other limit than powerlessness. He has sold his son, his wife, all who had fallen into his clutches. . . . their hearts and their brains for money. (228–29)

His ruin is called for not only in the interests of drama but by metaphysical principle. Yet even in ruin, Saccard retains the

1. Detotalization in Naturalism

irrepressible energy that allies him with nature. Visiting him in his cell, after his arrest, Mme Caroline becomes "conscious of an overflowing force, a resplendency of life: the eternal illusion of hope, the stubborn obstinacy of the man who does not wish to perish" (416).

For Saccard, the Middle Eastern enterprise is chiefly an investment promising vast returns; for Caroline and her brother, it is the realization of a dream characterized wholly by the idea of eternal renewal:

> From all the ruins, still warm, she already felt a complete florescence germinating, budding in the sunlight. Although the Turkish National Bank had fallen after the collapse of the Universal, the Steam Navigation Company remained erect and prosperous. Again she beheld the enchanted coast of Beyrout, where, in the midst of huge warehouses, stood the managerial buildings. . . . Marseilles had been brought close to Asia Minor, the Mediterranean was being conquered, nations were being drawn together, and possibly pacified. And in the Carmel gorge . . . a whole people had grown up. . . . The village of five hundred inhabitants, at first nestling round the mine, had now become a city of several thousand souls, with roads, factories, schools, a complete civilisation, fertilising the wild, dead nook. . . . life was already flowing in from every direction, the soil of the ancient cradle of humanity had just been sown with a new crop of men. . . . was not this the reawakening of a world, humanity enlarged and happier? (427)

Fecondité (1899), the first "évangile," with its appeal for colonization to propagate the "French race" and spread its culture and civilization, confirms Zola's sympathy with this vision, which may have had its source in the writings of Prevost-Paradol. Had Zola lived in a later age, he would no doubt have written his "Algerian novel"—a novel that, we suspect, would end with hope but not before revealing some of the bleaker realities of his subject.

In the Rougon-Macquart series Zola offers no genuinely social solution to the problems of mankind. Socialism (as I have said) dictates that all human problems are social; naturalism, that all social problems are "natural." As late as 1890 Zola could produce a work that would reassert his commitment to biologism as the basic way of explaining behavior. I shall conclude with a brief look at this novel, *La Bête humaine (The Human Beast)*.

Although the subject of *La Bête humaine* is the railroad, the treatment is qualitatively different from that of the coal-mining industry in *Germinal*. Virtually the only reference to labor conditions is the comment that the engineer's trade is a hard one, "finishing a man in twenty years." Psychology, abetted by heredity—to the almost complete exclusion of sociology—pervades the work: though seeming to live normal lives, the principal characters are all driven by obsessions with various kinds of homicide. That they all happen to be railroad employees (or associated with them) is of no social consequence.

Zola repeatedly explains that the problem of Jacques Lantier, the locomotive engineer and main character, has its origins in a kind of racial unconscious; thus the murder of Severine, Lantier's mistress, is described this way:

> Jacques, without turning, felt behind him with his right hand, for the knife. For a moment he held it tight in his fist. Was it again that thirst to avenge every ancient wrong of which he had lost exact recollection, that bitterness amassed from male to male from the first infidelity in the caves? He stared at Severine with mad eyes. He only needed now to throw her dead across his back, like a prey torn from another. The door of terror opened on the black gulf of sex, love even to death, to destroy to possess the more. (*Human Beast*, 345)

That this is scarcely a sufficient explanation of Lantier's psychopathic sexual impulses is not important; what is important is that his condition, whatever its source, has nothing to do with any other aspect of his life. He is a highly responsible man who takes pleasure in his work and suffers no apparent frustrations in it. He is not taking surrogate vengeance against a society that has wronged him.

1. Detotalization in Naturalism

Roubaud, Severine's husband, an assistant station master, who on learning that his wife had been violated as a child by her guardian, Grandmorin, the president of the railroad, flies into a jealous rage and plots and carries out the slaying of the old man. Roubaud had heretofore greatly profited, in terms of advancement and protection, from having married Grandmorin's ward, and though he is given to occasional "republican" (and therefore subversive) sentiments, it is obvious that his act is a *crime passionnel* and of no political significance. Flore, the gate attendant, out of jealous rage, wrecks Lantier's train in an attempt to kill him and his mistress; Misard, the signal man, slowly poisons his wife in the hope of finding and claiming the thousand francs she had buried; Severine herself plots with Lantier the slaying of Roubaud; and Pecqueux, Lantier's friend and fireman, pushes him off the speeding locomotive (and is himself pulled off) when he discovers that Lantier has been sleeping with his mistress, Philomene.

The novel concludes with the runaway train (Lantier and Pecqueux crushed beneath its wheels) carrying drunk and unsuspecting soldiers off to war with Prussia. A symbol of the approaching doom of the Second Empire, the wild locomotive is also a projection of the blind and uncontrollable forces that rule the universe and men.

It is true that the investigation of Grandmorin's murder is an instance of the corruption prevalent in the Second Empire (it includes the suppression of evidence by the secretary-general of the Ministry of Justice so as not to create a scandal around the life of the president of the railroad and the complicity of the struggling examining-magistrate, who is promised a promotion if he cooperates). The question remains, however, whether the empire is anything more than the sum of the people who inhabit it, the social and political expression of human nature as Zola understands it.

Whatever its attempt to find in individual heredity the "physiological" sources of one's behavior, as with Jacques Lantier, *La Bête humaine* in particular, like naturalism in general, strongly implies that all men are potential criminals—

indeed that the man devoted to making the trains run on time is the same man, who, in a jealous rage or under some other irresistible urge, deliberately pulls the wrong switch or lays the boulder on the tracks. For Zola, as for Schopenhauer, evil is omnipresent and suffering inevitable. People could be saved only by forces or laws beyond themselves or by saintly renunciation.

Far from being an eccentric excursion into psychopathology, *La Bête humaine* is a paradigm of Zola's view of social reality and his techniques for expressing it. Thus Boris Suchkov asserts that a

> typical feature of Zola's naturalism was his tendency to illustrate a particular social process by the actions and fortunes of his characters, rather than treat them as an organic part of the process, presenting man and environment as the indivisible whole they are. He thus often sacrificed historical perspective, substituting biological causality for social causality, thereby obscuring the real causal links in psychological and social phenomena. (*History of Realism,* 165)

To the Marxist, totality means "the indivisible whole" of man and his environment, the two in dialectical interaction and reaching a synthesis. For the naturalist, totality can be no more than the collection of parts hopelessly alienated from one another by the very nature of things. In depicting that endlessly detotalizing totality, that morally crumbling "synthetic" world of the Second Empire, Zola rose to the limits of his powers. We cannot bemoan the fact that the Rougon-Macquart novels, far from presenting a totality in definitive reply to the chaos and corruption of the visible world, take their life from the very detotalizing elements that they decry.

Part Two
The Totalities of Existentialism

4 Sartre I
The Scandal of Plurality

"I am not an existentialist," Albert Camus insisted, and only half-jokingly said that he and Jean-Paul Sartre thought of publishing a statement in which they declared that they had nothing in common. Still, the stereotype that yokes them is not wholly inaccurate. Even in his adverse review of Sartre's *La Nausée,* Camus's main philosophic objection was one that Sartre would soon heed; namely, the idea that life is absurd cannot be an end, as it seemed to be in *La Nausée,* but only a beginning. This is, of course, a sectarian quarrel, not a clash of radically different visions of life: Camus believes that the world is meaningless but that the life of the individual man is not; Sartre believes that the world is meaningless and he creates a hero who is increasingly disabled the more aware of that fact he becomes. *La Nausée* appeared in 1938; Camus had not yet written *L'Etranger*; it was an early time in the philosophic and literary development of both men, and when the war came, it taught both an identical lesson, one through his experience in the Resistance movement, the other through his in a prisoner of war camp. The two, who met and became friends in 1944, had a falling out in 1952 when Camus replied to an unfavorable review of *L'Homme révolté (The Rebel)* in Sartre's journal, *Les Temps Moderns,* and Sartre answered in a pamphlet-length open letter that could only terminate their relationship. The dispute

2. The Totalities of Existentialism

is illuminating because, regardless of whether he is right or wrong, Sartre can speak Camus's language.

Indicting Camus not only for the way in which he had attacked the reviewer but for what Camus "had become" or failed to become, Sartre made it clear that the causes of the rupture went far deeper than the immediate circumstances. What is ironic (in terms of the present discussion) is that Sartre praises the "old Camus," the Camus of 1945, for possessing the very same positive qualities that Camus had accused Sartre of lacking in 1938. "You united," Sartre writes, "the joy of life to the sense of death. . . . you were of the opinion that 'all negation contains within it a flowering of *yes*,' and you wanted to find consent in the heart of refusal." Sartre had moved away not only from the nihilism of *La Nausée,* but, under the influence of Marx, away from its wholly individualistic and metaphysical approach, or so it seemed. Moreover, he had thoroughly repudiated the absurdist view of history, outlined in the novel, in favor of the materialist, so that he could now blame Camus for asking the same "meaningless" question that Roquentin, the hero of *La Nausée,* had believed crucial, "Is history meaningful?" Had Sartre forgotten this point? Or was he being hypocritical? Or did he mean to imply that Camus had not only not grown since 1945 but, at least in one important way, was still where Sartre himself had been in 1938? No matter. My aim is not to judge Sartre or Camus but simply to show that both were nihilists who tried to transcend their nihilism by affirming certain social values—an elementary conclusion, perhaps, but still the only basis for a coherent view of the development of each.

By 1952 Sartre was no longer writing fiction; thus none of his novels reflects his encounter with Marx and whatever social thought it generated. They do reflect, however, that critical change from nihilism to affirmation, although what is affirmed is so ambiguous and so difficult to realize that it can scarcely be associated with an optimistic view of life: the idea or fact of "metaphysical" freedom, which proved to be a mixed blessing, and its "commitment" to some problematic form of social action. Paradoxically, this conception, the pivotal one in Sartre's attempt to move beyond the "man alone theory" of which he himself said *La Nausée* was the culmination, initially entailed an atomistic view of social life in which human relations are based on the clash of individual wills or "freedoms" or centers of consciousness that attempt to dominate or "capture" each other. In its emphasis on conflict it could have been a vision inspired by Schopenhauer, although its actual source is in part Hegel's theory of the recognitive self-consciousness and the master-slave relationship. This theory, which greatly influenced Marx and provided Camus with material for several pages in *The Rebel,* sheds so much light on the questions we've been discussing, it demands at least a brief consideration.[1]

In Hegel's *Phenomenology of Mind,* which is concerned with the ascending stages of consciousness measured by its relation to objects, the recognitive consciousness is a dialectical synthesis of the contradictions of the preceding form of consciousness, the "Understanding," just as the Understanding resolved those of "perception," and perception those of "sense-certainty." As the most primitive form of knowledge or certainty, that provided by sense-certainty for the sensuous consciousness was limited to an impression of the mere existence of things; its contradiction lay in the fact that if "nothing is said of a thing except that it is an actual thing, an external object, this only makes it the most universal of all possible things." Sense-certainty thus being illogical, consciousness rises to "perception," in which things are perceived both as particulars and universals or part of a class of objects: "perceiving takes the object as it inherently is in itself, or, put generally, as a universal. Singleness, therefore, makes its appearance there as true singleness, as the inherent nature of the one, or as reflectedness into self." This form is also seen to provide contradictory knowledge in that singleness and universality are logical opposites existing in one object. Perception then yields to Understanding, which takes universals as its object; it thus posits two worlds, that of multiplicity, the senses, and phenomena, and that of unity, "laws," and "noumena." This division also proves inadequate since it turns universals into mere ideas or forms without substance, and phenomena into a lawless and ungoverned turmoil. (This is Hegel's critique of Kant.)

It is with self-consciousness, says Hegel, "that we have passed into the native land of truth" (*Phenomenology of Mind*, 219). At this stage, the object, reflecting the universal process in which the Idea (subjectivity) seeks to objectify itself into the many while retaining its identity as a unity, becomes a "concrete universal" in which subject and object, unity and plurality, are identified with one another. In this new relationship, consciousness, or subjectivity, sees itself in the object. In its first phase, however, self-consciousness feels a contradiction insofar as the object as object retains a partial independence and therefore partly asserts itself as "other" or alien; correspondingly, the self-conscious here is still partly consciousness. This contradiction can be resolved only when the independence of the object is totally eliminated—hence the impulse to destroy or absorb (devour) the object so that it becomes totally identified with the subject.

In the penultimate stage, the self-conscious recognizes the existence of other selves, as well as objects, in the world. Since its nature is self-contemplation, it cannot destroy the "other" without destroying itself; it therefore seeks only to "capture" him or render him wholly subservient. This is the ontological basis of the master-slave relationship; it, too, has contradictions that emerge when the master discovers that his independence depends upon the slave, who is independent to the extent that the master depends upon him. The master thus must recognize the self-consciousness of the slave. In this mutual recognition and acceptance, the self-conscious becomes universal and passes over to Reason, which provides the highest and final form of certainty or truth.

When Camus interpreted Hegel in *L'Homme révolté*, he was committed to a thesis; namely, that metaphysical rebellion, which began in the interests of solidarity, almost invariably ended by authorizing terror and mass executions for the sake of a future society. In first defying and then denying God, it was a form of nihilism that could appeal only to the historical process for values, and therefore it was inevitable that it should forget its original inspiration and be guilty of the excesses that accompany an overweening pride. Listing Hegel among the "deicides," then, Camus offers this interpretation of the forms of the self-conscious:

> What distinguishes consciousness of self from the world of nature is . . . the desire it can feel with regard to the world. . . . Consciousness of self is therefore, of necessity, desire. . . . It therefore acts in order to gratify itself and, in so doing, it denies and suppresses its means of gratification. . . . To consume is not yet to be conscious. Desire for consciousness must be directed to something other than unconscious nature. . . . Self-consciousness must be gratified by another form of self-consciousness. . . . [A man] must be acknowledged by other men. All consciousness is, basically, the desire to be recognized and proclaimed as such by other consciousnesses. (*Rebel,* 138)

Camus then draws these conclusions:

> Fundamental human relations are thus relations of pure prestige, a perpetual struggle, to the death, for recognition of one human being by another. . . . The entire history of mankind is. . . . nothing but a prolonged fight *to the death* for the conquest of universal prestige and absolute power. . . . *each separate consciousness, to ensure its own existence, must henceforth desire the death of others.* (139; my italics)

All this seems accurate enough until we realize that Camus has not included in his description of the recognitive self-consciousness the crucial paradox or contradiction that differentiates it from the lower form of self-conscious, which indeed seeks to destroy (absorb, consume) the object as thing. The recognitive self-conscious cannot destroy the object (as person) without destroying itself in the object and in fact all possibility of recognition along with it. This situation, we remember, makes it imperative that the "other" not be killed but rather reduced to subservience or made into a "thing." Thus Hegel:

> [The] trial by death, however, cancels both the truth which was to result from it, and therewith the certainty of self altogether. For just as life is the natural "position" of consciousness, independence without absolute negativity, so death is the natural "negation" of consciousness, negation without independence, which thus remains without the requisite significance of actual recognition. . . .
> In this experience self-consciousness becomes aware that *life* is as essential to it as pure self-conscious. (*Phenomenology of Mind*, 233-34)

Camus's deduction that the entire history of mankind is a fight to the death for prestige and power is patently misleading as a complete description of Hegel's theory.

This problem is reflected in Camus's account of the master-slave relationship in which apparently minor discrepancies have a profound effect on the meaning. Here Camus reveals his awareness that there are contradictions. He tells us that mastery is at an "impasse," that the master's independence is not absolute since he is recognized by "a consciousness that he himself does not recognize as autonomous" (*Rebel*, 140). He then concludes that "the eternal destiny of masters is to live unsatisfied or to be killed." This is not the only case—yet it is clear from what follows that it had to be the case for Camus if not for Hegel:

> The master serves no other purpose in history than to arouse servile consciousness, the only form of consciousness that really creates history. The slave, in fact, is not bound to his condition, but wants to change it. Thus, unlike his master, he can improve himself, and what is called history is nothing but the effects of his long efforts to obtain real freedom. . . . The very agony of death experienced in the humiliation of the entire being *lifts the slave to the level of human totality. He knows, henceforth, that this totality*

exists; now it only remains for him to conquer it through a long series of struggles against nature and against the masters.(140-41; my italics)

This is simply a restatement of Camus's theory of rebellion in Hegelian terms. (The totality of which he speaks is that created by human solidarity, in whose name, the slave rebels.) In giving this account, Camus has ignored the exact nature of the contradictions and, despite his frequent reference to it, the actual dialectical process at work. He points out that by his labor, "by his transformation of the natural world into a technical world," the slave "manages to escape from nature which was the basis of his slavery in that he did not know how to raise himself above it by accepting death" (140). But, repeating the omission he made in regard to the distinct character of the recognitive self-consciousness, he doesn't say that the slave, through work, in shaping an object, puts himself into it and thereby rises to self-consciousness and independence, that here as everywhere a dialectical process is at work. Thus, says Hegel, "just as lordship showed its essential nature to be the reverse of what it wants to be, so, too, bondage will, when completed, pass into the opposite of what it immediately is: being a consciousness repressed within itself, it will enter into itself, and change round into real and true independence" (*Phenomenology of Mind,* 237).

Accordingly, through this dialectic, recognitive self-consciousness becomes universal self-consciousness, the final stage, in which the ego recognizes and accepts the existence and independence of others. The implication, then, is that on the epistemological and ontological level, the master is compelled by inherent contradictions in his own and the slave's nature—not by a deliberate effort on the part of the slave to rebel against and destroy him—to recognize and accept the slave's independence and self-consciousness.

For Camus, on the other hand, it is precisely in the act of rebellion that the slave acquires his identity as a man—and not only the slave as such, but all men, whose ultimate rebellion is against God. History for him is characterized by an eternally recurring opposition, not by a dialectical process in which contradictions are perpetually being resolved at higher stages. He is (as we have seen) a self-avowed mythmaker and rebellion is his principal archetype. That is why when he discovers in Hegel a single stage that more or less corresponds, or can be made to correspond, to his own vision, he can generalize it to all history and thereby regard it not as part of an ongoing process but *sub specie aeternitatis*.

It is the appearance of oneself in the other that makes rebellion against him a logical impossibility. This phenomenon is translated in Schopenhauer into the expression of the Will in all things, "that one inner being which is everywhere the same." Now, the conflict of self-consciousnesses and the master-slave relationship in Hegel occurs in Schopenhauer, as in Camus, as part of a permanent human condition. That is, it is the same kind of conflict but without the internal contradictions that will lead to a qualitative change. Life is a perpetual internecine war, says Schopenhauer, in which each man "only possesses what [he] wrested from others"; and each "presses and urges in vain; yet, by reason of its nature, it cannot cease; it toils on laboriously until this phenomenon perishes, and then others eagerly seize its place and its matter" (1:309). Endless struggle without possibility of triumph or reconciliation is the way of the world; unlike Hegel's contending self-consciousnesses who must recognize themselves in others and are compelled by dialectical logic to mitigate or transcend a blind struggle to the death, Schopenhauer's men remain blind to the ultimate truth that "the tormentor and tormented are one" (285).

Curiously—ironically—to appreciate the kind of salvation that Schopenhauer does offer, we must descend to what in Hegel's system is an earlier stage of consciousness—that of the Understanding, in which a world of universals or noumena is distinguished from the world of phenomena. (Hegel, remember, was refuting Kant, who was the source of this conception.) For Schopenhauer, then, the Understanding provides the kind of knowledge that makes it possible for the will in man to negate itself and therefore rise above the struggles of the (phenomenal) world. The inferior form of knowledge in this respect is associated with "sufficient reason," a mode of thought directed only toward action and therefore "in the service of the will." Self-conscious knowledge, the "pure will-less knowledge" of which it will become the "subject" is achieved in the contemplation of Ideas. Since the idea of Ideas or the idea of the existence of a noumenal realm ("the kingdom of laws" in Hegel) is itself an Idea, contemplation is here a form of Hegel's Understanding.

Camus and Schopenhauer give us a perspective on a fundamental issue in Hegel, just as this issue tells us something important about Camus and Schopenhauer. Still, the "Hegelian problem" was more implicit than explicit in one, and wholly external to the other. Sartre will meet this problem head on, for his whole conception of human relations and their possibilities, during his purely existential period, was involved. To begin with, in his belief that "Conflict is the original meaning of being-for-others," Sartre accepts what is obviously Hegel's view of the struggle of self-consciousnesses that results in the master-slave relationship: "While I attempt to free myself from the hold of the Other, the Other is trying to free himself from mine; while I seek to enslave the Other, the Other seeks to enslave me" (*Being and Nothingness,* 364). Now, Sartre can cite with full approval Hegel's theory that the self requires recognition from the Other in order to come to full awareness of itself ("I must obtain from the Other the *recognition* of my being," "I find that being-for-others appears as a necessary condition for my being-for-myself" [237, 238]). But he accepts this relation only in the conflict phase, not in the resolution phase; and he thereby denies the fundamental condition that makes that resolution a logical necessity. It is the very condition that Camus, moving in the same direction as Sartre, omitted from his account; namely, the existence of self-consciousness in the Other.

Thus charging Hegel with "epistemological optimism,"

2. The Totalities of Existentialism

Sartre attempts to show that the Other can never be seen as anything but an object; what he is doing, in effect, is denying the existence of the recognitive self-consciousness:

> The Other is not a *for-itself* as he appears to me; I do not appear to myself as I am *for-the-Other*. I am incapable of apprehending for myself the self which I am for the Other, just as I am incapable of apprehending on the basis of the *Other-as-object* which appears to me, what the Other is for himself.

Then he concludes,

> How then could we establish a universal concept subsuming under the name of self-conscious, my *consciousness* for myself and (of) myself and my *knowledge* of the Other. (242)

With this question Sartre is doing nothing less than challenging the existence of the universal self-consciousness, the mode in which the contradictions of the recognitive self-consciousness are resolved, and along with it the whole dialectical process.

Thus Sartre affirms his own nihilism, and he affirms it yet again when he charges Hegel with the parallel error of "ontological optimism." This argument reveals the essentially atomistic view of society that will reappear in Sartre's fiction. Ontological optimism is simply the belief that "plurality can and must be surpassed toward totality." This principle is at the very core of dialectical logic in which all things move perpetually toward synthesis. Hence, Sartre asserts that

> The multiplicity of consciousnesses is on principle unsurpassable, for I undoubtedly transcend myself *toward* a Whole, but I cannot establish myself in this Whole so as to contemplate myself and to contemplate the Other. No logical or epistemological optimism can cover the scandal of the plurality of consciousnesses. (244)

The *scandal* of plurality? A cause for moral outrage? If it involves us all, who is left to be indignant? And who is to blame?

Sartre doesn't say, but we can guess: in both cases, only God, and God doesn't exist. And that, I think, is exactly the point; God has caused this scandal by his disappearance, taking with him all possibility of totality in the universe. Thus we find Sartre writing elsewhere: "Everything happens as if the world, man, and man-in-the-world succeeded in realizing only a missing God." And he makes the connection explicit: "Everything happens therefore as if the in-itself and the for-itself were presented in a state of disintegration in relation to an ideal synthesis. Not that the integration has ever *taken place* but on the contrary precisely because it is always indicated and always impossible" (623). Even though Sartre is talking here about the hiatus between the for-itself (self-consciousness) and in-itself (the object, the Other), the principle is no different from that regarding individual consciousnesses as such. In concluding his discussion of Hegel, Sartre could state plainly and unequivocally, "So long as consciousnesses exist, the separation and conflict of consciousnesses will remain; we shall simply have discovered their foundation and their true terrain" (244). With this truncated Hegel, we are back to Schopenhauer.

Not entirely. Sartre has—and knows he has—arrested the Hegelian dialectic, and his theory takes this situation into account. This is what is meant when he speaks of an integration *always indicated* though never attained. The synthesis is "indicated" by dialectical logic for multiple self-consciousnesses (or for the self-conscious and the Other) but the process has been "short-circuited"; the elements "are held together without being able to be united in a synthesis which surpasses them and justifies them"; each element remains individually autonomous (623).

The idea of God as *en sui causa,* a totality in which the for-itself and in-itself are fused into a true unity (the In-itself-for-itself), represents an ideal. Accordingly, disillusion on the loss of God reveals the world as a "disintegrated ensemble" or "detotalized totality." In a sense this conception is analogous to Camus's theory that the Absurd is a result of man's regarding the world with an *expectation* of order while actually perceiving it as a chaos; because of his "nostalgia" or memory of a past unity, the world appears to him, as well, as a disintegrated whole—or better, since the process of questioning the world is continuous, it appears as a perpetually disintegrat*ing* whole.

Whatever the case, the implications for social thought are clear: Sartre's world remains predicated on the individual, who being irreducible to identity with any other individuals, cannot be synthesized into a community or social whole. But this was not to be Sartre's last word on the subject. Interestingly enough, during his monumental attempt to "update" Marxism or "correct" its deficiencies, in *Critique de la raison dialectique,* the whole conception was reduced to merely a stage in the development of individuals into groups and groups into communities. In the "lowest" form of organization, individuals are united only as a series of Others by an "inert object which gathers [them] about itself, and holds them there as inert and alienated from themselves."[2] Such unity, primitive as it is, is possible only because in this situation individuals, originally autonomous and irreducible to one another, are all treated as objects and therefore are in fact made reducible.

Seriality has some fundamental characteristics in common with Heidegger's idea of the inauthentic form of "being-with," (*Mit-Sein*) an ideal that Sartre had to refute, along with Hegel's, for its ontological optimism. As Sartre explains it, *Mit-Sein* is the mode of being (or being-in-the-world) that characterizes "human-reality": it "expresses. . . . a sort of ontological solidarity for the exploitation of this world. . . . The Other is not an *object.* In his connection with me he remains a human-reality" (245). For Sartre, who challenges the validity of substituting being-with for being-for (cooperation for conflict, to put it simply) as the basis of human relations, all Heidegger has done is to make "a simple affirmation without foundation." It is not enough that Heidegger asserts that authentic *Mit-Sein* must be earned, that in the inauthentic mode (ordinary life) being-with reveals itself "not as the relation of one unique personality with other personalities equally unique. . . . but as a total interchangeability." One is an Everybody whose anonymity is reflected in a world of "ready-made clothes, common means of transportation, parks, gardens, public places . . ." (246). As I have suggested, in the *Critique* Sartre could see this condition as one that would be surpassed, but here in *L'Etre et le néant,* it had only an ontologically useless ideal as an alternative. How could it under these circumstances be called "inauthentic" or do anything but reaffirm, if only by default, that conflict, not *Mit-Sein,* was the mode of being of human reality?

Ontological analysis led Sartre to the same general conclusion to which metaphysics led Schopenhauer—that life is characterized by endless conflict. As we have seen, Schopenhauer, by positing a noumenal in contradistinction to a phenomenal world, could envision a personal salvation, in which one achieved serenity through ascetic or aesthetic contemplation, while the rest of the world was left to go its own way. He resolved the ethical questions that rose from the fact of injustice and suffering with the principle of Eternal Justice, the notion that men created their own hell and that each could receive only what he deserved. Sartre, on the other hand, maintaining that mankind and each man was absolutely responsible for its and his actions, seemed to be taking the opposite course, and in fact he was, except that once again his logic would bring him full circle, at least for the moment.

If conflict is the "mode of being of human reality," so is "freedom" and its ontological equivalent "nothingness." Just as for Schopenhauer the will in man must negate itself as will to separate itself from the world of phenomena and to become pure thought, so for Sartre "consciousness" must "nihilate" (*néantiser*) itself as a being in order to contemplate or reflect upon being in general. That is, being (being-in-itself, things) cannot reflect upon itself; that which reflects upon it therefore must be separate, and to be separate from being is to be nothing. Thus reflective consciousness (being-for-itself) is a nothing; to be nothing is to have an indefinite number of possibilities to choose among, and that is one of the primary definitions of freedom. The ramifications of this conception are both far-reaching and profound.

I shall not attempt to reconstruct Sartre's account, in all its intricate and paradoxical logic, of the ontology of freedom; it will be enough to deal with those aspects that have either a bearing on the fiction we'll be discussing or implications for his social thought at this time.

Now, although Sartre would never accept the Kantian distinction between phenomenal and noumenal worlds, he does, up to a point, distinguish between a world of things or Being (a world in which there is the appearance of determinacy and stability) and the world of (reflective) consciousness or Nothing (associated with contemplation, freedom, and contingency). As I have implied, the division between these two worlds is nowhere nearly so sharp as between that of noumena and phenomena; indeed it would probably be better to regard them as "modes" rather than worlds. In any case, Sartre is not concerned here with Schopenhauer's saints or artists who transcend the world of action to live exclusively in contemplation; for him "to be is to act and to cease to act is to cease to be." Far from shutting out the world of action, the consciousness of freedom is the necessary condition for one's truly acting and not simply undergoing a "series of movements." This situation can be regarded from the viewpoint of the man "immersed" in action or from that of the man given to reflection; here lies the way to the heart of the matter.

For freedom to be freedom, nothing in the world of being can be taken as a cause or motive of action. Men do not act, says Sartre, without having a conception of their situation; it is only when the oppressed worker can "conceive of a different state of affairs" that he "decides" that his sufferings are unbearable. Before he does that, "he suffers without considering his suffering and without conferring value upon it" (435). "It is by a pure wrenching away from himself and the world that the worker can posit his suffering as unbearable suffering and consequently can *make it the motive* for his revolutionary action"

(436). In this way Sartre transfers all motives of action to the reflective consciousness where freedom and nothingness prevail:

> The motive is understood only by the end; that is, by the nonexistent. It is therefore in itself a negatité. . . . Thus the motive makes itself understood as what it is by means of the ensemble of beings which "are not," by ideal existences, and by the future . . . . *It is only because I escape the in-itself by nihilating myself toward my possibilities that this in-itself can take on value as cause or motive.* (437; my italics)

One need not be a Marxist to recognize the phenomenon that Sartre is describing in his example. Is this whole exotic argument reducible to the principle that the consciousness of the workers must be raised before revolutionary action is possible? If so, Sartre has made of this fundamentally social act a personal and individual one, for freedom that does not reside in the individual consciousness is not freedom, just as social consciousness seen in terms of purely individualistic motives is not social consciousness. That this is no casual observation becomes apparent as soon as we examine Sartre's conception of "anguish" (*angoisse*), the mode of being of the reflective man considering his possibilities.

The everyday world, the "immediate" world in which men act without reflection, is filled with requirements, demands, and exigencies that are accepted as such. Nothing is "put into question" in any significant way; we "act before positing our possibilities" and our acts "cause values to spring up like partridges" (38). In reflection, on the other hand, consciousness is the consciousness of freedom: we know that an exigency or a value exists only because in freedom we have chosen to recognize it as such. One is aware, in other words, that his "freedom is the unique foundation of values and that nothing, absolutely nothing, justifies [him] in adopting this or that particular value." As "a being by whom values exist," Sartre adds, "I am unjustifiable." With this knowledge comes "anguish," for in the realization that a given act or project is justified by nothing more than one's free choice to make or pursue it, all is "put into question." We become aware that nothing can compel us to choose or pursue any of our possibilities and that nothing stands in the way of our destroying anything we have done or abandoning any project on which we may be working:

> I emerge alone and in anguish confronting the unique and original project which constitutes my being; all the barriers, all the guard rails [that is, the requirements, demands, and exigencies of the social world] collapse, nihilated by the consciousness of my freedom. I do not have nor can I have recourse to any value against the fact that it is I who sustain values in being. Nothing can ensure me against myself, cut off from the world and my essence by this nothingness which I *am*. I have to realize the meaning of the world and of my essence; I make my decision concerning them—without justification and without excuse. (39)

But not all men can live with the anguish that such responsibility brings, and they attempt to flee from it by reestablishing contact with the world of Being and all the fixity, stability, security, authority, identity, and necessity it offers in exchange for one's freedom. As we shall see shortly, this issue is the mainspring of existential psychoanalysis.

Insofar as it denies that values have any foundation in being, Sartre's theory of freedom is a total rejection of all thought that assumes or refers to the authority of transcendent or established values. Logically, this would include all forms of humanism, not excepting socialism. For it is not only the bourgeois man, Sartre's favorite target, who can be infected with the "esprit de sérieux" in which one "apprehends values in terms of the world and resides in the reassuring materialistic substantiation of values." The social revolutionary, as well, believes he is acting in accordance with higher principles. Thus, Camus, taking the opposite tack, argued that even the isolated and apparently solitary rebellion of a single slave against his master appealed to a principle that transcended the immediate situation; namely, that of solidarity. In positing the individual mind as the source of all meaning and the foundationless foundation of all values, Sartre could recover social values only by a forced marriage of freedom and necessity, and that was a contradiction that no dialectical process could resolve.

In his psychoanalysis of Baudelaire (1947), Sartre alludes to an ideal that he believes has an analogue in the writings of certain social philosophers:

> About 1848 the combined actions of the Saint-Simions, the Positivists and Marx gave birth to the drama of anti-nature. The expression "anti-nature" was actually invented by Comte; and in the Marx-Engels correspondence we find the term *antiphysic*. The doctrines may be different, but the ideal was the same: it was to inaugurate a human order which would be directly opposed to the errors, injustices and blind mechanical forces of the natural world. . . . (*Baudelaire,* 103)

For Baudelaire, Sartre tells us, nature "was a vast, warm abundant force which penetrated everywhere. He had a horror of this damp warmth, this abundance." And Sartre elaborates the principle behind this condition: "If a man becomes frightened in the presence of nature, it is because he feels he has been trapped in an immense, amorphous, gratuitous existence which completely freezes him by its gratuitousness. He no longer has *his* place anywhere; he is planted on the earth without a goal, without a *raison d'être"* (106).

What Sartre is describing here is not precisely "anguish" if one means by this term the consciousness of freedom and the self-doubt that arises with the realization of one's total responsibility in judging the meaning and value of one's acts. Rather it is anguish once-removed, just as, in a sense, the consciousness of gratuity (*la contingence)* is at one remove from the consciousness of freedom. The condition is *nausea,* well-named in that unlike anguish it begins as a revulsion from the physical world. As a malady it can lead nowhere; it ends where anguish begins. Thus whereas anguish is a prelude to action founded on the knowledge of gratuity-as-freedom, nausea is no more than the result of the apprehension of gratuity as such (contingency). It is true that Antoine Roquentin, the complex hero of *La Nausée*, takes a certain joy in experiencing the gratuity of objects in that he gains a knowledge of reality denied the pragmatic bourgeoisie, whom he despises. Sartre himself, as Simone de Beauvoir tells it, delighted in wandering through Le Havre observing the surrealistic transformations of the things around him. Unlike the surrealists, however, who could abandon themselves to a "derealized" world and idealize the realms of dream and madness, Sartre was too much the rational man to deny the horror of what was happening to Roquentin. And indeed it is Roquentin's essential rationality—apparent, for example, in his scholarly sensitivity to historical and geographical details—that makes his encounter with gratuitous existence all the more severe while paradoxically offering one of the few means of relief.

Like Camus's Meursault, Roquentin both speaks for and enacts a philosophy that is the author's own. His hallucinations and apathy can no doubt be regarded as the manifestations of a psychotic personality, but, again, since Sartre was not concerned with presenting a character that was merely a case history, the judgment is irrelevant. This does not mean, however, that we cannot question, through Roquentin (as through Meursault), the philosophy itself in the light of what it purports to be. Lukács, for example, has argued that "modernist" writers, among whom he includes all writers who portray the world as a chaos with "angst" as a prevailing response, not only distort human nature and relationships, but attribute the distortion to reality itself. "It is easy to understand," he argues, "that the experience of the contemporary capitalist world does produce, especially among intellectuals, *angst*, nausea, a sense of isolation, and despair." The trouble comes from making these feelings universal or part of a human condition. Whatever reservations one might have about this position in general, it does at least suggest, I believe, a legitimate approach to Roquentin.

For one thing, metaphysical nausea is in fact an intellectual's malady; Sartre himself indicated as much when he had Baudelaire turn to work per se as a means for relieving his pervasive sense of gratuity. But this is as it should be since anguish, which as we have seen goes beyond nausea, is identified with "reflective consciousness." On the other hand, *Baudelaire* appeared in 1947; Sartre's perspective was no longer what it was in 1938 when he wrote *La Nausée*. Furthermore, he was presenting Baudeliare as the subject of a biography, not as a fictional hero who was intended to be wholly sympathetic and whose discoveries about the nature of the world and himself were to be seen as authentic.

In this sense, who and what Roquentin is does matter. It matters, for instance, that he is not only *de trop* in that all men are superfluous, that all existence is without justification, but also in that he has literally never participated in socially purposeful activity and therefore has no basis for making an authentic generalization. Thus we learn that he first experiences nausea in the office of a functionary in Indochina, but that he doesn't really know what brought him to the colony or kept him there. "When I left France," he tells us, "there were a lot of people who said I left for a whim. And when I suddenly came back after six years of travelling, they still could call it a 'whim' [*un coup de tête*]" (*Nausea*, 12). The source of nausea is a "little Khmer statuette," which "seemed to me unpleasant and stupid and I felt terribly, deeply bored. I couldn't understand why I was in Indo-China." Obviously, this statement was intended neither by Sartre nor Roquentin to raise any questions about the French presence in Indochina; the sensation is wholly metaphysical and personal; the statue is gratuitous and induces an ennui associated with meaninglessness. That is why we can ask legitimately whether Roquentin's response does not bespeak his own simple ignorance. Has he learned anything at all about the culture in which he finds himself? Has he done anything that is worth remembering? I do not think I am begging the question here or missing the point. If his past is meaningless, it is so not only because all human pasts are meaningless, but because his specifically has been so. If he cannot confer meaning upon it, the fault lies not in the human condition but in himself.

The same situation pertains in Roquentin's futile efforts with the biography of the Marquis de Rollebon, an adventurer and diplomatic intriguist of the Napoleonic era. The life of this figure is scarcely an adequate test for the view that all history is irrecoverable or that accurate knowledge of it is impossible. It is certainly no criterion for the thesis that history is gratuitous. We know that Roquentin's labors are more formal than substantive. His research, at least temporarily, places him in the realm of logic, necessity, and reason that represents an escape from the contingency of the world that surrounds him. The biography is intended to be the same antidote to nausea as the song, "Some of These Days," that, played repeatedly on a café phonograph, induces a sense of necessity. Roquentin's effort to piece together Rollebon's story is really an intellectual exercise and reflects no deeper commitment than curiosity. It is merely a puzzle that, able to be completed but imperfectly, can be abandoned and relegated to contingency. Roquentin's historical descriptions of Bouville and his sketches of those enshrined in the muncipal museum are, in their irony, far from implying that nothing significant can be said about the past. Even so, these do not represent any salvation, metaphysical or otherwise, for the author.

Roquentin's mistress, Anny, from whom he has been separated for four years, has followed a parallel course in that she, too, has come to see life as wholly gratuitous. She also seeks to order the past ("I live in the past. I take everything that has happened to me and arrange it" [204]) and has had a theory of "privileged situations" and "perfect moments," inspired by a selection of illustrations in Michelet's *History of France,* that corresponds to Roquentin's notion of "adventures." Both conceptions are founded on the idealist view that historical reconstruction (order) is imposed by the reflecting mind and never recaptures what was actually lived. Or better, instead of trying to find significance in the events of the past, Roquentin and

Anny both try to "invent" highpoints that are an inherent source of enjoyment (or else an antidote to nausea). The "privileged situation," the situation in Michelet's *History* selected as the subject of one of the few full-page illustrations, has for Anny a self-contained "grandeur," "a rare and precious quality," accentuated by its separation in the volume from the text that describes it. Such situations in one's life become the material for "perfect moments." Thus lifted out of the chaos that is historical reality, elements of the past are redeemed from gratuity.

Anny, no less than Roquentin, knows that she is dealing in illusions. Her career as an actress and her current life as a woman of dubious means travelling aimlessly throughout the world reflect a sense of lost identity and a general cynicism even more profound than that of her former lover. Roquentin himself is to her no more than a measure or a constant, a mere antidote to anxiety over gratuitousness, an ex-lover whose image is worth more than his person. Capable of saving him—for his feelings toward her are still strong—she plunges him even deeper into his metaphysical quagmire.

Indeed, love returned might have offered Roquentin more than the merely formal and temporary antidote afforded by "Some of These Days," although such a denouement would have made a shambles of the whole philosophic structure of the novel. Still, by his defense of the Self-Taught Man in the library, Roquentin does illustrate that he is capable of acting with both passion and compassion. Does this act hold the real solution to his agony? The metaphysical solution—he is going to acquire an identity and achieve a sense of necessity by writing a novel—does not represent much of an advance over the Rollebon biography; failing to show any commitment to subject matter, its proposal remains within the limits of a formal exercise. But when Roquentin grabs the "Corsican" by the neck and lifts him up after the latter has driven his fist into the face of the Self-Taught Man, he is never more sound of mind and body, nor less superfluous as a human being. Camus might have seen in this deed a declaration of Roquentin's "solidarity" with other men. This is the very lesson that the Self-Taught Man had learned when he was a prisoner of war and of whom Roquentin was contemptuous. Thus the incident, far from revealing anything to Roquentin about himself and the social world, bespeaks nothing more than an "adventure" soon to be forgotten. Roquentin would go on to his final antidote for nausea and it would turn into poison. Sartre would go on to his own prison camp and new discoveries about the human condition.

5 Sartre II
Perpetually Disintegrating Ensemble: France, 1938-40

In 1964 Sartre lamented that when he wrote *La Nausée* he was lacking a "sens de la réalité." "I've changed since then," he told his interviewer. "I've had a slow apprenticeship to the real. I've seen children die of hunger. Compared to a dying child, *Nausea* is without significance." Next to social ills, he added, metaphysical ones are a luxury (Contat and Rybalka, 64). Apparently, this slow apprenticeship to the real actually began when Sartre was called up in September 1939. "This was what made the social aspect enter my mind," he explains in "Self-Portrait at Seventy":

> I suddenly understood that I was a social being when I saw myself torn from where I was, taken away from the people who mattered to me, and put on a train . . . with other fellows who did not want to go any more than I did. . . . I saw something I shared. . . . Through this mobilization I had to encounter the negation of my freedom in order to become aware of the weight of the world and my ties with all the others and their ties with me. (*Situations,* 48)

But it was the war itself and his experiences in a prison camp that taught him the full significance of solidarity: "It was then . . . that I abandoned my prewar individualism and the idea of the pure individual and adopted the social individual and socialism. That was the turning point of my life" (48). Yet even as early as 1938 Sartre had concluded that nihilism alone was not enough and he envisioned in the trilogy he was planning a "profonde reconstruction morale de l'individu, d'une véritable resurrection, de la nausée à l'ardeur, du suicide au goût de la vie, de la vie unique, irréversible, libre" (65). Roquentin would indeed learn the meaning of metaphysical freedom and social commitment, even though he would first have to surrender his personal freedom in a social unheaval to do so.

In his literary magnum opus, *Les Chemins de la liberté* (*The Roads to Liberty*), a series of novels he abandoned in the middle of the fourth volume, Sartre attempted to mark out the paths to what salvation, personal and social, was possible in a gratuitous world—paths that proved to be circular or tortuous until an overwhelming social crisis clarified one's course of action. True to the idea, elaborated in *L'Etre et le néant,* that conflict is "the mode of being of human reality," these novels presuppose that the natural condition of men is egocentricity and that relations are marked by struggle and misunderstanding. This is the context in which the problems that had their origins in ontological freedom were dramatized.

In *L'Etre et le néant,* as we have seen, Sartre had asserted that to be conscious of freedom meant that a person was aware that he alone was responsible for whatever acts he projected, since he alone could confer value and meaning on them; to reflect was to put all in question, including oneself—hence, the inevitability of anguish. Ideally, consciousness of freedom is a prelude to action, but it can lead to paralysis and the "flight from anguish" in which one attempts, by various subterfuges, to find the security offered by the world of laws, necessity, and clear-cut judgments. Even from the purely ontological viewpoint, then, freedom not only offers a multitude of choices, but requires that a choice be made. As Sartre put it succinctly in *Qu'est-ce que la littérature (What Is Literature?),* "Freedom is not enjoyed by its experiencing its free subjective functioning, but in a creative act required by an imperative" (48). This is how he saw the problem in regard to *The Roads to Liberty:*

> *Age de la raison* and *Le Sursis* [the first two novels] are only an inventory of false, mutilated, and incomplete forms of freedom, a description of the *aporia* of liberty. Only in *La Dernière chance* are the conditions of true liberty defined. (Grisoli, "Interview"; see also Contat and Rybalka, 115)

As the stories of Mathieu and Daniel clearly illustrate, pure subjective freedom, unable to find a route to action, is a nightmare of perpetual uncertainty and indecision—of anguish, in short. Yet the distinction between "false liberties" and "true liberation" suggests that there is something more at issue here than the presence of anguish. Indeed, Sartre is referring not just to Mathieu's inability to act in general, but his failure to find, and commit himself to, a socially purposeful cause. Thus Sartre envisions the redemption of Mathieu in his eventual participation in the Resistance and sees his willingness to die under torture as his definitive commitment.

As Simone de Beauvoir said in her outline of the projected last volume, Mathieu was "héroique non par essence mais parce qu'il s'était fait héros" (Contat et Rybalka, 221). We cannot but agree with this doctrinally correct observation. The question then becomes is Mathieu heroic because he makes himself a hero or because his act is inherently heroic? Is the way in which one decides to act the critical factor in determining whether one has acted in true freedom, or does the nature of the act itself have something to do with it? If the latter, is Sartre implying that certain acts are self-evidently good or evil? And if that is the case, aren't such acts a limitation on freedom, since, if the situation arises, freedom is limited to a single choice and therefore ceases to be free? Or can freedom refuse to choose good and still be "véritable"?

Thus, we learn from both de Beauvoir and Sartre that there are indeed "unambiguous" situations—the German occupation of Paris, for example, during which, as de Beauvoir says, "on avait su sans équivoque comment se conduire." Yet this fact devalues Mathieu's achievement precisely because it indicates that his choice was obvious. "The situation was too simple," Sartre explained to Kenneth Tynan, who had asked him whether it was true he had abandoned his novel about the Resistance (*La Dernière chance*): "One's allegiances were obvious. . . . To write a novel whose hero dies in the Resistance committed to the idea of liberty would be much too easy. Nowadays, commitment is altogether harder to define." Thus "libération véritable" is negated by its own contradictions.

We can appreciate Sartre's dilemma. Logically, he had to posit an ideal form of freedom if he were to account for his experiences during the war, and even from a general philosophic viewpoint. But like any ideal actually achieved (only more so), that of "libération véritable," representing as it does "total deliverance," is fundamentally incompatible with Sartre's tenet that no man can be judged or "totally delivered" so long as he is alive and therefore still making choices. As we shall see shortly, man cannot *be* anything—cannot acquire a fixed identity or character or be wholly equated with a function —since to do so would be to exist only in the realm of things. And that includes being a hero. With the return of the world to normality, freedom reenters the gray area of ambiguity, its proper environment, and heroes made during the war are in danger of unmaking themselves. Thus like the multiple consciousnesses through which it is expressed, although it constantly seeks to surpass itself in a final, ideal synthesis, freedom, by its own nature, can never transcend the "detotalized totality" that makes it what it is and what it is not.

And, in fact, as *Le Sursis (The Reprieve)* makes clear, Sartre still viewed society as the "disintegrating ensemble" that detotalized totality was:

> A vast entity, a planet, in a space of a hundred million dimensions; three dimensional beings could not so much as imagine

it. And yet each dimension was an autonomous consciousness. Try to look directly at that planet, it would disintegrate into tiny fragments, and nothing but consciousness would be left . . . each constructing its destiny on its own responsibility. And yet each of these consciousnesses, by imperceptible contacts and insensible changes, realizes its existence as a cell in a gigantic and invisible coral. (*The Reprieve,* 252)

Coral is an accurate enough image to describe an amorphous existant actually definable only as a collection of atoms and not as an organic unity. The characters of *Le Sursis,* purportedly a cross-section of France in 1939, are united only in their anxiety over imminent war, a negative phenomenon depicted as a contingency that bears no relation to forces inherent in the society.

It is one thing to view social disunity from a perspective that has a relatively clear idea of what constitutes a cohesive society possible of attainment; it is quite another to view social disunity as an inevitable part of the human condition, as did Sartre during this period. Here, for example, is a sociological explanation of the divisiveness that literally exists in French society:

> If the peoples of northwestern Europe appear to be blessed with the gift of pragmatism and cooperativeness, and the French afflicted with the disease of "intellectualism" and "individualism," the reason may be found less in their respective national "characters" than in their contrasting social structures and the different sets of values these structures have evolved. Political consensus—the absence of political extremism—can be viewed as a reflection, rather than a cause, of social cohesion; conversely, lack of consensus betrays lack of social equilibrium and harmony.

What is really lacking in France—as opposed, for instance, to the Scandinavian countries—is an

> integration of individuals and groups into society both through participation in the life of the collectivity and through adequate

2. The Totalities of Existentialism

channels of communication and of promotion, whether individual or collective. (Micaud, 20)

The detotalization that characterizes France, adequately portrayed in *Le Sursis,* can be seen, then, as a particularly cultural, and not necessarily a metaphysical or universal, phenomenon. But neither explicitly nor by implication does Sartre's novel present an ideal of social cohesion that would make the situation of *Le Sursis* primarily historical and national rather than an inevitability of human life in general.

It is de Beauvoir's thesis that "an ethics of ambiguity will be one which will refuse to deny *a priori* that separate existants can, at the same time, be bound to each other, that their individual freedoms can forge laws valid for all." But this belief was contained in Sartre's *L'Etre et la néant* and de Beauvoir develops no genuine social theory beyond the view that individual freedoms authentically realized will result in some ideal condition. The point of departure is still the human atom. In his critique of Sartre, Herbert Marcuse implied that the logical point of departure was quite elsewhere:

> The activities, attitudes, and efforts which circumscribe [man's] concrete existence are, in the last analysis, not his but those of his class, profession, position, society. In this sense is the life of the individual indeed the life of the universal, but this universal is a configuration of specific historical forces, made up by the various groups, interests, institutions, etc., which form the social reality. The concepts which actually reach the concrete existence must therefore derive from a theory of society. (*Studies in Critical Philosophy,* 188)

But *The Ethics of Ambiguity* inverts this view; de Beauvoir argues that the existentialist is not interested in man "merely as a member of a class, a nation, or collectivity, but as an individual man." She says, for example, that if "the satisfaction of an old man drinking a glass of wine counts for nothing, then production and wealth are only hollow myths; they have meaning only if they are capable of being retrieved in individual and living joy." That may well be, but can such an appraisal distinguish between a universal old man, who is socially neutral, and one who is, say, a mine owner sitting down to a sumptuous lunch while his workers are starving (as in Zola's *Germinal*)?

Whatever the case, *Le Sursis,* a novel adapting the techniques of Dos Passos to provide a kaleidoscopic view of France during the last week of September 1938, is a work of individual situations affected by the threat of war. As we might expect, human relations are regarded not from a sociological point of view, but from that of existential psychology and ontology, which offers, as one of its archetypes, the master-slave conflict in which one attempts to dominate (captivate, transcend the freedom of) the Other by fixing him in a stare or look (*le regard*) that reduces him to an object. (The Other will attempt to reassert his freedom and his humanity by returning the look, thereby "transcending the transcendence.")

Again, this phenomenon is not a matter of class, race, or group; it is universal among men. The case of Charles, the invalid, whose situation in a social novel could be regarded as eccentric, here represents, in extremis, a fundamental human problem. Sartre has described him this way:

> Il est un object, il est un pot de fleurs. Sa vie sans avenir est une vie morte, privée de sans dimension essentielle: celle des actes. Voilá pourquoi il est tenté d'établir avec ces verticaux [normal persons] qui sont comme le visage de sa servitude des rapports qui les réduisent eux-memes au rang d'instruments, des rapports humiliants, des rapports par le bas. (Grisoli, 7)

Aboard a freight train on which a sexually mixed group of invalids is being evacuated, Charles refuses to give in to his bodily needs by calling for a bed pan. Sartre explains this act as an effort "pour vaincre sons corps, pour en surmonter les besoins . . . pour accéder à l'humain." Although he is here successful, his story ends with a defeat: he is carried off the train without having learned the last name of Catherine, a fellow invalid with whom he had begun to develop a relationship that made him feel like a complete man. He is tossed about like a parcel by the stretcher-bearers, who ignore his pleas.

That this is a prototypical situation is made clear in the story in Phillipe Grisaignes, a feckless adolescent pacifist, who rebelling against his oppressive stepfather, General Lescaze, plans to flee to Switzerland to avoid mobilization. His adventures include a frenzied encounter with a working-class couple, whom he overhears making love in the hotel room next to his own, during which he attempts to persuade the man to flee with him rather than obey his conscription orders; a detour to a nightclub brothel where he is taken to bed by a black girl and later, while asleep, shown off to her friend and temporarily held captive by being deprived of his clothes; and a street-corner denunciation of war in which he barely escapes a beating at the hands of an irate crowd. Consistently treated with contempt, just as Charles is consistently treated as an object, Phillipe struggles vainly for manhood, identity, and freedom in an oppressive environment. He suffers a culminating humiliation when, trying to give himself up as a deserter, he is merely turned over to the general. The inability to act, to exert one's freedom or will in the world, is endemic up and down the social scale. It characterizes the illiterate shepherd, Gros-Louis, who, having come to Marseille, survives beating and robbery only to discover he has been called up; and it characterizes the prime minister, Daladier, who finds himself forced by circumstances and irresolution into committing France to the Munich agreements.

The political situation in 1938 follows the prototype of the personal situation. Reneging on their commitments to Czechoslovakia, the allied diplomats are forced to regard the country as no more than a political entity or object that can be carved up. (With a heavy hand, Sartre simultaneously describes the treatment of one of the female characters, Ivich, as a sexual object.) Equally significant is that we are led to believe that France, in the persons of Daladier and his cabinet, is, in a sense, trying to realize its own freedom (further its interests, maintain its honor, exert its will) in its negotiations with Britain and Nazi Germany. Just as all the characters in the novel fail, France fails. Sartre is faithful to the historical circumstances, but it just so happened that the historical circumstances could be made to fit the existential description of personal conduct. Daladier's remark on being given a hero's welcome when he returns from Berchtesgaden ("Les cons"—"The Goddamned fools!") is historically accurate but no less does it reveal the lucidity and impotence that he shares with other men in Sartre's world.

I don't mean to suggest here that Sartre was personifying France. He explicitly said that he wanted to avoid "speaking of a crowd or a nation as a single person by lending it tastes, wishes, and displays, as Zola did in *Germinal*." In *Le Sursis* he set out to write a social novel: one in which individual histories, clearly partitioned in *L'Age de la raison*, became part of a greater context through the war scare. But, again, he could view that context only by the metaphor of coral. He succeeded in his aim to describe "le marasme français des années entre deux guerres" and the disarray apparent in the "sursis dérisoire de Munich." But he saw this whole as the sum of individual parts; he did not analyze the historical and social conditions that made the individuals what they were. How could he have when the principle of freedom meant that historical and social conditions didn't make individuals what they were in the first place, that it was just the other way around?

In his obsession with freedom, Mathieu Delarue, the central character of *L'Age de la raison*, cannot accept his brother Jacques's accusation that, for all his notions, he lives like a bourgeois and in fact is no more than a hypocrite. The matter is left ambiguous. Sartre characterized the bourgeoisie in *La Nausée* by its self-deluded "seriousness"—its false belief in its past, its conventions, and its "right to command." A bourgeois was a man who believed in established authority and the absolute nature of middle-class institutions, was ignorant of the gratuity that lay behind all things, and had no idea of the real meaning of freedom. Putting nothing into question, especially

100   2. The Totalities of Existentialism

not himself, he existed wholly on the level of being-in-itself. A Marxist would say definitively that Mathieu is a petit-bourgeois intellectual—and so indeed would a bourgeois, like his brother. But in existential terms Mathieu is everything the bourgeois is not and nothing that he is. For he is not only conscious of freedom but is the very personification of reflective consciousness: "he saw himself exposed and as he was: thoughts, thoughts about thoughts, thoughts about thoughts of thoughts" (*Age of Reason,* 189). Accordingly, "he could not sink his consciousness [by getting drunk] . . . if he lost grip of himself for an instant, he would suddenly find within his head, astray and drifting like a summer haze, the thought of a fly or a cockroach" (188–89). Mathieu's mental grip on himself is the substitute for action to a man who lives chiefly a life of the mind, and to lose that is to be hurled into oblivion in the fullest sense of the word, since there is nothing else by which he can be defined.

"Condemned forever to be free" means "condemned to decide without support from any quarter" (276), but for Mathieu it also means condemned not to decide and never to know certainty of self, a state of perpetual anguish in which freedom cannot be completed by act or nothingness by being. Thus, Mathieu projects upon the world no apprehensible character or identity; his being-for-others is an enigma. Lola Montero, the cabaret singer, aptly says of him, "Mathieu makes everyone uncomfortable because he's neither fish nor fowl, you don't know how to take him" (27). His friend Daniel Sereno completely misinterprets his nature: "Here was a man who found it quite natural to exist, he did not ask himself any questions, that light, so Greek and so impartial, that uncorrupted sky, were made for him, he was at home, he had never been alone" (67). As we have seen, Jacques defines his brother wholly in terms of appearances:

> I should myself have thought . . . that freedom consisted in frankly confronting situations into which one has deliberately entered, and accepting all one's responsibilities. But that, no

doubt, is not your view: you condemn capitalist society, and yet you are an official in that society; you display an abstract sympathy with Communists, but you take care not to commit yourself, you have never voted. You despise the bourgeois class, and yet you are a bourgeois, son and brother of a bourgeois, and you live like a bourgeois." (118)

In a bout of uncertainty, Mathieu concludes that "the sole freedom left to me is the desire to be what I am." But not really knowing what he is, he tries to come to a decision in his relations with his pregnant mistress:

"My sole freedom is—to want to marry Marcelle." He was so weary of being tossed about among conflicting currents that he almost felt relieved. He clenched his fists, and addressing himself with the gravity of a grown-up person, a bourgeois, a man of the world, and a family man, said: "I *want* to marry Marcelle."
Pah! These were words, it was a childish, empty choice. "This, too," he thought, "this too is a lie." (244)

That Mathieu's problem is an exaggerated version of that endured by all men is implied in Sartre's distinction between the consciousness of external objects (the prereflexive cogito) and consciousness of one's own consciousness (authentic reflection) to explain one of the major patterns of "bad faith," an elusive conception that bears the same relation to "falsehood" that anguish bears to mere "fear." When one acts with self-reflection, he sees himself in a certain role and to do so is in effect to impersonate that role. That is, when a man is too conscious of what he is doing, he begins to play-act, but more, as observer and actor, he suffers a bifurcation that would not be suffered by a creature acting without self-consciousness—a dog, for instance, who acts spontaneously and without the awareness that he is a dog. "If a man is what he is," asks Sartre in *Being and Nothingness,* "bad faith is forever impossible. . . . But is a man what he is? And more generally, how can he *be* what he is when he exists as a consciousness of being?" (58–59).

2. The Totalities of Existentialism

For Mathieu the problem is acute, since he is not only aware of himself as he acts, but fully understands the ontology involved. That is, a defining characteristic of bad faith is that one does not know he is acting in bad faith—at least most men don't. But Mathieu does, or rather he is capable of posing the question, with the result that he is in a perpetual state of anxiety over whether he is impersonating or acting authentically, that what in most men would be a flight from anguish is in him yet another source of it:

> "Am I not impersonating a wash-out? . . . And yet," he thought, "it's quite true I'm a wash-out." Around him it was just the same: there were people who did not exist at all, mere puffs of smoke, and others who existed rather too much. The bartender, for instance. A little while ago he had been smoking a cigarette, as vague and poetic as a flowering creeper; now he had awakened, he was rather *too much* the bartender, manipulating his shaker, opening it, and tipping yellow froth into glasses with slightly superfluous precision: he was impersonating a bartender. . . . "Perhaps it's inevitable; perhaps one has to choose between being nothing at all and impersonating what one is. That would be terrible," he said to himself; "it would mean that we were naturally bogus."[1] (195)

Mathieu's hyperintellectuality and its consequences are thrown into relief by the response to the world of Ivich, the sister of Boris Serguine, a student of Mathieu at the lycée who has developed a friendship with his teacher. Mathieu has a vague romantic interest in Ivich but she is inconsistently responsive to him, and it is precisely his intellectuality that puts her off. Unlike Mathieu, whose "thoughts about thoughts of thoughts" keep him at a remove from the facticity of the world, Ivich is a creature of feeling who has no mental protection against the impact of being-in-itself. Rather she is like Roquentin, whose own rationality began to crumble, wholly susceptible to the encroachment of objects:

> Mathieu eyed the glass with irritation, he set himself to observe the thick, ungraceful agitation of the liquid, the turbid

whiteness of the ice cube. In vain. For Ivich it was a little viscous delight that made her sticky down to her fingertips; for him it was nothing. Less than nothing: a glass full of mint. He could *think* what Ivich felt but he never felt anything; for her, objects were oppressive, insinuating presences, eddies that entered into her very flesh, but Mathieu always saw them from a distance. (62-63)

And when asked, typically, by Mathieu, "What are you thinking about?" she typically replies, "You're always asking me that. Nothing definite. Things that can't be expressed, there are no words for them" (63). Thus Mathieu yearns to feel things, yearns to be of use, yearns for authentic commitment. On reading of the bombing of Valencia in Spain, for example, he wants to be angry:

> There were thousands of men in France who had not been able to read their paper that morning without feeling a clot of anger rise in their throats, thousands of men who had clenched their fists and muttered: "Swine!" Mathieu clenched his fists and muttered: "Swine!" and felt himself still more guilty. If at least he had been able to discover in himself a trifling emotion that was veritably if modestly alive, conscious of its limits. But no: he was empty, he was confronted by a vast anger, a desperate anger. . . . But it was inert—if it were to live and find expression and suffer, he must lend it his own body. (123-24)

A genuine emotion begins to stir in him, only to collapse, and he concludes, pathetically, "One can't force one's deeper emotions."

The basic plot of *L'Age de la raison* concerns Mathieu's futile attempts to acquire the money for a reliable abortionist for his mistress, Marcelle. He broods over the question of whether or not he ought to marry her but finally steals the money from Lola, and presents it to Marcelle, who meanwhile has been made to realize by Daniel that she really wants the child and marriage. She is led to believe that Mathieu will accede but when he appears with the money, this illusion vanishes and she turns him out. The truth is that Mathieu does not know whether he loves the woman with whom he's been sleeping for seven years, and she, knowing his temperament, will not make any demands upon him. This is precisely Mathieu's fate in general: the man who does not know whether to commit himself is not counted on by others; not being counted on, he feels unneeded and is all the more confirmed in his lack of commitment.

Thus, like Roquentin, Mathieu is the superfluous man. Brunet, the communist, uses exactly the wrong arguments in his attempt to get him to join the party: " 'And let us get this quite clear: the party doesn't need you. To the party you represent nothing but a little capital of intelligence—and we've got all the intellectuals we want. But you need the party' " (130). This restates the familiar problem: "So you think I need to commit myself?" Mathieu replies, and he knows what he has to gain: "flesh, blood and genuine passions." The circle remains unbroken; Mathieu requires passion to commit himself in the first place; ratiocination alone will bring him neither to Spain nor to the party. In his case, freedom chooses freedom; that is to say, *nothing*. Had Brunet been able to convince him that he was really needed by the party, rather than the opposite, the appeal might have been more effective (though it would have gone against the policy of the party, which at this time did in fact mistrust the intellectuals). When he feels he is needed, Mathieu (like Roquentin) is quite prepared to spring into action. It is he who retrieves Boris's love letters to Lola when she is believed dead and it is he who tries to rescue Ivich from herself when she learns she has failed her examinations.

The first act requires mere daring and is negated by Lola's turning out to be alive after all. The second requires compassion and, in light of Mathieu's relation with Ivich, something more. Mathieu offers to support Ivich in Paris so that she will not have to return to the intolerable conditions of provincial life with her family—and this offer can only be interpreted as a commitment. But even here the combination of his uncertainty and Ivich's response to it makes a shambles of the matter. After making his offer to her, he announces that he will marry Marcelle. Ivich reacts with rancor, and he rushes from the apartment to steal the money for the abortion. He brings the money to Marcelle and is rejected; he then returns to the apartment to find Ivich still present. Encouraged by her sympathy for his forlornness, he draws her to him but suddenly releases her, asserting, "I don't know what I want from you" (321). She responds accordingly and explains away her willingness to yield to him: "You looked so proud of having made a decision, I thought you had come for a reward." "But I love you, Ivich," Mathieu replies, still unconvincingly. And Ivich answers, more convincingly, "I don't love you." Ivich cannot love a man who lacks feeling and decision; Mathieu cannot have real feelings when he is not deeply loved or needed or otherwise motivated to give up his freedom. Condemned to freedom, he is condemned to superfluity: "this life had been given him for nothing, he was nothing, and yet he would not change: he was as he was made" (342).

By this assertion Mathieu means, I assume, that his essence is freedom or nothingness (the only "essence" possible in Sartre's thought), but whatever that signifies in the Paris of 1938, it will signify something else in the Lorraine of spring 1940 (*Morte dans l'âme*) when Mathieu decides to participate in a virtually suicidal, rear-guard action against the invading Germans. War is not really the recommended solution to anyone's problems, but only something as momentous could break the closed circle of freedom that was Mathieu's consciousness.

"In the field of my reflection," writes Sartre, "I can never meet with anything but the consciousness which is mine. But the Other is the indispensable mediator between myself and me. . . . By the mere appearance of the Other, I am put in the position of passing judgment on myself as an object, for it is as an object that I appear to the Other" (*Being and Nothingness*, 221-22). And farther on he tells us, "It is through the mediacy of the world that they ["thinking substances"] communicate. My body as a thing in the world and the Other's body are the necessary intermediaries between the Other's consciousness and mine" (223). The problem Sartre is talking about here is "shame," a feeling in which "I recognize that I *am* as the Other sees me." The exposure of one's nudity to the gaze of the Other is a prototype of human relations in general, in which persons struggle to reduce each other to objects by means of a judging "look."

There is, however, a psychological complication, more explicit in *L'Age de la raison* than in the above passage. Since one can never know exactly how the Other sees him, he can experience shame by *imagining* how the Other sees him. Thus instead of the Other actually judging him, he in fact judges himself through the Other. Here is Mathieu torturing himself after he has left Marcelle's room on hearing of her pregnancy:

> Marcelle had not let him go: she was thinking of him, and this was what she thought: "The dirty dog, he's let me down. He forgot himself inside me like a little boy who wets his bed." . . . It was intolerable to be judged, and hated, away back in that room, and in silence. Without power to defend himself, or even to hide his belly with his hands. If only in the same second, he had been able to exist *for others* with the same intensity. (*Age of Reason*, 17)

Mathieu needs to judge himself through others because, as we have seen, others cannot "pin him down" or judge him directly. This is true of all men insofar as judgments are, like motives and causes, determinants and no determinant can originate in the external world. In this refinement, we can say that one responds only to those judgments he chooses to respond to—that is, those judgments he accepts as valid or imagines himself. (Hence, the Other transcends my freedom only because I recognize his doing so. Even if I am exposed to the gaze of the Other, I may not feel shame, just as I may feel it by simply imagining myself exposed to the Other. In a word, shame is the consciousness of shame, just as the suffering of the worker must be the consciousness of suffering before it acquires any meaning or power over the individual. Or as Hegel said, and Sartre noted, the slave must accept his slavery before there can be a master-slave relationship.)[2]

In Daniel Sereno this phenomenon has become virtually pathological. Ashamed of his homosexuality, Daniel craves the judgment and punishment that an oblivious or tolerant society withholds. His tragedy is that "animals and people never succeeded in hating him" (105). For a man thirsting for opprobrium, admiration is agony. Thus the encounter with the concierge's daughter:

> Every morning on her return from school she laid flowers outside his door. He kicked the flowers downstairs. . . . and now he must submit to the admiring gaze of this deplorable child, who was just at the puffy stage of puberty. (89)

Daniel chooses to act in a hateful or perverse way to elicit the response he so desires. When Mathieu comes to borrow the abortion money from him, he not only refuses but makes certain Mathieu realizes that his refusal is arbitrary. But attractive, successful, and always forgiven, Daniel undertakes to judge and punish himself, supplying self-hatred to meet the lack of hatred by others. Like Baudelaire in Sartre's interpretation, he interiorizes the Other:

> It was odd, he thought, that a man could hate himself as though he were someone else. . . . When he despised himself he had the feeling of detachment from his own being, as though he were poised like an impartial judge above a noisome turmoil; then suddenly he found himself plunging downwards, caught again in his own toils. (93)

It is in this schizophrenic condition that he attempts to drown his cats ("He would walk down to the water and say: 'Farewell to what I love most in the world' "), only to be saved by a sudden reintegration of his personality:

> He got a smear of tar on his tweed jacket and looked at it.
> He saw the black smear on the brown material, and suddenly he felt that he was one person and no more. One only. A coward. A man who liked his cats and could not chuck them in the river. (99)

"I am a truly evil man," thinks Daniel (168), playing at being evil. And he can say elsewhere, "it must be very entertaining to do the exact opposite of what one wants to do. One feels oneself becoming someone else" (106).[3]

As with Baudelaire, schizophrenic self-contemplation and the flight of the self from the self are exercises in futility and "boredom"—the boredom that results from the sense of one's own contingency. Daniel is eventually driven to contemplate the ultimate act: not suicide, but what amounts to the execution of the homosexual within him that he so loathes. His attempt to castrate himself is no more successful than his attempt to drown his cats, and he finally decides to martyrize himself by marrying Marcelle, whose trust he has won at Mathieu's expense.

Daniel is no more capable of saving himself than is Mathieu, and it is not until he has a religious epiphany (*Le Sursis*) that he can find satisfaction or rest. The letter that he sends to Mathieu reveals that he has accurately interpreted his own condition: "I have often wanted to hate myself and, as you know, had good reasons for so doing. But my attempted hatred of myself was absorbed into my insubstantiality and was nothing but a recollection (*Reprieve*, 313). He describes the theory of the look, in which he apprehends the futility of self-reflection and realizes that one can sense one's own reality only through the reality of the Other.

> You *saw* me, in your eyes I was solid and predictable; my acts and moods were the actual consequences of a definite entity. And through me you knew that entity. . . . I then understood that one could not reach oneself except through another's judgment, another's hatred. (313–14)

The letter then makes a leap of faith, a flight from anguish, that disgusts Mathieu. The human Other is inconsistent and inadequate, unable to render a final judgment. Neither, as we have seen, is there any help from within. For Daniel, the circle can be broken only by grace, the intervention of God, who becomes the Other:

> God sees me, Mathieu; I feel it and I know it. . . . I adapt for my own use, and to your disgust, your prophet's foolish wicked words: "I think, therefore I am," which used to trouble me so sorely, *for the more I thought, the less I seemed to be* [my italics]; and I say: "I am seen, therefore I am." I need no longer bear the responsibility of my turbid and disintegrating self; he who sees me causes me to be; I am as he sees me. . . . At last I am transmuted into myself. Hated, despised, sustained, a presence supports me to continue thus forever. . . . Before God and before men, *I am*. (314-15)

For Mathieu, the letter is no more than "trite rambling," and he throws it away in disgust. The Cartesian Man will continue to exist in his own nothingness and freedom until he attempts to find his own salvation not in a church but on a church tower with a gun.

Daniel's pathetic condition is the result of the absence not of God in the world but of a social order—any source of stable, generally acceptable values. The collapse of the French army in May 1940, no less than the collapse of French diplomacy two years earlier, could readily lend itself to existential interpretation; both reflected the detotalized nature of the world. In the first part of *La Morte dans l'âme (Troubled Sleep)* we find Mathieu, a soldier in the rout, trying but not entirely succeeding to be one of the men. Deserted by its officers, the unit is itself in a state of disintegration, and the men are whiling away their time waiting for the Germans to round them up. They are really united only in their anxiety:

> At first there had been the exhausting intoxication of brotherly love; there they were, fellow soldiers, sharing a glow of affection under the light of the moon, and life had seemed worth living at that moment. And then the torches were extinguished; they hit the hay because there was nothing else to do and be-

cause they were as yet unused to the claims of mutual affection. Now was the morning after and they felt like committing suicide. . . .

Their faces seemed to say: "Beware of the madness of the moon and of the ecstasies of midnight; each man for himself, and the Devil take the hindmost; we're not in this world for fun." (*Troubled Sleep,* 98-99)

The truth is, as Sartre says, that Mathieu remains uncommitted even as a soldier. He has accepted the war but "he does not claim it as his own. He feels himself excluded from the historic adventure which plays about him. He thinks of his fellow reservists as the dead or the surviving and therefore separates himself from them. . . . Mathieu is not free; he is nothing because he is always outside" (Grisoli, 8).

This is the context of Mathieu's decision to join a group of professional soldiers who decide to make a stand while the reservists are hiding in a cellar. The chasseurs have made their decision because they see it as a professional obligation. Pinette, Mathieu's friend, joins them because he wants "to kill a heinie"; Mathieu simply joins. "He thought, I am going to die for nothing," and he proceeds to rationalize that the secret of his life is that he had lived only for the purpose of dying (*Troubled Sleep,* 180).

Firing upon the Germans from a church tower, Mathieu feels an exaltation that Sartre, after Hegel, calls "liberté terroriste." Each shot eliminates a scruple that hindered his freedom in his peacetime life:

> One for Lola, whom I dared not rob, one for Marcelle, whom I ought to have ditched, one for Odette, whom I didn't want to screw. This for the books I never dared to write, this is for the journeys I never made, this is for everybody in general whom I wanted to hate and tried to understand. . . . He was firing on his fellow men, on Virtue, on the whole world: Liberty is Terror. . . . He fired: he was cleansed, he was all-powerful, he was free. (200)

This nihilism no more represents freedom than Mathieu's joining the chasseurs does true commitment. It calls to mind André Breton's infamous remark that the "simplest Surrealist act consists in dashing down into the street, pistol in hand, and firing blindly, as fast as you can pull the trigger, into the crowd." The existential act differs only in that one doesn't fire blindly but in rational control, and that makes it even worse. Actually, an even more apt parallel to Mathieu, in this situation, is Richard Wright's Bigger Thomas (*Native Son*), who, as the totally alienated American black, can exert his will, perform a meaningful act, only in murder. For all its legality, Mathieu's act is no less antisocial than Bigger's and indeed is less pardonable, if motivation is any consideration. Bigger is a victim of social oppression and his revenge on the world is more understandable than that of a French lycée teacher with a philosophic obsession.

If anything is certain in the existential world it is that no one, by dint of class, occupation, or temperament, has an unobstructed path to freedom. Total commitment brings as many problems as total lack of it; if Mathieu suffers from excessive subjectivity, Brunet, the communist, is wholly oriented to values that are "transcendent, written in the sky, intelligible, independent of human subjectivity and posited as [having the solidity of] things." Brunet "manque sa liberté," Sartre declared. In *Communism and the French Intellectuals* David Cauté noted that "Drôle d'amitié" portrayed the dilemma of the French communists in coming to terms with the Soviet-Nazi Pact of 1939 and its ideological consequences after the spring of 1940. But the second half of *La Morte dans l'âme* and the two succeeding installments in *Les Temps Modernes* that develop Brunet's story give a specifically existential view. Sartre, again, is not interested merely in the historical situation; he is interested in it only as it impinges upon Brunet's personal situation. Captured along with thousands of other soldiers, Brunet will find himself faced with conditions that seem to be beyond the pale of his verities. He embarks on the task of organizing the men and he follows the prescribed method of raising consciousness. Here is an exchange between him and the mysterious Schneider (later to be identified as Vicarios, who bolted the party on the signing of the pact):

> One by one [thought Brunet] with infinite patience, we shall have to destroy their hopes, prick their illusions, make them realize the hideous condition of their lives, see it naked and unadorned as it really is, disgust them with everything and everyone, beginning with themselves. Only then. . . .
> This time it was Schneider who looked at him, as if he were reading his thoughts. . . .
> "That'll be difficult," said Schneider. . . .
> "What'll be difficult?"
> "To give us a sense of solidarity. We're not a class; we're little more than a herd. Not many workmen; just peasants and middle-class riffraff. We haven't even got jobs; we're just human beings in the abstract." (223)

The prison camp conditions, as put by Schneider, unmistakably conform to the existential description of the general situation of men. Detotalization is a fact of human existence. After recounting the internal conflicts that have torn apart French society, an eloquent priest asks the men, "And what, my very dear brothers, was the cause of all this discord, of all this conflict of interests, of all this degradation of public conduct?" His answer is that it was a "sordid materialism" that represented a "turning away from God." Since in existential thought there is no God to turn away from, its answer would be that the condition is inherent.

The Marxist has another answer, of course, but it is really of dubious value in a prison camp. Brunet initially succeeds in organizing a cell but ironically its vitality and high morale are based upon beliefs that appeal to national and personal pride, capped by the faith that Russia will enter the war against Germany. From his own point of view, Brunet has been conducting himself as a communist should, but since he has been doing so without contact with the party, he really has been acting according to his own lights and therefore with full personal responsibility. He is troubled by this freedom and is ready to welcome Chalais, a party member who arrives with up-to-date information. He muses to the man who has announced Chalais's appearance:

> I am delighted to have him [here]. Very happy. Always deciding alone is very pleasant, but. . . . Look, in regard to free France, what attitude should be taken? I have told you how that is preoccupying me. Well, he ought to know; he has his contacts.

Confronted by Chalais, Brunet will learn that all his calculated manipulations of the men and his apparent successes have been based on an ideological deviation. The party has actually been advocating a detente with the Germans and stressing that France's worst enemy is the imperialism of the French generals and the two hundred families. Brunet yields up his abstract freedom virtually at once: "Brunet listens, fascinated, to this voice of fashionable speech. It is no longer the voice of someone. It is the voice of the historic process, the voice of truth." Not only does he surrender his authority to Chalais, but he ousts his friend and confidante Schneider-Vicarios, whom Chalais has recognized as a renegade. When the men refuse to accept Chalais in place of Brunet, the latter decides to escape with Vicarios, whose life is threatened once he has been identified. The escape is arranged but there has been a leak, probably deliberate on the part of the cell; Vicarios is killed and Brunet allows himself to be recaptured. He will eventually succeed in escaping and return to Paris, where he will try to clear Vicarios's name before the party, whose line has changed once again.

It is Vicarios's suffering and death that brings Brunet to an awakening to the human condition. "This absolute of suffering; no victory of man can eradicate it. It is the Party that breaks it, even if the U.S.S.R. wins, men are alone." And he adds, "I don't give a damn about the Party; you are my one friend." The solitude that Brunet is speaking of pertains to more than the immediate experience; it is actually apparent as early as his encounter with Maurice and Zezette, the working class couple, in *Le Sursis,* with whom he finds it difficult to communicate and it is sharply defined by his frequent contempt of the men throughout the second part of *La Morte dans l'âme* and his pride in the personal physical discipline he imposes on himself. Even after the organization is effected, he holds the lonely position of leadership, accentuated, as we have seen, by his severance from the outside world. His only intimacy has been with Vicarios, a "strange friendship" based both on intellectual antagonism and personal warmth. It is fitting that only when he witnesses his friend's death does Brunet come to appreciate what that friendship, spurned in the interests of the party, was really worth.

The story of a communist in an existential world, then, is not the story of a communist in a capitalist or a socialist world. For all his struggles, the latter operates among certain fixities and tangibles, given forces and conflicting groups and classes. None of this is at issue in "Drôle d'amitié." The dichotomy of patriotism and class consciousness is in this microcosm a secondary matter. Indeed in the world of the trilogy, the Germans appear chiefly as vague menacing abstractions only occasionally manifesting themselves as human beings and there is no portrayal of explicit class exploitation. (The mobilization, for instance, affects peasant, worker, and bourgeois alike.) Brunet, then, is an individual among other individuals and all that matters is how he responds to his own situation—his own anguish and his own freedom.

Simone de Bouvoir has said that in 1944 "Sartre thought that any situation could be transcended by subjective effort; in 1951, he knew that circumstances can sometimes steal our transcendence from us; in that case, no individual salvation is possible, only a collective struggle" (*Force of Circumstance,* 254). Sartre's political evolution and the controversies to which it gave rise have been adequately traced by others and it need only be reiterated here that his quest for collective ideals, his fellow-travelling with the communists, his grand effort, culminating in *Critique du raison dialectique,* to "revise" Marx in terms of existential psychology, had no substantial issue in imaginative literature.

The two plays that can be said to represent his major literary work over the last three decades, *Le Diable et le bon dieu (The Devil and the Good Lord,* 1951) and *Les Séquestrés d'Altona (The Condemned of Altona,* 1959), bear no special evidence of Sartre's readings in Marxism. The former is concerned with a sixteenth-century German mercenary, Goetz von Berchlingen, who, attempting to live by absolutes, devotes himself first to Evil and then to Good. As an "anarchist of evil," Sartre states in an interview, Goetz "destroys nothing when he thinks he is a great destroyer. He destroys human lives but fails to destroy either society or the bases of society"; he merely benefits those in power. His efforts to do good are no more successful; by distributing his land to the peasants, he foments a war; his pacifist utopia is destroyed primarily because it cannot or will not defend itself.

Concluding that God is dead, Goetz abandons a morality of absolutes that can end only in "anti-humanism" and accepts "the limited morality which befits the human destiny: he replaces the absolute with history." By freeing himself of the belief in God, Goetz correspondingly is delivered of the pride underlying his behavior; by agreeing, as he does in the final scene, to take charge of the peasant armies, he redeems himself as a positive existential hero—one who has "committed his freedom" in the right way. Again, what is important here, if Sartre's comments are any indication, is not the discovery of a collective ideal as such; rather it is the quintessential existential attempt to base a morality not in God but in oneself ("if God existed, man would find favor in his sight by being himself, by accepting himself and accepting other people in their finiteness").

Inspired partly by the war in Algeria and partly by Nazi atrocities, *The Condemned of Altona* deals with Franz, the eldest son of a German family of aristocratic industrialists, who,

2. The Totalities of Existentialism

recoiling from his participation in the torture of partisans, has returned from the Russian front only to lock himself in his room for the subsequent decade and a half. Sartre says that he was trying in this play to reach the level of myth, this being the means by which the audience could identify itself with Franz and thereby realize its own "complicity"—that all men are capable of torturing others, French in Algeria no less than Germans in Russia ("We are living in an age of blood and violence and . . . we have, so to speak, interiorized this violence and injustice. The problem is therefore to present what we are today"). Elsewhere, he sees the play in terms of clearly existential themes: thus he develops an interviewer's observation that the characters are Protestants and speaks of their direct "accountability" for their sins, their having, unlike the Catholics, no "intercessor" or "defense" against what they take to be an "absolute fault." Sartre then moves on to the theory of history that adds another dimension to the anguish of the characters. Franz imagines that the ceiling of his room is covered with crabs, who are judging him—this becomes an analogue of the way History will judge the actions of the present. "We shall be judged," says Sartre, by beings whom we cannot understand and on the basis of principles that are not entirely our own.

In other words, one can no more appeal to History than to God for justification of one's existence or absolution for one's acts. Thus we are brought full circle to the basic existential contradiction between the knowledge that life is ambiguous and the need to distinguish between good and evil. For if we are judged by alien principles (Sartre's argument continues) we shall also be judged, no doubt, as we judge, on the basis of principles we have (277). In a sense the whole edifice of Sartre's thought is reducible to the reply he gave when asked what particular emotion he wanted to convey in *The Condemned:* "The feeling of the ambiguity of our age. Morals, politics—nothing is simple anymore. There are some acts, however, which are unacceptable" (268).

6 Camus
Detotalizers and Monologists

For Arthur Schopenhauer, blind Will was the essence of life; through human consciousness and knowledge, this will was objectified in the phenomenal world. Man was will made conscious; his knowledge was knowledge wholly in the service of the Will. To be Will meant to strive endlessly; to strive endlessly was to endure endless frustration or restlessness. Suffering and pain were a part of a human destiny. In a world in which all was Will, in which competition was universal, the distinction between victim and victimizer lost all meaning. "As the will is, so is the world," and only it can bear the responsibility for what it is: "Eternal Justice reigns." This is not the Eternal Justice of God's will, a will whose purposes are beyond human comprehension, but that of an absolute nothingness that lies behind phenomenal reality.

Although he never had much to say about Schopenhauer, Albert Camus would have appreciated this vision even while rejecting its conclusions. He would have appreciated most of all its recognition of the pervasiveness of human misery and its acceptance of that misery, without any appeal to a higher or external force, as a wholly human phenomenon. And he would have appreciated, I believe, Schopenhauer's notion of Eternal Justice insofar as it can be considered neither an apology for nor defense of suffering but rather a description of "things as they are"—a response that does not lead to complicity in suffering but, on the contrary, to the total renunciation and psychological transcendence of the world in which it occurs. The pre-1940 Camus, for whom the chief issue was to recognize the "Absurd" and its consequences in a world that clung to illusions about God, might have found in Schopenhauer's vision an example of that rare "lucidity" associated with the ability to see the world as and for what it is. Conversely, Schopenhauer might not have objected strenuously had this passage from *Le Mythe de Sisyphe* been applied or ascribed to him:

> [The mind must meet the night] Yes, indeed, but not the night that is born under closed eyelids and through the mere will of man—dark, impenetrable night that the mind calls up in order to plunge into it. If it must encounter a night, let it be rather that of despair, which remains lucid—polar night, vigil of the mind, whence will arise perhaps that white and virginal brightness which outlines every object in the light of the intelligence. (*The Myth of Sisyphus*, 48)

That is, Schopenhauer would not have objected, except on one point—and that point will, of course, make all the difference. For Schopenhauer, the "vigil of the mind" involves an ultimate mode of thought, a higher knowledge in which Will negates itself and the thinker becomes the pure will-less subject. That "white and virginal brightness which outlines every object" is the illumination achieved during an aesthetic contemplation that, as a means of transcending the phenomenal world, is an end in itself. How far Camus stands from Schopenhauer on this matter is evident in his conclusion: "The preceding merely defines a way of thinking. But the point is to live." "To live"—the double meaning pertains in both the English and French: to live on or survive ("There is but one truly serious philosophical problem, and that is suicide," begins the essay); and to live fully ("What does life mean in such a universe? Nothing else . . . but indifference to the future and a desire to use up everything that is given" [44]). To commit oneself to life in the phenomenal world when its meaninglessness should invoke a suicidal despair is, for Camus, a mode of "revolt," something that occurs when one has "the certainty of a crushing fate, without the resignation that ought to accompany it." The Absurd Man is inherently a rebel; Schopenhauer, in his renunciation and transcendence, a suicide.

But rebellion in *Le Mythe de Sisyphes* (written in 1940) did not mean exactly what it came to mean a decade later in *L'Homme révolté*, after an intervening war and enemy occupation had deepened and matured Camus's social and moral awareness. Or to be more specific, rebellion against despair and meaninglessness in the earlier work was not explicitly rebellion against suffering and injustice. It was a solitary act that could be seen as having social consequences, but which was a mode of salvation ultimately no less personal than that of Schopenhauer's contemplative man. "No," wrote Camus in 1945, "everything is not summed up in negation and absurdity. We know this. But we must first posit negation and absurdity because they are what our generation has encountered and what we must take into account" (*Resistance, Rebellion, and Death*, 59). Camus had done just that in *L'Etranger*.

Whether or not, even in 1941 when the novel appeared, Camus was beginning to outgrow his hero, Meursault, it is clear that negation and absurdity had in fact not summed up everything. In fact, as a version of *Néant*, the Absurd was by nature a wholly "detotalized" totality, an antitotality, that bore the same relation to synthesis that antimatter bears to Being. As a negative personality, Meursault will find himself "at home" in this dimension of reality, in tune with "the benign indifference of the universe," just as he is a stranger in the positive world of bourgeois Algiers. The point, however, is that in Camus's vision the "positive world" (colonial Algeria) is the ethically absurd world, while the metaphysical Absurd is a phenomenon of the cosmos that the lucid man recognizes and learns to live with.

Now, Meursault's character is such that to the untutored eye

—or to the eye tutored in a different philosophy—he might appear to be anything from merely eccentric to psychopathic. No psychiatrist is called upon to testify during Meursault's trial, but that has not kept actual psychiatrists from delivering an opinion. In what is no doubt one of the most ingenious of such studies, Nathan Leites would almost have us convinced did we not realize that Meursault is not a living person but a fictional character whose actions, as we've seen, take their significance from the specific context the novel provides. Leites's analysis is worth consideration both for what it tells us and what it does not.

Meursault's apathy ("affectlessness"), we learn, is a reaction "to the guilty rage induced by the severe deprivation imposed by an absent father, an indifferent mother, and a withholding wider environment." Leites lists the various forms of Meursault's affectlessness, all representing a repression of that rage, essentially murderous, which breaks to the surface during his encounter with the Arab and again with the prison chaplain. Those who hold this view admire Camus for creating, both consciously and unconsciously, a character of high psychological plausibility. Meursault's virtues—lucidity, simplicity, honesty, and self-reliance—emphasized by many critics, are discounted; his neurotic condition is deemed responsible for his fate, since it leads him to "aggress his environment and provoke it into aggressing him, thus alleviating his guilt."

"Alleviate his guilt?" It would, I'm certain, be virtually inconceivable to Leites that Meursault should be wholly without a sense of guilt, conscious or repressed. Yet, for Camus, that is the essence of his character as it is that of the Absurd Man in general, who "does not understand the notion of sin":

> An attempt is made to get him to admit his guilt. He feels innocent. To tell the truth, that is all he feels—his irreparable innocence. This is what allows him everything. Hence, what he demands of himself is to live *solely* with what he knows, to accommodate himself to what is, and to bring in nothing that is not certain. (*Myth of Sisyphus*, 39)

Meursault's qualities are meant to be thrown into relief by the failures of the social world around him. What Leites blandly refers to as the "withholding wider environment" actually includes Camus's caricature both of the legal system and the society it represents. Leites has nothing to say about examining magistrates suffering from hypocritical religious sentimentalism, self-important murderous prosecutors carried away by their own rhetoric, prison chaplains manipulating the emotions of the men to whom they minister—nothing about the institutions nor the rules of conduct that make life in an Absurd Algeria what it is, an Absurd Algeria that Leites must take to be normal if he is to pronounce Meursault "maladjusted."

Ironically, it is the very qualities condemned by Leites as antisocial that make it possible for Meursault to "adjust" to an absurd universe. We are told, for instance, that his affectlessness is often an attempt to avoid "fantasied dangers of involvement and also a means of aggression against those who [rightfully] expect a fuller response from him." One such example is Meursault's reply to his boss's invitation to transfer him to Paris: "I told him I was quite prepared to go; but really I didn't care much one way or the other." Leites omits the philosophic justification: "one never changed his way of life; one life was as good as another and my present one suited me quite well" (*Stranger,* 52). This absence of expectation—viewed by the psychiatrist as a potentially destructive "negative motivation"—is precisely what makes it possible for Meursault to "live without appeal," to surrender hope without falling into despair. It is also what will eventually give him the strength to adjust to the difficult conditions of prison life and to those of life in general: "I've often thought that had I been compelled to live in the trunk of a dead tree, with nothing to do but gaze up at the patch of sky just overhead, I'd have got used to it by degrees" (95). It even paradoxically underlies the epiphany that gives him more than ample strength to face his execution: "It was as if that great rush of anger had washed me clean, emptied me of hope, and, gazing up at the dark sky spangled with its signs and stars, for the first time, the first, I laid my heart open to the benign indifference of the universe" (154). Camus spelled out the full meaning of this experience:

> The divine availability of the condemned man before whom the prison doors open in a certain early dawn, that unbelievable disinterestedness with regard to everything except the pure flame of life.... The absurd man thus catches sight of a burning and frigid, transparent and limited universe in which nothing is possible but everything is given, and beyond which all is collapse and nothingness. He can then decide to accept such a universe and draw from it his strength, his refusal to hope, and the unyielding evidence of a life without consolation. (*Myth of Sisyphus,* 44)

Absurd indifference, then, is by no means the same thing as "affectlessness" and to reduce one to the other, as Leites does, is obviously to miss the whole point of the novel. On the other hand, if Meursault can be wholly exonerated by an appeal to absurdist philosophy, then absurdist philosophy, at least in its ethical aspects, is also in need of exoneration. For the same "indifference" that lends Meursault his strength and the same sense of "irreparable innocence" that accompanies his lucidity allow him to commit murder, keep him aloof from human attachments, and perpetuate his social naïveté along with his contentment. In saying this, I may seem to be falling into the same error Leites did—judging Meursault as though he were an actual person and doing so with irrelevant criteria. To repeat, what I am actually doing is judging the absurdist argument, as did Camus himself when he said that everything was not summed up by negation and absurdity.

Overcome by the heat and light of midday sun, Meursault shoots an unnamed Arab, the brother of the mistress of Meursault's demimonde friend, Raymond. The Arab has been harmlessly threatening Raymond for having maltreated his sister and has no real connection with Meursault. The shooting is motiveless and the four extra shots fired by Meursault are wholly without meaning. It is the sun, throughout the entire novel an image and force of the absurd universe to which

Meursault was particularly sensitive, that has killed the Arab, Meursault being merely its passive instrument. This argument is acceptable because the novel seems to argue that society's "legal" intent to execute Meursault, ostensibly for the murder but actually for his candid nonconformism—for not playing the game, as Camus later put it—is a much greater crime than the one Meursault committed. Because the examining magistrate, a warped representative of justice, is so intent upon effecting an emotional surrender in Meursault, we may well find ourselves applauding Meursault's assertion to him that he felt no remorse, only vexation ("un certain ennui"). In sympathizing with the murderer, the reader accepts the crime.

This is made easier by the nature of the victim: a faceless, unnamed Arab—and one with a knife at that. We accept the argument that the sun killed him and we reaffirm the innocence and lucidity of Meursault, who, during his trial and incarceration, appears to be the one sane and honest man in a society of madmen and knaves. Now, Camus was to write in *L'Homme révolté* that "a mind imbued with the idea of the absurd will undoubtedly accept fatalistic murder [le meurtre de fatalité], but it would never accept calculated murder [le meurtre de raisonnement]." Obviously, this notion can explain Meursault's act, but can it really justify it? Suppose, for instance, that Marie had been the victim of Meursault's sunstroke—or even Raymond or Masson. Could we then have judged Meursault anything less than temporarily insane? In this case the absurdist thesis would have received its true test. As it stands now, the reason we don't consider Meursault a homicidal maniac is not simply that he had no motive and that the murder was "fatalistic" but that his victim was never presented as anything but a shadow.

Perhaps in this deceptively simple way the French Algeria of the thirties enters the novel and the metaphysical determinants take on a social cast. Leites's "withholding wider environment" now looms as the paramount influence in shaping Meursault, not the Oedipus complex or the sun. The society in *L'Etranger* is revealed only through Meursault's eyes, which are sensitive to the natural but not the social realities around him. Camus's intense concern for the plight of the Arabs under French colonial rule is wholly unreflected in Meursault's narration. But even if colonial injustice has made no impression on Meursault, the society in which he lives can neither hold out meaningful values nor inspire its citizens with genuine purpose. The absurd relation of Salamano and his dog, the ludicrous pride of Raymond betrayed by his mistress, the obsessive attention to radio programs of the woman whom Meursault calls "the little robot"—to say nothing of the quirky attitudes and sentiments of the higher administrators—are not simply eccentricities but symptoms of a detotalized and solipsistic citizenry. The society being what it is, it is not surprising to find that Meursault is what he is: a stranger in his candor, self-acceptance, and horror of making judgments; a typical citizen in his disorientation, lack of constructive values, and finally what can only be called his indifference to Arab life, sun or no sun.

I am not at all certain that Camus would have approved of this reading, for it reduces absurdist thought and behavior to a social phenomenon and thereby undermines its metaphysical status. That is, Camus's central concern was to portray the Absurd Hero, not the various forms of social alienation in Algeria, and especially not the form of which absurdism was thought to be a part. This brings us back to the Arab again who, apparently confirming his shadowy nature, refuses to die. I offer no solution to the moral issue raised by his role in the novel. That the episode might have been modelled upon an actual case has nothing to do with its fictional implications. We cannot accuse Camus himself of an implicit contempt for Arab life when the facts are wholly to the contrary, and that is what we must do if, as the logic of the novel requires, we reaffirm Meursault's innocence, and are unperturbed by his lack of remorse. The only alternative to that is for us to willingly suspend disbelief.

Our appreciation of the social limitations of absurdist thought does not require that we reduce it to a social phenomenon. Nor does it require any ingenious interpretation of *L'Etranger*. As we have seen, negation and absurdity never meant for Camus the kind of nihilism that he was to attack in *L'Homme révolté*, a nihilism that didn't merely excuse an unpremeditated murder committed as a result of sunstroke (fatalistic murder), but philosophically and ethically sought to justify massacre (calculated murder). They really meant in part a modern form of Greek stoicism; what they failed to "sum up," at least in social terms, was what any philosophy of extreme individualism failed to sum up. As an ethic, it called for inner discipline at the expense of social consciousness (but did not preclude the hedonistic enjoyment of life)—an inner discipline predicated upon self-protection and therefore the very antithesis of social consciousness. In 1940 Camus could write in his notebook,

> More and more, when faced with the world of men, the only reaction is one of individualism. Man alone is an end unto himself. Everything you try to do for the common good ends in failure.... Withdraw into yourself completely, and play your own game. (*Note Books* 1:171)

A nobler but no less egocentric version of this view underlies the triumph of the Absurd Hero, who achieves absolute self-reliance by denying all hope for external aid, either universal or social. It is a triumph that is meaningful to Sisyphus, alone with his rock, and to prisoners awaiting execution. The world outside neither knows nor cares nor is in any way changed for the better.

Camus, his notebook editor informs us, wrote "idiotic" across the entry just quoted. This is no surprise. If it were not a response made long after the item was inscribed, it at least pointed to the future when, having accounted for nihilism, Camus would make "the common good" his primary concern. By 1945 he could see the need for a "coexistence of negation and a positive morality" as the great problem of the epoch. "If there is one fact that these last five years have brought out," he said in an interview, "it is the extreme solidarity of men with one another." And asked whether the individualism of the French didn't make it difficult for them to have a real experience of this solidarity, he replied:

> That remains to be proved. And besides, in a world whose absurdity appears to be so impenetrable, we simply must reach a greater degree of understanding among men, a greater sincerity. We must achieve this or perish. To do so, certain conditions must be fulfilled: men must be frank (falsehood confuses things), free (communication is impossible with slaves). Finally, they must feel a certain justice around them. (*Lyrical and Critical Essays*, 346-47)

During the war Camus joined the Resistance and lived the ideals that would provide the ethical basis of *L'Homme révolté* and *La Peste*. His *Lettres à un ami allemand (Letters to a German Friend)* reveal the intensity of personal feeling underlying the transformation of the Absurd Hero into the Rebel, of Meursault, the man of solitude, into Rieux, the man of solidarity. In these letters, Camus continues to believe that the universe holds no meaning—he does not repudiate this fundamental principle of nihilism. What he does reject is the conclusion drawn by "the German friend," now the Enemy, that "man was negligible and that his soul could be killed, that in the maddest of histories the only pursuit for the individual was the adventure of power and his only morality, the realism of conquests" (*Resistance*, 27). Camus says that he once saw "no valid argument to answer you except a fierce love of justice which . . . seemed to me as unreasonable as the most sudden passion." That was what saved him:

> Because you turned your despair into intoxication, because you freed yourself from it by making a principle of it, you were willing to destroy man's works and to fight him in order to add to his basic misery. Meanwhile, refusing to accept that despair and that tortured world, I merely wanted men to rediscover

their solidarity in order to wage war against their revolting fate. (28)

Camus now speaks in the plural whereas he has previously spoken in the singular. Once, he had conceived of adverse fate (mainly death) in terms of the individual man who, like Meursault, rebelled against it by refusing to despair. It was a struggle man could not win except psychologically. But now, with the German army in Paris, fate takes on a social and historical reality that can and must be challenged, and the values of solidarity begin to reveal themselves. These letters to a German friend, published in the Resistance journal *Combat,* are charged with all the emotion that an authentic patriotism can generate. Philosophically, they are Camus's farewell to that hypothetical "German friend," Arthur Schopenhauer, and the whole ideology in which the only revolt against suffering and misery in the world is that of the individual man who seeks his salvation through a special act of the mind.

They are, however, no farewell to metaphysics. Not only will the conception of "metaphysical rebellion" dominate his second major venture into philosophical writing, *L'Homme révolté* (1951), but its patterns will be applied to "historical rebellion." Camus's mind, in other words, will continue to work in terms of a universal principle, an Idea, that he will see manifested in all the particular instances of rebellion—philosophic, political, aesthetic—that he discusses. The true significance of this procedure will become apparent shortly.

From the beginning Camus had to think "solidarity" where he had always thought "solitude," especially in regard to "revolt," that central (metaphysical) act by which, to Camus, man defines himself or acquires his identity. Even a single slave rebelling against his master is demonstrating his awareness of certain rights due him as a man and therefore is acting in the name of a "common good." Indeed, he is not only acting in its name but actually risking his life for it in the all-or-nothing situation that is his rebellion. "We see that the affirmation implicit in every act of rebellion is extended to something that transcends the individual in so far as it withdraws him from his supposed solitude and provides him with a reason to act" (16). "When he rebels, a man identifies himself with other men and so surpasses himself, and from this point of view human solidarity is metaphysical" (17). Thus Camus makes the critical philosophic leap that establishes the direction for his entire argument.

In abandoning strict individualism, however, he did not repudiate the absurdist experience; he simply collectivized it:

> In absurdist experience, suffering is individual. But from the moment when a movement of rebellion begins, suffering is seen as a collective experience. Therefore the first progressive step for a mind overwhelmed by the strangeness of things is to realize that this feeling of strangeness is shared with all men and that human reality, in its entirety, suffers from the distance which separates it from the rest of the universe. (22)

Is it logically possible for the Stranger to negate himself and become Everyman? Do all men feel the same kind of strangeness—and in the same kind of way? And what about all the other qualities that constitute absurdist experience and the absurdist character (the sense of guiltlessness, for example)—are they all collective? I shall not pursue these questions. For even if we were to prove the illogicality or futility of trying to socialize the absurdist experience, all we would have is another indication of how urgently Camus was following the logic of his own vision, a logic that required that solidarity be the essence of all forms of rebellion, even the most seemingly individualistic. Why this had to be so is obvious from the principle that Camus derives from it:

> Man's solidarity is founded upon rebellion, and rebellion in its turn, can only find its justification in this solidarity. We have, then, the right to say that any rebellion which claims the right to deny or destroy this solidarity loses simultaneously its right to be called rebellion and becomes in reality an acquiescence in murder. (22)

A touchstone by which we will judge all rebellion and revolution, this principle makes it possible for Camus to accept on ethical grounds the idea of revolt while condemning the invariable results of actual revolutions. For any rebellion to be true to its nature and origins, he says, "it must respect the limit it discovers in itself" if it is not to plunge "into a mire of tyranny or servitude." On this idea rests the whole intricate structure of Camus's thought, which, with all its correspondences, counterpoints, contradictions, and reconciliations, is in essence a critique of unrestrained nihilism and calculated murder.

As the "movement by which man protests against his condition and against the whole of creation," metaphysical rebellion is originally a denunciation of God and ultimately a refusal to recognize his existence. "When the throne of God is overturned," Camus explains, in formulating the prototypical situation,

> the rebel realizes that it is now his own responsibility to create the justice, order, and unity that he sought in vain within his own condition, and in this way to justify the fall of God. Then begins the desperate effort to create, at the price of crime and murder if necessary, the dominion of man. This will not come about without terrible consequences. . . . (25)

Put this way, it seems that "crime and murder" are, indeed, an inherent part of metaphysical rebellion. But this is the very point Camus must deny if his whole argument is not to be put in jeopardy. Thus he asserts that these consequences occur "only to the extent that the rebel forgets his original purpose" and "abandons himself to complete negation or total submission." And that "original purpose" is fundamentally the same as in the rebellion of the slave: human solidarity and freedom. Camus's metaphysical rebels are, for the most part, mythological figures (Prometheus, Lucifer, Cain), philosophers (Lucretius, Nietzsche), and writers (Sade, Lautréamont); but they have defined the context for the historical or political revolutionaries as well. One form of rebellion is continuous with the other:

130   2. The Totalities of Existentialism

> Now that God is dead, the world must be changed and organized by the forces at man's disposal. The force of imprecation alone [that is, the mode of metaphysical rebellion] is not enough; weapons are needed and totality must be conquered. Even revolution, particularly revolution which claims to be materialist, is only a limitless metaphysical crusade. (108)

Thus, drawing to a conclusion, Camus restates the metaphysical ethos in historical terms:

> We now know . . . that rebellion with no other limits but historical expediency signifies unlimited slavery. To escape this fate, the revolutionary mind, if it wants to remain alive, must therefore return again to the sources of rebellion and draw its inspiration from the only system of thought which is faithful to its origins: thought that recognizes limits [la pensée des limites]. (294)

This *pensée des limites, pensée de midi,* or *pensée solaire* ("thought at the meridian," "noon" thought, solar thought) emerges as an ideal, associated with the Mediterranean mind, that Camus fittingly enough sets against the "German ideology" with its idealization of the State, absolutist society, rational tyranny, and colonization of the masses (299). In all the revolutions that Camus has examined, only one seems actually to have objectified this spirit of moderation, revolutionary Syndicalism, a movement, Camus argues, that "is responsible for the enormously improved conditions of the workers from the sixteen-hour day to the forty-hour week." What appeals most to Camus in this movement, and what accordingly offers an idea about the specific nature of *pensée solaire,* is its "realism," its reliance on "the most concrete realities—on occupation, on the village, where the living heart of things and of men is to be found" (298). Unlike "Caesarian" revolution, which, lacking the sense of limits, imposes a doctrine upon reality and is given to violence, Syndicalism seeks to advance history and alleviate suffering without resorting to terror, and therefore acts on "behalf of life, not in defiance of it" (298).

This argument is probably more noteworthy for what it tells us about Camus than for its persuasiveness. The Algerian sun, which in *L'Etranger* was associated with an absurd universe and "fatalistic murder," now assumes a more traditional meaning, symbolizing as it does reason or intellectual and moral "enlightenment" and maturity. (In the Mediterranean, says Camus, "intelligence is intimately related to the blinding light of the sun"—"l'intelligence est soeur de la dure lumiere" [300/370].) These two opposing meanings do have a common denominator in the idea of "lucidity," which includes both the intellectual apprehension of absurdity in the universe and the knowledge that understands limits. Perhaps it is appropriate that a single image should include, if not reconcile, these opposites for, as we have seen, Camus did not wholly dispense with his original nihilism. To the contrary, without a meaningless universe (a universe in which there is no apparent justification for suffering) there would be no metaphysical rebellion, in the first place. Camus's humanism or rationalism, then, has not only its origin but its very inspiration in negation. It is true that Camus uses Manichaean imagery when he speaks of Mediterranean light in conflict with European (German) darkness but it is also true that the Mediterranean sun can be blinding and Mediterranean night pellucid with stars.

I have already briefly discussed the personal dimension of these ideas expressed in *Lettres à un ami allemand* and elsewhere. If his experience with the Resistance gave impetus to the development of his philosophy of rebellion, then, conversely, Camus himself fits the description of the ideal metaphysical rebel—the lucid Mediterranean man, the nihilist possessed of solar thought, the solitary with communal feeling, the sick but energetic man sharply aware of his own mortality yet believing in life. There are times when Camus sees the same phenomenal world Schopenhauer did:

> The world I live in is loathsome to me.... There are ambitions that are not mine, and I should not feel at ease if I had to make

2. The Totalities of Existentialism

> my way by relying on the paltry privileges granted to those who adapt themselves to this world. (*Resistance,* 83)

But I have deleted above what Schopenhauer would not have said, and perhaps only Camus could have: "[The world I live in is loathsome to me,] *but I feel one with the men who suffer in it.*" And following the passage quoted, he writes, "But it seems to me that there is another ambition that ought to belong to all writers: to bear witness and shout aloud, every time it is possible, insofar as our talent allows, *for those who are enslaved as we are*" (my italics). Could Camus's personal metaphysical rebellion, with its nihilist's appeal to solidarity, be any more faithful to type?

"Bearing witness" is the way of rebellion of the writer; it is at once a mode of protest against a universe or government and, as a form of communication, a means for both establishing and expressing solidarity. And since, if he is to remain true to his original revolutionary inspiration, the witness must be guided by the solar thought of moderation, so his language—the language of Reason—must be rigorously and indeed courageously clear. That these ideas are not mere platitudes is evident when we see them in their personal and political contexts. In "Why Spain?" (1948), for example, Camus is replying to Gabriel Marcel, who had criticized him for using Spain rather than Eastern Europe, in the play *State of Siege,* as the setting for political terrorism:

> For you are willing to keep silent about one reign of terror [he tells Marcel] in order the better to combat another one. There are some of us who do not want to keep silent about anything. It is our whole political society that nauseates us. Hence there will be no salvation until all those who are still worth while have repudiated it utterly. (82)

Thus the voice of the rebel. That same year, before an audience of monks, he brings up the question of the Pope's failure, during the war, to condemn Fascist and Nazi atrocities—that the Pope did condemn them in the obscure style of the encyclicals was inadequate:

> It seems that that voice did speak up. But I assure you that millions of men like me did not hear it and that at that time believers and unbelievers alike shared a solitude that continued to spread as the days went by and the executioners multiplied. (71)

In the terminology of *L'Homme révolté* the Pope should have rebelled by bearing witness in a language that was unmistakably clear; only then would his words have given those millions of men who "shared a solitude" a sense of solidarity and the inspiration to resist the calculated murder perpetrated by the enemy. Camus's own language before such an audience exemplifies what it preaches:

> Christians should speak out, loud and clear, and . . . they should voice their condemnation in such a way that never a doubt, never the slightest doubt, could rise in the heart of the simplest man . . . they should get away from abstraction and confront the blood-stained face history has taken on today. The grouping we need is a grouping of men resolved to speak out clearly and pay up personally. (71)

Obviously, Camus is here taking as his model the Resistance group, that collection of solitaires like himself who in an all-or-nothing situation were indeed willing "to pay up personally" for the common good.

Ten years later, during the Algerian crisis, we find that neither Camus's ideas nor feelings have changed. He is committed to reconciliation and he sees his task to be that "of clarifying definitions in order to disintoxicate minds" made drunk by political rhetoric, of "calming fanaticisms," and, in short, of helping to distinguish "the respective limits of force and justice" (121). Both philosophically and personally, this was a role that seems to have been made for Camus: solar thought called for the knowledge of limits, for moderation, for the absolute refusal to commit murder in the name of any cause; that he himself was a French Algerian and could appreciate what was legitimate in the *colon*'s argument was counterbalanced by his profound and outspoken sympathy for the Arabs. He saw justice on both sides and therefore he was sensitive to its excesses —the justice of retaliation, for instance, that led to an endless cycle of torture and massacre by one side and terrorism and massacre by the other. Camus's efforts, we know, were futile and he fell silent—reason could recognize the limits of reasoning, and in this instance was not silence the most powerful form of protest?

When challenged by an Algerian member of the audience during his speech accepting the Nobel Prize in 1957, Camus included in his reply the now famous utterance, "I believe in justice, but I would defend my mother before I would justice." Of course he would! For the justice that would require the killing of his mother would be the justice of terrorism or calculated murder and therefore it had to be resisted as the false justice that it was. But, again, this is the viewpoint of the metaphysical rebel, of a man who sees social problems invariably in metaphysical and personal terms; it could not be the viewpoint of the Algerian social revolutionary for whom Camus's ideas of solidarity and solar thought meant nothing and liberation everything. And finally it was the social revolutionaries who were to determine Algeria's fate, not the militant reformers like Aziz Kessous, to whom Camus could appeal as the man of reason speaking to a man of reason (126).

Because his thought is so much of a piece, the issues raised here shed a curious light on Camus's most elaborate novel, *La Peste (The Plague)*, which appeared in 1948, about a decade before the Algerian situation turned critical. Now, there is no particular social or political reason for the setting of this work to be an Algerian city. Indeed what characterizes Oran, a commercial center of predominantly European inhabitants, is its cultural similarity to the average French provincial town. The narrator himself, Rieux, calls it "merely a large French port on the Algerian coast," a "negative place" marked by ugliness and banality. "But," he adds significantly, "social unrest is quite unknown amongst us" ("on ne connâit pas chez nous le désordre"). The Oran of Rieux's chronicle, like the Algiers of Meursault but for its one fatal exception, is devoid of Arabs. The battle against the plague and the suffering endured because of it are chiefly European matters. If the novel is allegorical, as Camus has insisted, and, at least on one level, refers to the German occupation and the Resistance, there are no signs whatsoever that Camus also had in mind a potential Arab struggle against the French presence in Algeria.

That *La Peste* is metaphysical in design and execution and that metaphysical rebellion is its real subject is no truism. For, in its broad canvas, its many different characters, its documentary atmosphere, and its realism in general, it gives every illusion of being the social novel that it is not, a novel in which the chief concern is to analyze and dramatize specific social problems. Inherently the plague is not a social problem; it is a natural problem that can without much difficulty be set in a metaphysical context. There is no need to become involved at this point in the complex theories of Georg Lukács on the inadequacy of allegory as a vehicle for social criticism; the weakness of this genre is visible to the naked eye. Not only is allegorical image or situation by nature too blunt to convey the details of social reality, but it can also acquire a life of its own. The more realistic in its detail and dramatization the struggle against the plague becomes, the less its ability to stand for another concrete reality, such as the resistance to the German occupation.

Philip Thody tells us that it was not unusual to argue, as Roland Barthes had done, that *La Peste* was an inadequate symbol for "the problems of the Resistance movement because Camus had replaced a struggle against men by a struggle against the impersonal microbes of plague" (*Literary and Critical Essays,* 338). Nonetheless, Camus replied to Barthes with disappointment, listing some of the ways in which the two situations were alike: forced separation from loved ones, perpetual state of terror, recognition of the need for solidarity, promise and acceptance of struggles yet to come. Camus argues that terror has many faces and he concludes, ironically, that he is being reproached with "the fact that *The Plague* can apply to any resistance against any tyranny." This is exactly what we'd expect Camus to say; it is a reply that all the more confirms his passion for universals. For in Camus's usage, "tyranny" and "resistance" are so generalized as to become absolutes or abstractions, and the novel itself, pure parable. It is at these heights that allegory functions best.

What all this comes down to is that in *La Peste,* as everywhere else in his writing, Camus reveals no interest in the specifically social origins of the problems that concern him, nor for that matter is he interested in social problems as social problems. He is not concerned, as the historical novelist would be, with the actual situation of and conditions in France between 1940 and 1945 or with the literal Resistance movement and its activities. *La Peste* is not primarily an attack on bourgeois society before, during, or after the Occupation—at least not any more than *L'Etranger* was—and it does not call for social revolution. On the contrary, the argument of the novel begins with an a priori condition, an Absurd universe, and the unjustified suffering that is part of it. And Camus's main concern is with how individual men respond to it, with community consciousness (which is not class consciousness), and with human solidarity (which is not the solidarity of workers or of the victims of colonial oppression). In other words, the subject of *La Peste* is metaphysical rebellion, Camus's recurring Idea and the common denominator in fighting plagues, Germans, and all the forces of tyranny.

If bearing witness is the way of rebellion of the writer, it is also the way of anonymity-loving doctors who chronicle their experiences in the fight against the plague. At the end of his account, Rieux speaks of the qualities that the ideal witness possesses (he is referring to himself in the third person):

> Summoned to give evidence regarding what was a sort of crime, he has exercised the restraint [il garde un certain

réserve] that behooves a conscientious witness [un témoin de bonne volonté]. All the same, following the dictates of his heart, he has deliberately taken the victims' side and tried to share with his fellow citizens the only certitudes they had in common —love, exile, and suffering. Thus he can truly say there was not one of their anxieties in which he did not share, no predicament of theirs that was not his.

And he continues,

> Whenever tempted to add his personal note to the myriad voices of the plague-stricken, he was deterred by the thought that not one of his sufferings but was common to all the others and that in a world where sorrow is so often lonely, this was an advantage. Thus, decidedly, it was up to him to speak for all. (*Plague,* 272)

The restraint, the honesty, the desire to say only what can be said in the name of solidarity—these are no more than extensions of the qualities Rieux has drawn upon as a leader in the actual struggle, a struggle in which the power he held could well have corrupted him but did not. In "fighting against creation as he found it" ["contre la création telle qu'elle était"] (116/100), in denying the existence of God, he might have become the typical nihilistic revolutionary did he not have that essential humility that has made him the true hero he is in Camus's eyes. "I assure you," he tells his friend Tarrou, "I've no more than the pride that's needed to keep me going. . . . For the moment I know this; there are sick people and they need curing" (117). Rieux is also humbled by his knowledge that the battle is a losing one, that the plague will end not by the efforts of men, but only after it has run its course. Acting in the face of this truth, Rieux says he is doing no more than he can and claims no glory—all the more showing that he deserves it.

Tarrou brings into the novel the whole conception of "calculated murder," an evil that the plague metaphor cannot really represent, unless one believes, as does Father Paneloux, that behind its advent is the inscrutable will of God. Since it justifies suffering of the innocent, Paneloux's belief, which will be thundered from the pulpit, is intolerable to Rieux and to Tarrou, who is no less sensitive. Thus, Tarrou eventually reveals his horror of a legal system in which men are judged and executed, and explains his own efforts to live without judging others. "I learned," he tells Rieux,

> that even those who were better than the rest could not keep themselves nowadays from killing or letting others kill, because such is the logic by which they live; and that we can't stir a finger in this world without the risk of bringing death to somebody. (228)

In this sense, all men are "plague-stricken," and constant vigilance is required if even the best of men are not to spread the "infection." Literally, Tarrou intended to have "no truck with anything which, directly or indirectly, for good reasons or for bad, brings death to anyone or justifies others' putting him to death" (228-29). He thus commits himself to inaction and a life of exile. The actual plague will prevent him from pursuing this "secular Sainthood."

To this line of reasoning Schopenhauer himself might have assented. What is natural is the microbe, Tarrou tells us. And like the Will, it is in every man. Just as will in men can negate Will through a renunciation made possible by contemplative knowledge, so sickness can cure itself by "tremendous willpower" and "tension of the mind" that Tarrou's kind of saint exercises in his own form of renunciation. "Health, integrity, purity . . . is a product of the human will," says Tarrou, and insofar as the human will is the only part of the Will that has sufficient consciousness and knowledge to negate itself, Schopenhauer would have agreed. That's where the similarity ends.

For Tarrou's renunciation is an ultimate outcry against injustice and suffering, whether caused by a literal plague or a moral one; it is but an extension of his participation in the activities of the "sanitary squads" in which, like the true rebel he was, he risked his life (and lost it) for the principle of solidarity. If he believed in the universality of evil, he did not believe that it was essential to life and that the world was such that men, in creating their own fate, received only what they deserved. Like Rieux, he knew that the hopelessness of the struggle was no reason not to struggle; that one was obliged to do what one could. Renunciation, in Tarrou's idea of it, involves a positive struggle that aims not at transcendent serenity, but at conquest, impossible though it may be, of evil and sickness.

This whole moral vision, we learn, was shaped by Tarrou's traumatic response to a trial, in which his father, the prosecutor, "spewed out long, turgid phrases like an endless stream of snakes," in "clamoring for the prisoner's death" (224). Again like Rieux, he thus understands the principle of bearing true witness and the moral imperative to use clear language in a society in which both Church and State, through sermon and political rhetoric, seek to intoxicate the citizenry. Camus was to write about yet another man who bore true witness but bore it in such a way that it ceased to be true. He was a Parisian lawyer turned judge-penitent—and he was not a metaphysical rebel.

In May 1950 Camus jotted down in his notebook this brief outline: "I. The Myth of Sisyphus (absurd)—II. The Myth of Prometheus (revolt)—III. The Myth of Nemesis." Slightly earlier he had written,

> My work during these first two cycles: persons without lies, hence not real. They are not of this world. This is probably why up to now I am not a novelist in the usual sense. But rather an artist who creates myths to fit his passion and his anguish. (*Note Books* 2:255)

There is no indication that these entries have any bearing on Camus's third and last novel, *La Chute (The Fall),* which was not to appear for another six years. Still, its single character, Jean-Baptiste Clamence, is a kind of Nemesis whose victim is none other than himself. Like Camus, he has created a myth to fit his own passion and anguish; he defines his own crime, judges himself guilty, and, as penance, goes into exile in Amsterdam, where he recites his tale to anyone who seems a promising listener. But even in sackcloth and ashes, he remains the Parisian lawyer whose very eloquence will betray him. "Holland is a dream," says Clamence; "sleep-walking in the fog's gilded incense," its people pray to the "grimacing gods of Indonesia." It "is not only the Europe of merchants but also the sea, the sea that leads to Cipango and to those isles where men die mad and happy" (*Fall,* 12). This curious fantasy, romantically oblivious to the realities of colonial rule, reveals much about a narrator who, obsessed with personal salvation, is himself a kind of sleepwalker in "the fog's gilded incense" of his own rhetoric. If Amsterdam is indeed the "middle class hell . . . peopled with bad dreams" that he says it is, he himself is one of its denizens, and what is true of the boat ride on the fog-bound Zuiderzee is true of his life in general as well as the account of it: "We are making progress and yet nothing is changing. It's not navigation but dreaming" (73).

The external points of reference required for moral navigation are missing; Clamence broods over his own vices and failures without any possibility of transcending his self-consciousness. His narration, fittingly cast in the form of a monologue addressed to a listener who turns out to be like himself, is in effect the work of a solipsist trapped by the same bourgeois habits of mind and values that he criticizes in others. For Meursault, it meant living without despairing; for Clamence, cynical and introspective, it meant judging himself and others without recourse to any established law or social ethos.

The absence of God implied total human freedom: for Camus, we recall, the revolutionaries, in replacing divine law with that of their own, rejected all principles but desire for power, and "rushed to suicide or madness and proclaimed the apocalypse." Accordingly, Clamence tells us:

> But actually there is no father left, no rule left! [Men] are free and hence have to shift for themselves; and since they don't

want freedom or its judgments, they ask to be rapped on the knuckles, they invent dreadful rules, they rush out to build piles of faggots to replace churches. Savanarolas, I tell you. (100)

Clamence's attempt to become "judge-penitent" (one who must constantly accuse himself in order to earn the right to accuse others) is one reply to the problem of judgment posed by Tarrou in *La Peste*. But it is clearly an unsatisfactory one, since, as the hypersubtle Clamence realizes himself, it still has its roots in self-love, vanity, and the desire for power:

> I haven't changed my way of life; I continue to love myself and to make use of others. Only, the confession of my crimes allows me to begin again lighter in heart and to taste a double enjoyment, first of my nature and secondly of a charming repentance. . . . How intoxicating to feel like God the Father and to hand out definitive testimonials of bad character and habits. (105)

The truth is that Clamence is a false prophet because he is wholly the bourgeois man who engages in moral exploitation in the very act of bringing aid. He proves that the egoism of the public defender, if less bloodthirsty, is no less bloated than that of the public prosecutor:

> Yet is was enough for me to sniff the slightest scent of victim on a defendant for me to swing into action. And what action! A real tempest! My heart was on my sleeve. . . . I am sure you would have admired the accuracy of my tone, the appropriateness of my emotion, the persuasion and warmth, the restrained indignation of my speeches before the court. (15)

Although the desire for business success and literal wealth would be too crass for Clamence, he is still thoroughly materialistic: "Life, its creatures and its gifts, offered themselves to me and I accepted such marks of homage with a kindly pride. To tell the truth, just from being so fully and simply a man, I looked upon myself as something of a superman" (23). His Eden is illusory because he inhabits it alone. The climactic moral incident in his life, his failure to come to the aid of a girl who has thrown herself into the Seine, reveals that he lacks not only courage but compassion as well, without which he never can achieve the salvation he eventually seeks.

Clamence's cynicism, therefore, provides a natural rationalization for his own deficiencies. His message is that self-love underlies all human action and attachments, that while "we cannot assert the innocence of anyone . . . we can state with certainty the guilt of all" (82). The difference between Clamence's expression of these sentiments and Tarrou's in *La Peste* is humility ("I know that I'm not qualified to pass judgment on . . . others," he says, "I've learned modesty"). Clamence remains the *judge-advocate* to the end. Comprehension of his own nature does not lead him to true penitence but to accepting himself on the grounds that all men are sinners: "we are in the soup together. However, I have a superiority in that I know it and this gives me the right to speak" (103-4). The confession is a means not only of self-accusation but of self-aggrandizement and intimidation of those whom he approaches. Perhaps a true justification of Clamence would be proof that he had wrought a conversion in his listener. But we are not even certain whether he had an actual listener or whether he was talking to himself—whether he could even in fact conceive that there were centers of consciousness other than his own:

> You practice in Paris the noble profession of lawyer! I sensed that we were of the same species. Are we not all alike, constantly talking and to no one, for ever up against the same questions although we know the answers in advance? Then tell me, please, what happened to you one night on the quays of the Seine and how you managed never to risk your life. You yourself utter the words that for years have never ceased echoing through my nights. (108)

The solipsist's rebellion is, in essence, wholly psychological. Clamence abandons his Eden when, after failing to rescue the drowning girl, he is haunted by the sound of mocking laughter.

He falls into petty vices that represent an attack on his normal style of living and later into debauchery; he eventually chooses Amsterdam as the site of his exile and new role as judge-penitent; it is a city he often compares to hell, but one which is really for him a limbo in which he suffers no pain other than that which he inflicts upon himself. That may be pain enough and perhaps his true punishment is that it should be futile.

Clamence is a detotalizer and a monologist, a term that I have elsewhere used in a special sense (see my *The Monological Jew*). Monologism or monologuery is a form of (non)communication that belongs to what Martin Buber has called the I-It relationship, one of whose attributes is that it holds the listener not as a "whole" human being whose presence the speaker feels and engages in the intimacy of "dialogue," but rather as an object or sounding board for the speaker's linguistic indulgences and the obsessions they betray. By the same token, Rieux is the very antithesis of Clamence; even though it is true that he narrates the story of the plague, he is not a monologist but a witness (in Camus's sense) who is anything but intoxicated with his own psyche or the sound of his voice. Far from being a detotalizer or force for social disorder, he is the epitome of the positive man in a detotalized society.

Rieux is a social hero, Meursault an Absurd one, who, while a kind of solipsist and in no way a force for social unity, is no true monologist, either. Rather, the real monologists in his world are the Magistrate, the priest, and the prosecuting attorney, each of whom is carried away by his own rhetoric both in private and in court.

In this chapter, I have been concerned mainly with philosophic abstractions, a necessary and rewarding subject, perhaps, but one that cannot give a total insight into Camus as a writer and thinker. Even though it may be true that the world is rational to the rational man (as Hegel and Lukács both believe), we can still ask, Is it sick to the sick man? And what of the rational man who is sick? Perhaps we are oversimplifying when we seek, in a writer's physical condition, the origins of his view of life, but certainly Camus's long bout with tubercu-

2. The Totalities of Existentialism

losis (dating from around 1930), which often kept him isolated and depressed, contributed much to the emotional side of his pessimism. Theoretically it may be so that once it strikes, plague cannot be conquered, but when one suffers from an incurable disease (the new drugs did not eliminate Camus's infection) that theory has the force of living, and lived, truth, imparting its certitudes even to those situations that are merely symbolized by disease. And because the sick man tends to become solipsistically involved with his own condition, Camus's creation of a Meursault or a Clamence may have been guided by more than philosophic abstraction. Yet, while Rieux, the doctor, the man of reason, has no cure, he does have a prescription for overcoming despair and loneliness: one summons all one's willpower to fight the plague. Like the slave who rebels, the sick man thus fights his own battle in the name of a principle that goes beyond himself—he chooses life and community. As did Camus—until Nemesis, growing weary or bored, turned to the final absurdity she had in store for him, and he himself became the Arab on the beach.

Part Three
Self-Detotalizing Heroes

7 Orwell's Unrevolutionary Rebels

The leap from Albert Camus to George Orwell is not so great as it may seem. Both were political leftists in their essays and nihilists in their fiction; both were preoccupied with the various forms of rebellion; both had profound, if ambivalent, feelings about colonialism; and both suffered from tuberculosis, a fact worth noting only insofar as the intensity of a writer's pessimism can be attributed to poor health. In short, Camus and Orwell have enough in common to make a consideration of their differences meaningful. Orwell does not, for example, share Camus's flair for philosophic speculation; there is nothing metaphysical about his pessimism, which is wholly derived from his perception of social and political realities. Whereas Camus saw himself as a mythographer and created characters who act out timeless dramas in modern dress, Orwell was a social critic whose heroes exist only in the specific situations in which they are found. Philosophy and myth may transfigure failed rebellion into something nobel or tragic; social criticism, without benefit of myth or ideology, can see it only as the pathetic thing it appears to be. Failed rebellion and failed revolution: ironically these themes are no less recurrent in Orwell than in Camus, for although Orwell is ostensibly a social revolutionary, his characters all carry out confused personal struggles against a system that invariably reassimilates or destroys them. The issue that emerges here is Orwell's commitment to socialism and its influence, or lack of it, on his fiction. This was not a problem for Camus, who, although briefly a communist, worked out a positive ideology of his own. On the other hand, given the problems that concerned him, Orwell could rely on no positive "doctrine" but the one socialist thought might have provided.

Although he had been an "anticapitalist" all of his adult life, it was not until June 1937, when he lay in a Spanish hospital recovering from a throat wound, that Orwell could proclaim himself a socialist. "I have seen wonderful things," he wrote to Cyril Connolly, "& at last really believe in Socialism, which I never did before" (*Collected Essays,* 269). He had not been able to say as much even the preceding year, when he wrote *The Road to Wigan Pier,* a survey of mining conditions in northern England that revealed his understanding of the psychology of the working class as well as the petty bourgeoisie. While in the last half of that book, Orwell affirmed the need for socialism, he was more concerned with the bad image and misdoings of English Socialists than he was with revolutionary philosophy. Even in *The Lion and the Unicorn* (1941), his most explicit exposition and advocacy of socialism, Orwell avoided theory and doctrine in favor of political psychology. Just as in *Homage to Catalonia* he had argued that a socialist revolution was necessary to the success of the Loyalists, so he argued here that it was essential to the British war effort against fascism; in both instances the working class had to have goals it could fight for if it was going to fight effectively.

Whatever his relation to the movement in England (he joined the Independent Labour Party in 1938), Orwell never wrote a novel that expressed the positive ideals of socialism, either in respect to the development of the individual or the progress of society. Rather, his characters are well known for their passivity and their impotence against a system that inexorably victimized them. Orwell's preoccupation with this condition, which lasted from his first novel, *Burmese Days* (1934), to his last, *Nineteen Eighty-Four* (1949), sprung from his own childhood experiences, if the retrospective essay "Such, Such Were the Joys" is to be taken as a literal account of his years at St. Cyprian's school. And this essay offers a special insight into the psychology of the Orwell hero, whether he is struggling against imperialist bigotry in Burma, commercialism in London, or Oligarchal Collectivism in Airstrip One. It is precisely the negative kind of psychology out of which socialism claims to offer a way.

The lesson of St. Cyprian's (Crossgates in the essay) is not simply that prep schools are oppressive institutions against which sensitive students rebel, but that true rebellion is impossible because there are no alternative values to those of the system. The child is forced to accept the validity of the very ideals he would defy and therefore cannot but feel guilty:

> A child accepts the codes of behaviour that are presented to it, even when it breaks them. From the age of eight, or even earlier, the consciousness of sin was never far away from me. If I contrived to seem callous and defiant, it was only a thin cover over a mass of shame and dismay. All through my boyhood I had a profound conviction that I was no good, that I was wasting my time, wrecking my talents, behaving with monstrous folly and wickedness and ingratitude—and all this, it seemed, was inescapable, because I lived among laws which were absolute. . . . (*Collected Essays,* 24)

The kind of schizophrenia that characterizes Winston Smith in *Nineteen Eighty-Four* has its origins in prep student psychology:

> The high-water mark of good favour was to be invited to serve at table on Sunday nights when Bingo and Sim [the headmaster and his wife] had guests to dinner. . . . one got a servile pleasure from standing behind the seated guests and darting deferentially forward when something was wanted. Whenever one had the chance to suck up, one did suck up, and at the first smile one's hatred turned into a sort of cringing love.

3. Self-Detotalizing Heroes

This state of mind coexists with its opposite:

> And yet all the while, at the middle of one's heart, there seemed to stand an incorruptible inner self who knew that whatever one did—whether one laughed or snivelled or went into frenzies of gratitude for small favours—one's only true feeling was hatred. (33)

The hatred is as impotent as the "cringing" love is pathetic; the rebel is in part possessed by the system, and the defiance by which he would free himself is not based upon any coherent values.

This situation recurred when Orwell (then Eric Blair), age nineteen, went to Burma as an officer in the Indian Imperial Police—and shot an elephant! As he informs us "he had come to realize that imperialism was an evil thing" and that the sight of native prisoners left him "with an intolerable sense of guilt." On the other hand, he was outraged by the frequent insults he and other Europeans endured from Burmese mobs. He concludes: "I could get nothing into perspective. I was young and ill-educated and I had to think out my problems in the utter silence that is imposed on every Englishman in the East." Sensitive enough to rebel but not politically or intellectually developed enough to give his rebellion a positive direction, he finds himself called upon to deal with an escaped elephant that had gone wild but has since calmed down.

There is no reason to kill the animal and Orwell does not want to kill him, but, as he interprets the situation, he has no choice:

> And suddenly I realized that I should have to shoot the elephant after all. The people expected it of me and I had got to do it; I could feel their two thousand wills pressing me forward, irresistibly. And it was at this moment . . . that I first grasped the hollowness, the futility of the white man's dominion in the East. . . . I was only an absurd puppet pushed to and fro by the will of those yellow faces behind. I perceived in this moment that when

the white man turns tyrant it is his own freedom that he destroys. ("Shooting an Elephant")

Fear of ridicule is the problem, and the English sahib, doomed constantly to impress the natives, must do what they expect of him.
This is a convincing argument, but it is not really definitive. A sahib who did not share Orwell's doubts about the British presence in Burma would not necessarily see the question of maintaining face before a crowd as paramount and would not necessarily have felt compelled to shoot. (Neither, on the other hand, might he have been moved by cruelties perpetrated upon native prisoners.)
Correspondingly, an Englishman who dissociated himself completely from the imperial administration, renounced the "white man's tyranny," would also have been free of compulsion—since as Orwell tells us, it is through his tyranny that the imperialist destroys his own freedom. But the man who shoots the elephant is one who feels the profound insecurity of his social position yet, instead of abandoning or trying to transcend it, finds himself upholding it precisely because he is ignorant of any constructive alternatives. He is, in fact, "young and ill-educated."
Blair resolved the issue by resigning his commission and quitting Burma permanently, but the crisis this episode expressed—that of the sensitive but isolated hero, thrown back on resources too limited for him successfully to defy the world or change it—was to reappear in one form or another in nearly all of Orwell's fiction. Flory, the hero of *Burmese Days,* understands his situation perfectly:

> Each year had been lonelier and more bitter than the last. What was at the center of all his thoughts now, and what poisoned everything, was the ever bitterer hatred of the atmosphere of imperialism in which he lived. For as his brain developed—you cannot stop your brain developing, and it is one of the tragedies of the half-educated that they develop late, when they are al-

ready committed to some wrong way of life—he had grasped the truth about the English and their Empire. (60)

He appreciates the consequences of isolation:

> It is a corrupting thing to live one's real life in secret. One should live with the stream of life, not against it. It would be better to be the thickest-skulled pukka sahib . . . than to live silent, alone, consoling oneself in secret, sterile worlds. (62)

In an ironic foreshadowing of things to come, Mrs. Lackersteen, one of the more outspoken *memsahibs* in the British colony at Kyauktada, writes to her niece, who is about to make the journey to Burma, "But really in some ways these small stations have their advantages for a young girl. . . . The unmarried men are so lonely that they appreciate a girl's society in a quite wonderful way" (84). Flory is suffering not from simple loneliness but from total alienation. While he tries to maintain appearances, avoid rows, and keep his membership in good standing at the club, he endures an inner rage over the bigotry and narrow mindedness of his countrymen:

> Dull boozing witless porkers! Was it possible that they could go on week after week, year after year, repeating word for word the same evil-minded drivel, like a parody of a fifth-rate story in *Blackwood's*. . . . Oh, what a place, what people! What a civilisation is this of ours—this godless civilisation. . . .

But he can still appreciate his own dichotomous position: "God have mercy on us, for all of us are part of it" (29).

Although Elizabeth Lackersteen turns out to be a shallow young woman who easily adapts herself to the habits and attitudes of the colony, Flory is wholly captivated by her:

> Elizabeth, by coming into his life, had so changed it and renewed it that all the dirty, miserable years might never have passed. Her presence had changed the whole orbit of his mind.

> She had brought back to him the air of England—dear England, where thought is free and one is not condemned forever to dance the *danse du pukka sahib* for the edification of the lower races. . . . Just by existing she had made it possible for him, she had even made it natural to him, to act decently. (130)

This is the fantasy of a man possessed by the very system against which he would rebel. Flory can achieve intimacy with the woman only when he reflects her values; when he expresses his own, she turns away. She abandons him altogether upon the arrival of a young cavalry officer of aristocratic birth. In turn deserted by this person, she effects a reconciliation with Flory only to abandon him again when he is publicly humiliated by the threats of his Burmese mistress, whom he has cast off.

The pathetic pursuit of Elizabeth is counterbalanced by Flory's friendship with the kindly, but essentially feckless, Indian doctor Veraswami. This relationship is frowned upon by the colony, although all it really consists of is a longstanding friendly debate on imperialism, with Veraswami as apologist. Like Flory, Veraswami is a victim, not a man of action or a moral guide who can provide his friend with the insight or values to lead him out of his quagmire, and he is eventually brought down by the local political boss, U Po Kylin, an unscrupulous self-made man, who represents what it means to be active and successful in this society.

Flory's greatest moment comes when, learning that membership in the club would give Veraswami the prestige he needed to protect him from the schemes of U Po Kylin, he puts up the Indian's name, knowing full well that a row will follow. But the meeting is interrupted by a Burmese mob, reacting to an incident that had occurred shortly before, and ironically Flory becomes a hero to the very people he detests by slipping out of the clubhouse and bringing help. After Elizabeth's final rejection of him, Flory commits suicide, thereby confirming his inability to resolve his situation in any meaningful way. This sense of hopelessness was to carry over into the story of Dorothy Hare, the main character in Orwell's next novel, *A Clergyman's Daughter.*

No rebel in any sense of the word, Dorothy accepts the drudgery of running her father's household on inadequate funds and of performing the endless social chores of her position. Repelled by the very idea of sexual intercourse, punishing herself with needle pricks and other "penances" when her thoughts diverge from rectitude, she seems destined for a life of arid spinsterhood. Then struck by amnesia, she finds herself on the London streets, joins a group of drifters, and eventually obtains work as a hop-picker. As her memory gradually returns, she learns that she has been repudiated by her father, who is under the impression that she simply ran off, but through family connections, she is given a position in a girls' school, which, run only for profit, represents the very nadir of the English education system. Here, for the first time in her life, Dorothy acts positively and creatively against the establishment by introducing a curriculum that the students find rewarding. But like all of Orwell's heroes, she is wholly isolated in her battle, and though certain that her educational values are superior to those she has tried to replace, she cannot stand up to the pressures of the narrow-minded parents and the crass headmistress to reinstitute the old, oppressive and worthless system. Her surrender, however, does not bring her the favor she seeks, and she is dismissed at the first convenient moment.

This episode bespeaks the hopelessness of Dorothy's position, just as it exemplifies the hopelessness of the sensitive but detotalized individual, who, partly a product of the system, and partly a would-be rebel, finds himself with no support and no apparent options. The only voice urging Dorothy on, at least to escape if not to positive rebellion, is that of Washburton, lecher and self-proclaimed atheist, whose offer of marriage Dorothy realizes is no solution. Yet Washburton's vivid description of the future awaiting her if she refuses—drudgery and sterility—is wholly accurate, and when she accepts this alternative, a return to the old life without the religious faith that gave it what little meaning it had, we know that she is lost.

The futility of the rebellion of the lower middle-class hero is really spelled out in *Keep the Aspidistra Flying*. In Orwell's world, failure is always personal: the hero suffers from "passivity" and self-consciousness; temperamentally he is a loner. And while he is sensitive to the weaknesses of the society in which he lives, he has no coherent ideas on how to correct them. Escape may or may not be possible for him, but social action clearly is impossible. Gordon Comstock, a young poet obsessed with the pervasiveness of money worship in the world around him, refuses to keep a job in which he can "get ahead" and takes work as an ill-paid clerk in a bookstore. He chooses squalor and suffers various humiliations, especially in regard to his girlfriend, Rosemary, who has refused to sleep with him. But even when she consents, during an outing, he is rendered impotent by the embarrassment suffered at the hands of a waiter during lunch.

The philosophic bankruptcy of Comstock's outlook is apparent in the line of reasoning that, toward the end of the novel, sums up his beliefs:

> To spend your days in meaningless mechanical work, work that could be slovened through in a sort of coma; to come home and light the fire when you had any coal . . . and get the stuffy little attic warm; to sit over a squalid meal of bacon, bread-and-marg and tea, cooked over a gas-ring; to lie on the frowzy bed, reading a thriller or doing the Brain Brighteners in *Tit Bits* until the small hours; it was the kind of life he wanted. . . . Life had beaten him; but you can still beat life by turning your face away. Better to sink than rise. Down, down into the ghost-kingdom, the shadowy world where shame, effort, decency do not exist! (208-9)

These are the alternatives of the nonpolitical, isolated aesthete.

Socialism is represented in the novel in the person of Comstock's friend and protector, the wealthy magazine editor, Ravelston. Ravelston is perhaps the type of the intellectual socialist, whom Orwell condemns in the second half of *The Road to Wigan Pier,* a man whose life style keeps him far from actual contact with the proletariat. Nonetheless, he speaks true when he tells Comstock,

> "The mistake you make, don't you see, is in thinking one can live in a corrupt society without being corrupt oneself. After all, what do you achieve by refusing to make money? You're trying to behave as though one could stand right outside our economic system. But one can't. One's got to change the system, or one changes nothing. One can't put things right in a hole-and-corner way, if you take my meaning." (211)

This theme is never developed; in any case, Ravelston is not taken seriously.

Comstock's philosophy works poorly enough for the single man; it is all but impossible for the man who is married. When he becomes responsible for Rosemary, whom he has made pregnant, Comstock gives in to the pressure to accept the bourgeois life, returns to his profitable job with an advertising agency, and buys an aspidistra, the plant beloved by the middle class. In this denouement the detotalized hero is supposedly reintegrated into the world he has repudiated, and Comstock's justification seems to imply a resolution to his problems—economic, moral, and spiritual:

> Our civilization is founded on greed and fear, but in the lives of common men the greed and fear are mysteriously transmuted into something nobler. The lower middle-class people . . . lived by the money-code, sure enough, and yet they contrived to keep their decency. The money-code as they interpreted it was not merely cynical and hoggish. They had their standards, their inviolable points of honour. They kept themselves "respectable"—kept the aspidistra flying. (279)

Is this Orwell speaking through the persona of his now redeemed hero—wherein we are meant to take the optimism seriously—or is Orwell ironically suggesting that Comstock has betrayed his principles and rendered his criticism of society meaningless? In any case socialism is not posited as an answer to the problems besetting Comstock as an individual or the society that he has condemned. It was not until 1937, in a foreign country with a living model before his eyes, that Orwell could explicitly identify himself with a socialist cause.

But did Orwell really discover socialism in Spain? In principle, yes; in doctrine, no. He had been exhilarated by his experiences in Aragon, where he had seen a de facto socialism at work:

> Many of the normal motives of civilized life—snobbishness, money-grubbing, fear of the boss, etc.—had simply ceased to exist. The ordinary class-division of society had disappeared to an extent that is almost unthinkable in the money-tainted air of England; there was no one there except the peasants and ourselves, and no one owned anyone else as his master.

But he made clear that he was not interested in ideology:

> In every country in the world a huge tribe of party-hacks and sleek little professors are busy "proving" that Socialism means no more than a planned state-capitalism with the grab-motive left intact. But fortunately there also exists a vision of Socialism quite different from this. The thing that attracts ordinary men to Socialism and makes them willing to risk their skins for it, the "mystique" of Socialism, is the idea of equality; to the vast majority of people Socialism means a classless society, or it means nothing at all. (*Homage to Catalonia,* 104)

Orwell could say that the effect of this experience was to make his "desire to see Socialism established much more actual than it had been before," but he was not concerned with precisely how a socialist society could be created in England, nor, as a novelist, with characters who were aware of the problems involved and could engage in creative social action.

Thus as late as 1939 Orwell could still write a novel like *Coming Up for Air,* the very title of which suggests the limited options available to his characters. Here we again find the hero, George Bowling, immersed in the routines of bourgeois life, sensitive enough to understand himself, but basically incapable of transcending his fate. As he tells us, he is very much a part of the world that frequently disgusts him:

> I'm vulgar, I'm insensitive, and I fit in with my environment. So long as anywhere in the world things are being sold on commission and livings are picked up by sheer brass and lack of finer feelings, chaps like me will be doing it. . . . But also I've got something else inside me, chiefly a hangover from the past. (23)

Much of the novel is taken up by Bowling's nostalgic recollection of his childhood and youth in Lower Binfield; coming up for air means for him a visit to the town, one that turns out to be crushingly disappointing: Lower Binfield has been industrialized and polluted beyond recognition.

Bowling's helpless disgust at the ravages of civilization has a counterpart in his political attitudes. He is tormented by the fear of imminent war and has a vision of a future police state in England. Still, he is unable to identify himself with any political group or conceive of any course of action. His response to the antifascist speaker at a meeting of the Left Book Club is wholly critical:

> The lecturer was rather a mean-looking little chap, but a good speaker. White face, very mobile mouth, and the rather grating voice they get from constant speaking. Of course he was pitching into Hitler and the Nazis. . . .
> "Bestial atrocities. . . . Hideous outbursts of sadism. . . . Iniquitous persecution of the Jews. . . . Back to the Dark Ages. . . . Act before it is too late. . . . Alliance of the democratic nations. . . ."
> You know the line of talk. These chaps can churn it out by the hour. (171)

That the speaker may be conveying an accurate picture is of no concern; Bowling is much more interested in interpreting the psychology behind the words:

I saw the vision that he was seeing. And it wasn't at all the kind of vision that can be talked about. What he's *saying* is merely that Hitler's after us and we must all get together and have a good hate. . . . But what he's *seeing* is something quite different. It's a picture of himself smashing people's faces in with a spanner. Fascist faces, of course. . . . The bones cave in like an eggshell and what was a face a minute ago is just a great big blob of strawberry jam. . . . And it's all O.K. because the smashed faces belong to Fascists. You could hear all that in the tone of his voice. (175)

The only outcome of the belief that antifascists are really as fascistic as the fascists is despair and paralysis. For all his scorn, however, Bowling is sufficiently unsettled to pay a visit to a retired school-master, a classicist, who represents to him the world of culture. Bowling asks him what he thinks of Hitler and receives the reply,

"Hitler? This German person? My dear fellow! I *don't* think of him."
"But the trouble is he's going to bloody well make us think of him before he's finished." . . .
"I see no reason for paying any attention to him. A mere adventurer. These people come and go. Ephemeral, purely ephemeral." (185)

This is obviously unsatisfactory. There is no real guidance for Bowling, who, we imagine, will go on brooding in isolation until events claim him.

Although the point is not made clear in *Coming Up for Air,* Orwell himself, after his return from Spain, insisted repeatedly that fascism was a product of capitalism, and that it was futile to oppose one without working for the overthrow of the other. "If one collaborates with a capitalist-imperialist government in a struggle 'against Fascism,'" he told Geoffrey Gorer, "one is simply letting Fascism in by the back door." In Spain, the enemy was not only the fascists themselves but the parties that "wanted to fight the Fascists in the name of 'democracy,' and

3. Self-Detotalizing Heroes

... when they felt sure enough of their position and had tricked the workers into giving up their arms, reintroduce capitalism." This view was elaborated in *The Lion and the Unicorn* (1941), in which Orwell admitted the failure of the various left-wing groups in England and called for a specifically "English Socialism." What this meant was the elimination of privilege without violation of basic English democratic institutions. Orwell believed that public opinion could force a "shift of power" that was essential if the war against Germany were to be waged effectively. "What is wanted," he wrote, "is a conscious, open revolt by ordinary people against inefficiency, class privilege and the rule of the old."

The Lion and the Unicorn is a cautionary essay, but insofar as it prescribes as well as diagnoses, it is also optimistic. Still, its values were never expressed in Orwell's fiction, which remained coldly pessimistic.

Thus, for all the cleverness of its allegory, *Animal Farm* (1946), perhaps Orwell's most acclaimed book, did not reflect the "socialist" development in his thought. The chief intention of this "fairy story," is to present the way in which a revolution is betrayed; its target is the hypocrisy of a leadership that comes to assume the qualities of the ruling class it has overthrown. Major, the horse who prophesies the revolution, sets the theme around which most of the irony centers:

> In fighting against Man, we must not come to resemble him. Even when you have conquered him, do not adopt his vices. No animal must ever live in a house, or sleep in a bed, or wear clothes, or drink alcohol, or smoke tobacco, or touch money, or engage in trade. All the habits of Man are evil. And, above all, no animal must ever tyrannise over his own kind. Weak or strong, clever or simple, we are all brothers. No animal must ever kill any other animal. All animals are equal. (22)

These are the very vices into which the boar, Napoleon, falls during the course of his dictatorship. In rewriting history, making a former hero into a scapegoat, maintaining a personal army, and the like, Napoleon is meant to be a comment on

Stalin, but the question of the overall significance of the satire persists.

Like all satire, *Animal Farm* exposes human weaknesses but in doing so gives us a view of society that is based wholly on personalities or personality stereotypes. Is Napoleon's corruption inevitable? If so, are we to believe that all revolutionary leaders are corrupt and that all revolutions are inevitably betrayed? Camus would affirm that this is indeed the case, though the malady goes deeper than mere hypocrisy or acquisition of the vices of one's enemies. Even so, foremost in both Camus's and Orwell's views of revolution is the idea that power corrupts and that human nature is weak. Conversely, both Camus and Orwell assert a rational ideal—"solar thought" and the principles of egalitarianism—to which revolutionaries must cleave if they are to remain true to their inspiration. Thus, while Orwell does have a vision, essentially implicit, of what Animal Farm should have been, he gives no indication of how such an ideal can be attained, if at all. Like Camus, he saw the necessity for revolution but he had an even sharper eye for its contradictions: the result is that *Animal Farm,* the story of a revolution, turns out to be no more optimistic than the previous stories in which revolution was not even a hope and defeat of the individual was inevitable.

We have already noted the limitations of allegory as a means of presenting social reality (see pp. 135–36). Like allegory, the animal fable is, finally, too simplistic to deal convincingly with the social, political, and psychological (as distinguished from the universal or broadly "human") aspects of actual revolution. Satire, I know, was never meant to be equated with realism, but its significance is still limited by the extent to which it is caricature. We delight in the correspondences and analogies of *Animal Farm,* but we are not given any greater insight into the complexities—or their impact upon the people who lived through them—of real social upheavals.

Orwell's concern with totalitarianism, a phenomenon that he apparently had begun to see as something distinct from the class struggle, was developed in *Nineteen Eighty-Four.* This novel, partly naturalistic, partly fantastic, as Orwell put it, dramatizes the principle that total power, exercised through ideological control and a secret police, is possible. The fact that the party is successful in its attempts to revise history, create a living language in which subversive abstractions are eliminated, and to maintain itself generally indicates that Orwell himself pessimistically believes in the efficacy of its methods. As O'Brien, the inner-party members, tells his victim, Winston Smith, the ruling class is engaged in "collective solipsism," the perpetual rerecording of events to conform with current policy, and that the "reality" they have established has all the potency of a real reality, since in the final analysis, "reality is inside the skull."

O'Brien goes on to prophesy a world in which the Party achieves omnipotence, "a boot stamping on a human face— forever" (220), and there is nothing in the novel, including Smith's protestations, to prove him wrong; to the contrary, Smith's conversion proves O'Brien wholly justified. This nightmarish vision, a product of idealism gone wild, is predicated on the assumption that not only men individually but societies as a whole can disengage themselves from history and reach stasis purely through intellectual machinations. Fortunes in war are the only gratuitous force acting upon the society and they apparently can be kept under control.

Orwell was fully aware that this view of history gave priority to precisely that element the Marxist view took as derivative: consciousness as manifested in the will to power. He wrote, for example, that Jack London showed "special insight" in *The Iron Heel*, a novel that envisions an oppressive state ruled by capitalist oligarchs, when he indicated that the capitalist class would not be passively defeated by "social forces" or "history," but would counterattack and attempt to seize total power. Orwell is really confirming his own reading of history when he says that although London accepted certain Marxist conclusions, he was temperamentally "very different from the majority of Marxists:" "With his love of violence and physical strength, his belief in 'natural aristocracy,' his animal-worship and exaltation of the primitive, he had in him what one might fairly call a Fascist strain. This probably helped him to understand just how the possessing class would behave when once they were seriously menaced" (*Collected Essays,* 2:30-31). One need not be a fascist to believe in the potency of the will to power in human affairs, and Orwell is certainly not suggesting that he himself has a fascist strain. What he is saying is that the Marxian socialists were blind on the point, that they "failed to foresee dangers that were obvious to people who had never heard the name of Marx."

Even so, *The Iron Heel* clearly is much closer than *Nineteen Eighty-Four* to socialist thinking. To begin with, it *is* concerned with the class struggle; it does present, in Ernest Everhard, a revolutionary hero whose Nietzschean strength is devoted to the service of socialism; it does envision the eventual triumph of the workers and the emergence of a socialist state. Most important is that it depicts a working class which, though oppressed, never loses its identity or gives up its revolutionary struggle; it embodies the positive ideals that survive and are a permanent source of hope.[1]

There is a qualitative difference between a capitalist tyranny and a totalitarian state, such as is imagined in *Nineteen Eighty-Four.* While the latter is believed to have somehow developed from an economic revolution, the oligarchy is not equated specifically with a traditional class, the capitalist, but with the Party, a semimystical organization that has emerged out of a raw and inevitable will to power that is assumed, when wakened by opportune conditions, to be an irresistible, if not all-consuming, instinct in human beings. The ranks of this organization, we are told in Goldstein's clandestine account, are filled solely by examination, and the positions of power, unlike those in capitalism, are not hereditary. The working class has been replaced by the "proles," a group that Winston Smith discovers to be more "human" in its relationships, but in whom there can be no hope for positive action. The entire society, we learn, is geared to maintaining the "hierarchical structure" of the party apparatus; it is a world, in fact, in which pure form has triumphed and become monstrous, a totality proof against detotalization, a synchrony free of all diachrony. Whereas the capitalist tyranny, as defined by socialism, is caught up in the dialectics of history and is constantly moving toward the qualitative change of revolution, the totalitarian state is a changeless, fixed entity dedicated to the elimination of history and the perpetuation of a power relationship that is an end itself.[2]

Some of the fundamental characteristics of the world of *Nineteen Eighty-Four* have been traced to James Burnham, whose books, *The Managerial Revolution* (1940) and *The Machiavellians* (1942), Orwell analyzed at length in 1946. The most striking thing about Orwell's study is not the indebtedness it reveals but rather its attempt actually to discredit Burnham's prophecies and indeed his character as well.[3] Orwell calmly summarizes Burnham's thesis that the new "managerial" society of the future will consist of

> great super-states grouped around the main industrial centers in Europe, Asia, and America. These super-states will fight among themselves for possession of the remaining uncaptured portions of the earth, but will probably be unable to conquer one another completely. Internally, each society will be hierarchal, with an aristocracy of talent at the top and a mass of semi-slaves at the bottom. (4:160–61)

"The power of the oligarchy," Orwell's paraphrase continues, "always rests upon force or fraud. . . . Politics consists of the struggle for power and nothing else." Then, conceding that this argument is plausible as the description of a current trend, Orwell castigates it as a long-range prophecy, asserting that in its vision of apocalypse it takes no account of the "slowness of historical change." "Burnham sees the trend and assumes that it is irresistible," says Orwell and then goes on to argue *ad hominem*, "rather as a rabbit fascinated by a boa constrictor might assume that a boa constrictor is the strongest thing in the world" (176). By this he means that Burnham is basically a power worshiper himself, and he concludes, "the huge, invincible, everlasting slave empire of which Burnham appears to dream will not be established, or, if established, will not endure, because slavery is no longer a stable basis for human society" (180).

George Kateb could well wonder what happened to change Orwell's mind so completely by the time he began writing the novel, and he comes up with a plausible if somewhat ingenious answer. In the manner of Swift, whom he admired for "a terrible intensity of vision, capable of picking out a single hidden truth and then magnifying and distorting it" (Kateb, 84), Orwell wanted to present an image of pure evil; by thus exaggerating, he would "sicken the decent man" and make him more attached to present political rights; the writer could therefore help defeat his own dire predictions by the very act of presenting them in the form he did. I'm not sure how far this argument takes us—and in fact neither is Kateb.

Perhaps closer to the truth is Alex Zwerdling's opinion that Orwell's attack on Burnham was an attempt to exorcise his own instinctive pessimism, yet this does not account for the fact that Orwell having exorcised his demons took them back in exactly the same form in which he cast them out—Burnham's very notions. That is, it would not account for this fact were Orwell indeed predicting the future. But, according to Zwerdling he is not; he is, rather, "trying to give his readers an idea of what it is like to live in a totalitarian state," and he draws upon childhood fantasies, terrors, and obsessions to do so. Thus "Orwell's plot records the unsuccessful rebellion of a prodigal son, a 'stubborn self-willed exile from the loving breast'" (96).

This view is very much to the point insofar as it shifts the interest away from Orwell's political intentions to his social, psychological, and literary ones. From this perspective it doesn't matter whether Orwell accepted or rejected Burnham's ideas as political prophecy; indeed they are useful to him literally because of the identical characteristic that makes them objectionable politically—their melodramatic and apocalyptic nature. Thus there is no contradiction in Orwell's condemnation of Burnham's notions in a political review and his subsequent use of them as the basis of an imaginative work.

Whatever the case, *Nineteen Eighty-Four* did not represent a new direction for Orwell as a novelist inasmuch as it centers upon but an extreme form of the relationship between the sensitive, would-be rebel and the oppressive system that appears throughout his work. Like Gordon Comstock, Winston Smith "feels" rebellious but cannot conceptualize the values that will enable him to act as a revolutionary; living in total intellectual isolation, he receives no reenforcement and must rely wholly on his own instincts, instincts that in regard to O'Brien prove to be fatal. Julia, the first authentic nonconformist he has met, offers him not revolution but escape:

> Any kind of organized revolt against the Party, which was bound to be a failure, struck her as stupid. The clever thing was to break the rules and stay alive all the same. He wondered vaguely how many others like her there might be in the younger generation—people who had grown up in the world of the Revolution, knowing nothing else, accepting the Party as something unalterable, like the sky, not rebelling against its authority but simply evading it, as a rabbit dodges a dog. (109)[4]

Smith's only real hope for acquiring a revolutionary identity lies with O'Brien, in whom he places his faith completely. Were O'Brien really the subversive that he appears to be to Smith, did the Brotherhood actually exist, were Goldstein's historical account of the origins and nature of Oceania genuine, *Nineteen Eighty-Four* might in some sense have been thought of as a novel in the socialist tradition. That is, it would have pointed a way out, certainly arduous, but at least possible. But that is not what Orwell wanted to say: as we have seen, his thesis was that totalitarian power is characterized by its totality and that, in effect, organization for revolution is impossible. As we have also seen, this was the very point he had sharply criticized James Burnham for making, even though it was in essence but a version of his own recurrent conception. Smith's fate is much more horrible than that of his counterpart in the preceding novels, but then so are the social and political conditions under which he lives.

The more thoroughly totalitarian the state, the more it enforces the detotalization of the populace. A systematic detotalization of language, consciousness, thought, the negation of family values, the perversion of all personal and social relations, the surrogating of sexual desire into state-directed hatred are but the paradoxical means to achieving the "perfect unity" of the undetotalizable totality that is the state of Oceania. Thus, the individual is at once "locked into loneliness" and isolation and made a part of "a nation of warriors and fanatics" all "thinking the same thoughts and shouting the same slogans . . . three hundred million people all with the same face" (64).

All of Orwell's heroes are defeated—by the overt pressures that their worlds apply against them, but, more important, by their inability to find coherent ideals to put in opposition. Smith's conversion to the faith of Big Brother was brought about by torture, but intellectually Smith never did have much of a chance.

Orwell's totalitarian society—a society in which no effective opposition to the order of things exists or can exist—is, in essence, but an extraordinarily brutal and more thoroughly regimented counterpart to the one-dimensional society described by Herbert Marcuse. In advanced capitalist or postindustrial society, argues the latter, the working class, having, like all other classes, been integrated into the social order by the all-pervasive ideology of consumerism, has lost its revolutionary character. What in Orwell's world is achieved through terror, massive propaganda, and all the techniques of the overtly tyrannical and repressive society is achieved in Marcuse's conception of the modern world by a technology that, "extended to a whole system of domination and coordination, creates forms of life (and power) which appear to reconcile the forces opposing the system and to defeat or refute all protest in the name of the historical prospects of freedom from toil and domination." "In this society," says Marcuse, "the productive apparatus tends to become totalitarian to the extent to which it determines not only the socially needed occupations, skills, and attitudes—but also individual needs and aspirations" (*One-Dimensional Man,* xii–xv).

3. Self-Detotalizing Heroes

It is particularly relevant to introduce Marcuse into a discussion of Orwell not only because Marcuse has shown a great deal of interest in *Nineteen Eighty-Four,* but because the same reasons that mainstream Marxism had for criticizing Marcuse's conception of the modern world could be applied to Orwell's. Thus the Soviet critic, Edward Batalov, attacks Marcuse on the grounds that the very idea of a one-dimensional society—that is, a society without internal opposition—flies in the face of the basic Marxist view that all societies develop and change as a result of internal contradictions in dialectical interaction. In that it fails to define "the revolutionary forces and factors within society," argues Batalov, Marcuse's "negation" of the system can lead only to a sterile pessimism or, if an alternative is proposed, to a childish utopianism (*Philosophy of Revolt,* 84). Batalov does not account for those counterforces that Marcuse did define (avant-garde art, for example), but that is of no concern here, for Orwell's Oceania does not offer even cultural opposition as a possibility for change; it therefore represents a view that is even less palatable to the Marxist than Marcuse's.[5]

I say this even though at one point Winston Smith experiences a "mystical reverence" for a proletarian woman who is singing as she hangs up clothes in the squalid courtyard outside his room in the working-class district. She strikes him as being "a solid, unconquerable figure," a symbol of the immortality of the proles, who are "storing up power that would one day overturn the world." Actually this vision reminds us of Zola's prophecy at the conclusion of *Germinal,* and, like Zola, Orwell is relying not on social analysis but on myth to justify his apparent optimism.

Judging from the fact that Smith had already come to believe that the "masses" would never revolt of their own accord, that they were without intellect, we can only conclude that Orwell's faith that a future is possible is a case of *doublethink,* and indeed Smith's concluding statement, as Orwell's last words in the novel, leaves no room for doubt about the depth and durability of his pessimism.

8 Sinclair's Socialite Socialists

In *The Radical Novel in the United States* Walter Rideout defended the long, didactic conclusion of Upton Sinclair's *The Jungle* by maintaining that the turn of the hero, Jurgis Rudkus, to socialism was carefully prepared for: Sinclair conducted Jurgis "through all the circles of the workers' inferno" and attempted to "show that no other savior except socialism exists."[1] The point is worth elaborating for it is crucial to an understanding of what Sinclair achieved in *The Jungle* and what he failed to achieve in most of his other novels.

Now, without the specifically socialist conclusion, Jurgis's story would be that of a naturalist man in a naturalist world. His repeated insights into the harsh terms of life in Packertown are never in themselves enough to free him. He arrives in America, for instance, with a naïve faith in the ways of the world and a pride in his own powers; in reaching the inevitably disastrous decision to buy a house, he reasons:

> Others might have failed at it, but he was not the failing kind—he would show them how to do it. He would work all day, and all night too, if need be; he would never rest until the house was paid for and his people had a home. (57–58)

He eventually gains an understanding of his situation:

3. Self-Detotalizing Heroes

> He had learned the ways of things about him now. It was a war of each against all, and the devil take the hindmost. . . . You went about with your soul full of suspicion and hatred; you understood that you were environed by hostile powers that were trying to get your money, and who used all the virtues to bait their traps with. (87)

This disillusionment does not make a socialist out of Jurgis. Quite the contrary, he accepts the state of affairs around him as a permanent reality, a given to which he must adapt himself. It is the naturalist, not the socialist, who declares the world a hopeless jungle. Thus Jurgis, still confident in his powers, goes no farther than is required by personal survival and the protection of his immediate family. His encounter with unionism teaches him that he has "brothers in affliction and allies. Their one chance for life was in union, and so the struggle became a kind of crusade" (107). But this sentiment, embryonic to begin with, does not withstand the despair that overtakes him as he lies convalescing from an injured ankle.

It is in the misery of his imprisonment for assaulting his wife's seducer, however, that the vision of the world as a jungle in which all that matters is personal survival overwhelms Jurgis. Sinclair makes it explicit that frustration and rage, not social consciousness, underlie Jurgis's "rebellion":

> These midnight hours were fateful ones to Jurgis; in them was the beginning of his rebellion, of his outlawry and his unbelief. He had no wit to trace back the social crime to its far sources—he could not say that it was the thing men have called "the system" that was crushing him to the earth. . . . He only knew that he was wronged, and that the world had wronged him. . . . And every hour his soul grew blacker, every hour he dreamed new dreams of vengeance, of defiance, of raging, frenzied hate. (192)

This response is as far as Jurgis can go; on the death of his son, the last member of his immediate family, he can feel only the same kind of rage:

> There should be no more tears and no more tenderness; he had had enough of them—they had sold him into slavery! Now he was going to be free, to tear off his shackles, to rise up and fight. . . . he was going to think of himself, he was going to fight for himself, against the world that had baffled him and tortured him! (253-54)

Thoroughly disillusioned but still unenlightened—trapped by ignorance as well as rage—Jurgis gains a temporary respite by fleeing to the countryside, but returns to a life of street crime and, when the opportunity presents itself, political corruption. Nor is he averse to strikebreaking, an activity that earns for him, for the first time in the novel, Sinclair's sarcasm.

Regarded from a socialist point of view, Jurgis is the very man who, because of his sufferings, can appreciate the truth once it is made known to him. His conversion is explained in the same oration that illuminates him:

> There will be some one man whom pain and suffering have made desperate. . . . And to him my words will come like a sudden flash of lightning to one who travels in darkness. . . . The scales will fall from his eyes, the shackles will be torn from his limbs—he will leap up with a cry of thankfulness, he will stride forth a free man at last! A man delivered from his self-created slavery! A man who will never be trapped—whom no blandishments will cajole, whom no threats will frighten; who from tonight on will move forward, and not backward, who will study and understand, who will gird on his sword and take his place in the army of his comrades and brothers. (361-62)

An important point is easily overlooked in the flow of the rhetoric: revelation is only the first step in a socialist education; it must be followed by hard study and experience. The conclusion of *The Jungle* is optimistic not simply because it envisions a socialist victory at the polls, but because it marks the socialization of a man who without the doctrine would be wholly lost.

Never committing himself to a specific social theory, Zola emphasizes the baffling multiplicity of socialist solutions, and at the end of *Germinal* he sends his hero, Lantier, off to Paris still uncertain of the path he should follow. Nothing is clear but the grim possibility of anarchic and apocalyptic uprising—the one sure means of ushering in a new world. Committed to socialism, Sinclair is anxious to show the diversity in socialist thought only to indicate that, contrary to the stereotype, socialists have no "cut-and-dried program for the future of civilization." And, as we have seen, he does go on to list the fundamental principles on which all socialists agree.

For Zola, "heredity" was as crucial an influence on character as environment: that fact was expressed in the belief that there existed a jungle within as well as without. Sinclair believed there was no jungle within except that created by the jungle without, that there was a specific criterion for enlightenment, and that socially conscious men, using rational means, could bring about change.

Unfortunately, the men and women whom Sinclair believed met these standards—his heroes and heroines—frequently turn out to be not proletarians or foreigners but upper-class Americans. The implications of this preference are startlingly evident even in *King Coal* (1917), an account of conditions in the unorganized coal industry that was intended to be another muckraking bombshell. The trouble with this novel is not that it insists on presenting socialist propaganda in the guise of literature; to the contrary, it is socialist merely by inference. Its real failure lies in its focusing upon the experiences of an upper-class hero (Hal Warner, a mine owner's son, who spends a summer working under an assumed name in a mining camp not owned by his father; he soon finds himself championing the miners' causes). As he was to do in many of his succeeding novels, Sinclair, though intent on exposing the oppression of the working class by an avaricious and tyrannical capitalism, chooses as his means of narration the romantic clichés of popular fiction. The education of Hal is so simplistically and obviously rendered that *King Coal* cannot be justified by one's calling it a *bildungsroman*. Although it is probable that Sinclair felt he could better enlist the sympathies of the bourgeois reader by presenting the story as he did—and in 1917 he may indeed have been right—an account of the heroic adventures and the noble, self-sacrificing behavior of a clear-eyed, red-blooded, rich young American among a group of downtrodden, confused, often inarticulate, and impotent foreigners not only appeals to the worst kind of sentimentality but confirms more prejudices than it dispels.[2]

"The book," comments Sinclair in a postscript to *King Coal*, "gives a true picture of conditions and events.... Practically all the characters are real persons, and every incident which has social significance is not merely a true incident, but a typical one. The life portrayed in *King Coal* is the life that is lived today by hundreds of thousands of men, women and children in this land of the free" (358). This description may be accurate enough from a journalistic point of view but only from that point of view. Unlike the characterization in *Germinal*, or even in *The Jungle*, that in *King Coal* is superficial and stereotypical. We are presented with a "representative" old Slovak, an Italian anarchist, a fiery Irish maid with an alcoholic father, and others—all of whom emerge precisely in their typicality, just as do the municipal and mine officials and their police.

We see these characters mostly through the eyes of a twenty-year-old youth, who is sensitive but inexperienced and still limited by many of the prejudices of his class. Sinclair seems to have a broader vision than his hero; here is his treatment of Hal's initial encounter with the poor:

> He had come with love and curiosity, but both motives failed here. How could a man of sensitive nerves, aware of the refinements and graces of life, learn to love these people, who were an affront to his every sense—a stench to his nostrils, a jabbering to his ear, a procession of deformity to his eye? ... After all, what were they fit for, but the dirty work they were penned up to do? So spoke the haughty race-consciousness of the Anglo-Saxon, contemplating the Mediterranean hordes, the very shape of whose heads was objectionable. (21)

3. Self-Detotalizing Heroes

Sinclair obviously disapproves of this attitude, but when Hal learns better, what does he learn?

> Thus, as always, when one understood the lives of men, one came to pity instead of despising. Here was a separate race of creatures, subterranean gnomes, pent up by a society for purposes of its own. . . . Coal . . . would go to the ends of the earth, to places the miner never heard of, turning the wheels of industry whose products the miner would never see. It would make precious silks for fine ladies, it would cut precious jewels for their adornment; it would carry long trains of softly upholstered cars across deserts and mountains; it would drive palatial steamships out of wintry tempests into gleaming tropic seas. And the fine ladies in their precious silks and jewels would eat and sleep and laugh and lie at ease—and would know no more of the stunted creatures of the dark than the stunted creatures knew of them. Hal reflected upon this, and subdued his Anglo-Saxon pride, finding forgiveness for what was repulsive in these people—their barbarous jabbering speech, their vermin-ridden homes, their bare-bottomed babies. (22–23)

The speciousness of this passage is apparent in almost every line. The mine-owner's son finds "forgiveness" for the people whose exploitation has made him the "superior" person he is! It is easy enough for him to deride the "fine ladies" on "palatial steamships," quite another for him to realize that he is no less implicated. All of Hal's fine heroics on behalf of the poor—including his imprisonment in his bid to become check-weighman (a representative of the miners who makes certain that each man is credited by the company with the proper weight of coal he has dug)—are, without this knowledge, little more than adolescent adventures.

What is more, this lack makes Hal's heroism dangerously misleading. Because he is "educated" and "American" he is chosen as a leader and spokesman, and we are led to believe that he alone, acting on his own initiative, has the consciousness and capability to take effective action. Even the organizer from the miners' union is relegated to a passive role. As for most of the miners, we learn, "it was impossible to work so hard and keep . . . mental alertness . . . eagerness . . . and sensitiveness." This may well be true, but the activities of a Hal Warner, disguised as Joe Smith, are, from any social perspective that goes beyond romantic sentimentalism, irrelevant.

Hal persuades his college classmate, Paul Harrigan, son of the owner of the mine in which he is working, to order the superintendent to expedite rescue operations after an explosion (the mine had been sealed to prevent further property damage) and eventually, on the advice of union representatives, persuades his fellow workers not to go ahead with their planned strike. After these exploits, he decides to return to his normal life and to marry the spoiled girl to whom he had been engaged; even from the beginning he had spurned the love of the Irish working-class girl whom he now leaves, as he leaves all his summer working-class friends, "with more than a trace of moisture in his eyes."

Sinclair means all this quite seriously; throughout the entire novel, Hal's idealism and nobility are contrasted with the insensitivity and avarice of his relatives, friends, and the institutions they control. But because it lacks the sophistication and insight to develop the full implications of class relations, the work fails in social vision. Because it creates a stereotyped hero and not a character who undergoes an authentic moral development, it fails as a novel and remains at best a piece of muckraking journalism, at worst a sentimental tale.

A decade after he published *King Coal,* Sinclair wrote an exposure of the oil industry (*Oil!,* 1927) and once again chose to tell the story of an upper-class boy, this time Bunny Ross, the son of an oil magnate, who is torn between a devotion to his father and to a working-class friend, Paul Watkins, who perpetually is victimized by and reveals the horrors of the capitalist system in America. Bunny lives a dual life: captivated by the romance of oil exploration and eventually involved with a movie star, he remains partly true to his class; still he engages in radical activities at the conservative college he attends and befriends and gives financial aid to a group of socialists. After his father dies, he gives himself over more fully to the radical cause by founding a labor college and offering marriage to a Jewish socialist girl.

Unlike *King Coal,* which centers upon the tyranny exercised over an isolated mining camp, *Oil!* is a sweeping novel, that, covering Bunny's life from boyhood in the 1900s through his youth in the 1920s, includes as part of its background the First World War and the Allied invasion of Russia in 1919, as well as the election of Harding and the subsequent oil scandals. Sinclair also comments on religious superstition in capitalist America through the story of Paul Watkins' brother, Eli (modelled on Billy Sunday), "Prophet of the Third Revelation," who rises to wealth and power. As always, Sinclair can be effective in describing social injustice, but he is still heavy-handed and unconvincing in creating a hero.

Bunny, it is true, is portrayed as an ambivalent figure—and as such is neither an outright hero or villain. Sinclair is explicit about Bunny's deficiencies: his extreme dependence on his father, his inclination to "lean on others," and his general fecklessness. On the other hand, he supposedly possesses the same "nobility" as Hal Warner in *King Coal;* he is depicted as being one of the rare men of compassion of his class and this quality is meant to redeem him. But unlike George Orwell, for example, Sinclair is interested in declassment not as a psychological, social, and ethical phenomenon but rather as a device for revealing the manners and conduct of the two classes through sensitive eyes. Bunny is chiefly an observer and sympathizer. Although he undergoes something of a socialist education, he is never made to experience the hardships of an oil worker; although occasionally baited by the press, he is never really brutalized. And like Hal, even when participating in radical activities, he holds the trump card of his identity as the son of a member of the ruling class.

That Sinclair is himself aware of these weaknesses in the position of his upper-class heroes is evident in *Boston* (1928), at once an account of the Sacco-Vanzetti case and a novel about the social and moral education of Brahmin Cornelia Thornwell, who, upon the death of her wealthy and powerful husband, renounces her family (and all it stands for) and attempts to transform herself into a working-class woman. This so-called "runaway grandmother" does, in fact, undergo all the hardships that an unskilled worker in a New England cordage factory in 1917 would, but it is still not enough, as she learns in an argument with a French socialist:

> "Understand me, Comrade Thornwell, it is good of rich and cultured ladies to take an interest in the exploited workers; but you suffer always from the fact that you can't possibly realize how they actually feel."
> "Don't forget, Comrade Leon, I worked for a year and a half in a cordage plant, and lived on the wages."
> "I know. . . . and I never heard anything like it. But all the same, if you will pardon me, it wasn't practically real, because if you had been ill or out of a job, you'd have gone back to your family; it wasn't psychologically real, because you always knew you could, and you had the moral support of knowing you were a lady. No worker has that." (231)

This revelation does not prevent Cornelia from committing herself to a socialist view of the world, nor does it in any way detract from Sinclair's obvious admiration for his heroine and her real-life models. What helps make her a sympathetic figure, not only to Sinclair but, insofar as she is credible at all, to his readers, is precisely what is lacking or at least unemphasized in the other heroes: a strength of character that perhaps goes deeper than politics or doctrine, and manifests itself in her desire to see and act upon the truth as it reveals itself. This trait goes against the grain of her entire Brahmin upbringing, in which decorum, maintained by repression and hypocrisy, is the chief value in social conduct, especially among women. Her education through the long ordeal that begins with her flight and culminates in the execution of Sacco and Vanzetti is intended to be that of the reader as well. *Boston* is Sinclair's *Verité*, Sacco and Vanzetti, his Dreyfus. Like Zola, he argues for "objectivity" and historical accuracy in the reconstruction of the circumstances. "An honest effort," he tells us, "has here been made to portray a complex community exactly as it is. The story has no hero but the truth." And he continues,

> I wish to make clear that I have not written a brief for the Sacco-Vanzetti defense. I have tried to be a historian. What I think I know, I have told the reader. What is uncertain, I have so portrayed—and have let the partisans of both sides voice their feelings and beliefs. My book will not satisfy either side completely; both have already expressed dissent—which I take to mean I have done my job. (vi)

But this statement scarcely characterizes a novel which, for all the research behind it, is impelled not by detachment but moral outrage. One can concede, I suppose, that Sinclair does explore certain morally ambiguous areas—as, for example, the dilemma into which Lee Swenson, the experienced, tough radical lawyer, leads Cornelia when he informs her that she (and she alone) has the power to destroy the prosecution's case against Sacco and Vanzetti if she'll commit perjury; the implications and ramifications of this problem occupy Sinclair for several pages. Nonetheless we neither expect nor find any sympathy whatsoever for those who have brought Sacco and Vanzetti to trial (the "rulers" of the Commonwealth of Massachusetts) or any hostility toward those who would defend them. By a "complex community," then, Sinclair in no way means one toward which, or in which, moral neutrality can have any place. What he does mean is a detotalized society divided into the oppressors and their henchmen and the oppressed. The former contains frequently antagonistic groups, such as the Back Bay aristocracy and the wealthy and politically potent Irish, but their commercial, legal, political, and social interactions are reducible to the common motives of avarice and lust for power. The latter are the poor, chiefly Italian, who are invariably portrayed in a favorable light; they are not Zola's Parisian poor (*L'Assommoir*) or his land-hungry peasants (*La Terre*). Whereas in Zola's work, family life on all social levels is dominated by envy and greed and therefore is in a state of disintegration, in *Boston* Italian family life stands in ideal contrast to that of the Brahmins. Tolerance, generosity, kindness—an openness to life—characterize the relationships of the Brinis, with whom, as a boarder, Cornelia finds more than adequate compensation for the hardships she must endure as a laborer.

If Sinclair has presented an oversimplified image of the Italian family, it is not necessarily out of sentimentality that he has done so. Such an image logically underscores the view that, along with self-interest, an almost psychopathic paranoia marked the "American" attitude toward the Italians, all of whom it held to be potential bomb-throwing anarchists. Accordingly, Bartolomeo Vanzetti, whom Sinclair describes as a man of words rather than action, emerges as the perfect Italian hero, a saintly man incapable of taking any life, to say nothing of attacking the paymaster of a shoe factory.

What is ironic in all this is that the socialist view of the anarchists—that is, the one expressed by Pierre Leon in his argument with Cornelia—actually justifies the anxieties of the capitalists who wish to jail, deport, or execute the "whole lot of them":

> All militant anarchists believe in bombs. Not all make them. . . . But the faith calls for it. . . .
>
> What you have to get clear is the central doctrine of anarchism, that property used for exploitation is theft. That makes capitalist society a gigantic bandit-raid, a wholesale killing; any killing you have to do to abolish it, or to cripple it, always is a small matter in comparison. (233)

That Vanzetti as a dedicated anarchist could have committed the crime with which he has been charged is a possibility that Cornelia cannot accept—nor, for that matter, can Sinclair himself, since the effectiveness of his attack on the Commonwealth, the capitalist state, depends on Vanzetti's innocence, not only as a bandit but as a bomber. Equally important is that such innocence, which carries with it an inability to act, reaffirms a notion that is ubiquitous in Sinclair's work: namely, that the oppressed cannot save themselves, that somehow their

3. Self-Detotalizing Heroes

salvation, if attainable at all, requires the appearance of enlightened American aristocrats who renounce or rebel against their class.

The wealthy, clean-cut American, sympathetic to the socialist cause but accustomed to privilege and material comfort, was to remain Sinclair's favorite hero to the end. Not only does he reappear in the simple propaganda piece about the Spanish Civil War, *No Pasaran,* but he is elaborated throughout the eleven-volume Lanny Budd series, Sinclair's epic and chronicle of the period 1913-49. Written between 1940 and 1953, these novels can scarcely be called proletarian literature since they deal mostly with the haute bourgeoisie, the aristocracy, high government officials and leaders, and with the diplomatic and political history of the West. Fascism, Nazism, and finally world communism emerge as the central evils; capitalism is attacked for generating these forms of tyranny or, at least, making it possible for them to flourish. Except for one episode concerning the slums of pre-World War I London, there is no attempt to delineate consistently the conditions that inspired the muckraking novels.

From the start Sinclair's reviewers were sensitive to the aesthetic weaknesses of the series.[3] Pedantry, sentimentality, and an irritating facetiousness permeate the entire work. Wholly unaffected by the stylistic innovations of the twentieth century, Sinclair writes in what is often the worst rhetoric of another age. His treatment of personal relations, including Lanny's pallid romances, is superficial and contrived and the dialogue of his characters often banal and awkward. He is repetitious to the point of distraction, not only in his recitation of facts or his use of epithets for his characters, but in the plotting itself. (Lanny's adventures fall into basic types that appear cyclically: the interviews with political leaders, the rescue of prisoners or victims of the fascists, the participation in seances, art agent dealings, dealings with socialists. The many visits to Hitler or Roosevelt are identical in form, if not in actual subjects discussed, as are the other adventures within their categories.) Yet, all these weaknesses conceded, there is no denying that

Sinclair's Socialite Socialists

Sinclair does have a genius for recreating historical events and portraying a seemingly endless variety of actual public figures. These portraits are not the ironic or idealized sketches that one finds in Dos Passos; rather they are convincing if limited life studies. In addition to Hitler and Roosevelt, Lanny Budd, playboy, art agent, and presidential spy, has protracted or numerous dealings with most of the major and many minor Nazi officials, Harry Hopkins, Hearst, Truman, Churchill, Laval, Petain; he has illuminating encounters with hundreds of others, including English, French, German, Italian, and Spanish aristocrats, industrialists, generals, scientists, and politicians. This plethora and scope led one reviewer to argue that Lanny was "an all-seeing eye, not a dramatic hero." From the viewpoint of technique Lanny is perhaps a device, but that does not mean we can avoid judging his character or considering his development as a socialist sympathizer and its actual significance.

The illegitimate son of Robbie Budd, an American munitions maker, and his first love, Mabel Blackless (called Beauty), whose marriage had been prevented by the Budd family, Lanny is born and raised on the Riviera by his socialite mother. He comes under the sway of his father, who visits him often and exposes him to his Darwinian views of society in the hope that Lanny will eventually take his place in the family business. Thus, justifying his trade, Robbie plants the seeds of a capitalist philosophy:

> "Men hate each other. . . . They insist upon fighting, and there's nothing you can do about it, except learn to defend yourself. No nation would survive for a year unless it kept itself in readiness to repel attacks from greedy and jealous rivals."
> (*World's End*, 39)

He sees the First World War as a "war of profits," in which the steel men were "selling to both sides, and getting the whole world into their debt" and international industrialists in general "had taken entire charge of the war so far as their own properties were concerned" (280).

3. Self-Detotalizing Heroes

But Lanny finally is convinced no more by his father's conclusions than by those of his uncle, Jesse Blackless, the spokesman for violent world revolution:

> The uncle and the father agreed upon the same set of facts, and they even drew the same conclusion—that nobody ought to be patriotic. The point where they split was that Robbie said you had to stuff your pockets, because you couldn't help it; whereas Uncle Jesse—Lanny wasn't sure what he wanted, but apparently it was to empty Robbie's pockets! (281)

Repudiating them both, Lanny sees himself at the age of eighteen, after his experience at the Peace Conference, as "the man who loved art and beauty, reason and fair play, and pleaded for these things and got brushed aside. It wasn't his world! It had no use for him! When the fighting started, he'd be caught between the lines and mowed down" (635).

Still, as he grows older, he continues to make discoveries that won't allow him peace of mind with his own class:

> No longer an innocent child, he looked about him at the idlers of this Côte d'Azur and they had ceased to appear glamorous. He saw gambling and drinking and assorted vices, and what seemed to him an orgy of foolish and profitless activity. . . . when he went into the great cities he was made sick by the spectacle of human degradation. (*Between Two Worlds*, 443)

The young Spanish socialist, Raoul Palma, urges him to make his first commitment:

> He was ready to teach a class in the [socialist] night school, and one in the Sunday school. He would tell the workers of the Riviera and their children about the great war which was already growing dim in the world's memory; he would try to explain to them the forces which had caused it, and what they could do by their collective efforts to prevent another such calamity from breaking upon their lives. (593)

If this sounds both presumptuous and ludicrous, it is pure Sinclair and we are meant to take it seriously. Lanny will eventually come to doubt his effectiveness, but having married the heiress Irma Barnes, who will prove to be a reactionary, he is unable, even if he so desired, to do any more: "Lanny Budd found himself in the midst of a social whirlwind; and it would have been cruelly unkind of him not to like it. Once more the ladies were in charge of his life, and what they considered proper was what he did" (*Dragon's Teeth*, 224).

Content to roll through life "in a well-cushioned limousine," Lanny is confronted in the years 1933-37 with the accession to power of the Nazis and the advent of the war in Spain. Through his boyhood friend, Kurt Meissner, pianist, composer, Prussian aristocrat, and Beauty Budd's former lover, he had come to know and love pre-Hitler Germany; he is fluent in the language and seems to be as much at home in upper-class German society as he is in French and English. In aiding the escape of another longtime friend—the Jewish speculator, Johannes Robin, one of whose sons has married Lanny's stepsister—Lanny is given a direct insight into the realities of the new regime, and the fate of another son, Freddi, only increases Lanny's horror.

His commitment now takes the form of financial aid to a socialist underground. Lanny makes several trips to Berlin to meet Trudi Schultz, a dedicated young socialist and art student. Even though she is increasingly intolerant of Lanny's leftist activities, Irma agrees to help him smuggle Trudi out of Germany. Characteristic of Lanny's double life is that part of the escape plan includes a prearranged visit to Hitler at Berchtesgaden, and here Irma's voluntary declaration of her admiration for the Nazis precipitates Lanny's final decision to divorce her.

What is thematically important in all this is that it signals the first real moral crisis in Lanny's life, and this crisis is accentuated when it becomes apparent that not only Irma, but most of Lanny's friends and acquaintances—the aristocracy and the ruling class of Western Europe—along with powerful groups in the United States, see in fascism and Nazism only a bulwark against the "Bolshevik menace." In *Wide Is the Gate* ("Wide is the gate, and broad is the way, that leads to destruction") this thesis is dramatized repeatedly and offered as the basic reason that the Nazis were unchecked in the thirties. Whether talking to French industrialists, Spanish landowners, or highborn persons in the British Foreign Service, Lanny knows just what politics will ingratiate him most quickly. But when he is sincere, as he must be with his father, now building aircraft, when after his experiences in Spain he comes to argue for a pursuit plane for the loyalist government, he finds himself in a hopeless deadlock with his own family. Robbie's intransigence, his bitter opposition to the Republican forces, is a graphic enough demonstration of the chasm that has opened between Lanny and his class.

Whatever the depth of his commitment, Lanny finds himself in a position that requires his continued existence as one of the privileged. As a "presidential agent," charged by Roosevelt with learning the intentions of the rich and powerful of Europe, he poses as a Nazi sympathizer pursuing his trade as an art agent. Aside from contact with Raoul Palma and the Côte d'Azur socialists, his only connection with the movement is through his continued relationship with Trudi Schultz, who refuses to give up hope that her husband, though captured by the Gestapo, is still alive (now in Paris she slavishly devotes herself to composing anti-Nazi propaganda to be smuggled to German workers). Lanny, after a less than romantic courtship, marries her, admires her, and, when she is kidnapped by Gestapo agents in France, moves heaven and earth to locate and rescue her, until he is given confirmation of her death in Dachau.

With the exception of boyhood friend Rick (Eric Pomeroy-Nielson), who was crippled while flying for the R.A.F. during World War I and has become a liberal journalist and playwright, there are few members of the aristocracy with whom Lanny can express his real feelings. As he is to reflect after the Nazis are defeated, "He had been living in the enemy's country, not merely physically but ideologically; he had been living capitalism and luxury, while cherishing democracy as a secret dream" (*O Shepherd Speak!,* 348). The fact remains, however, that despite some mental anguish and the personal risks involved in espionage, Lanny is never called upon to make any real sacrifices, never suffers unduly, and never abandons the habits, instincts, and outlook of the man of privilege. He tells Trudi that the force of property is "so overwhelming that only a small fraction of mankind has any chance of resisting it. I am not sure if I myself am among this number; I feel myself struggling in a net, and just when I think I am out of it I discover that another fold has been cast over my head and I am as helplessly entangled as ever" (*Wide Is the Gate,* 423). This is a genuine insight, but its implications are not pursued. To Sinclair, Lanny is a wholly creditable hero whose essential high-mindedness is seriously presented: "No, he was not a Socialist, he didn't know enough to say what he was, but he knew human decency when he met it, and he had learned what it was for a modern state to be seized by gangsters and used by them to pervert the mind and moral sense of mankind" (*Between Two Worlds,* 382). Lanny always speaks for "human decency," for the sound mind and moral sense of mankind. Thus, even though Sinclair has created a dichotomous position for his character, one that invites further inquiry into his motives and behavior, the subtleties involved have no part in Sinclair's design.

For example, it is of no thematic consequence that Lanny is a man who lives to ingratiate himself with others and that deception and manipulation are second nature to him; that he is sanctimonious, condescending, and passionless; that his charm, his "famous smile," his ready wad of cash, his inside knowledge, and his possession of credentials with intimidating signatures are his chief means of getting along in the world. Perhaps affected most by Trudi's kidnapping, and then not because he loved her but because he felt guilty for not having loved her enough (again the Moral Hero), he emerges physically and emotionally unaltered from every perilous adventure

3. Self-Detotalizing Heroes

he has had, including torture by the Russians after the war. It is true he has risked much in helping relatives, friends, and allies escape from Germany, but he is wholly capable of turning down an appeal by strangers without much more than apt reflection on the sadness of the situation and perhaps a "tear in his eye."

The lack of psychological dimension in Lanny's character is no mere technical failing; it is a reflection of Sinclair's view of the world, which to its core is rationalistic and moralistic. It is not the schizoid world of Zola's *La Bête humaine,* where the id of heredity can, under the right conditions, transfigure the most virtuous and reasonable of men; rather it is the dualistic world in which virtue and villainy, forever distinct from one another, are forever locked in combat. Reason is virtue's weapon, social consciousness its inspiration, justice its goal.

This is putting the matter in its most simple terms, terms that tell us nothing about Sinclair's insight into specific social problems or his ability to describe actual events and persons. On the other hand, they do tell us a great deal about his fictional characters and the unifying themes of his narratives. Here is a typical example of Lanny's speculations on the universe:

> Presumably . . . Providence or God wanted each human to do his best; and for Lanny that could only mean a great deal of puzzling or worrying. Perhaps this puzzling and worrying was part of the process; perhaps God meant for each of the two billion creatures to go on striving until it learned to think more clearly, and to organize and cooperate with its fellows. . . . Why couldn't they have learned to cooperate from the beginning? Why couldn't they have been born with enough sense in their heads—instead of with a desire to dominate and oppress, to rob and kill.
>
> . . . If they were ever going to stop dominating and oppressing, robbing and killing, it would be because some among their number had sufficient intelligence to persuade others to settle down and produce wealth for themselves instead of trying to take it away from their neighbors. (*Presidential Agent,* 558)

"Think more clearly, and so to organize and cooperate," "sufficient intelligence to persuade others"—these ideals are clearly the inspiration for the kind of liberal socialism that Sinclair espouses. They assume a simple human psychology and ethos in which reason and passion, intelligence and stupidity, are easily distinguishable from one another, as are good and evil, and they are founded on the hope that men can change themselves and the world by rational decision. One of the major problems, as formulated by Rick as early as the round of futile international conferences after World War I, is that of education and communication:

> There just wasn't enough intelligence on the poor tormented planet; not enough statesmanship, not enough ordinary decency. The people weren't able to control the forces which modern industrialism had created; they didn't even have the means of getting the facts. There were a few honest papers, but they reached only a small public; the big press was in the hands of the big interests, and told the people whatever suited the purposes of the masters of steel and munitions and oil. (*Between Two Worlds,* 148)

The passage expresses Sinclair's own purposes throughout a lifetime of writing.

Although, whatever its relation to capitalism, fascism presented its own forms of oppression and required a shift in perspective, it made a Manichaean view even more credible. With the emergence of the Nazis, dragons appeared on the earth and dragon-slayers would have to be called upon:

> It was Lanny's fond dream that the whole people were wiser than any self-appointed leaders; that if they could once get power and manage to keep it, they and the products of their toil would no longer be at the mercy of evil creatures spewed up from the cesspools of society. So long as such existed, so long as they could seize the wealth of great nations and turn them to fanaticism and aggression, they had to be fought. (*O Shepherd Speak!,* 210)

3. Self-Detotalizing Heroes

Elsewhere, Lanny reasons,

> It was really not the German people who were perpetrating [the atrocities of Nazism], but a band of fanatics who had seized a nation and were perverting its youth and turning them into murderers and psychopaths. Germans would awaken someday as from a nightmare, and contemplate with loathing and dismay the crimes that had been committed in their name. (*Presidential Agent,* 640)

In this view, "evil" is not in the normal order of things and certainly not within oneself; it cannot belong to a whole people but only to the fanatics among them or to specific "creatures" who can be so designated. Wholly "other," it can be isolated and fought by the forces of reason and the men of "human decency."

These sentiments are perhaps more adequate as a call to action than as an explanation of the Nazi phenomenon. They are, in fact, too simplistic even for Sinclair's own portrayals of Nazi officials. In his dealings with these figures, Lanny is so often caught up with them as personalities that he must remind himself that they are perpetrators of atrocity. They come from all walks of life, represent a variety of temperaments, and more often than not are "typical Germans." Ironically, one of the most fanatical of them is Lanny's old friend, Kurt Meissner.

The defeat of the Nazis did not, of course, satisfy Sinclair's moral sense; after bringing the series to a conclusion with *O Shepherd Speak!* (the tenth volume) in 1949, he added a new volume in 1953, *The Return of Lanny Budd,* a work permeated with the attitudes of the Cold War. The shepherd to whom Sinclair is referring is Roosevelt, whom Lanny has adulated and whose death he sees as leaving the world without strong moral leadership.

Having for over a decade regarded the idea of "the Bolshevik Peril" as a Nazi-propagated illusion, Lanny, after a flirtation with pacifism, now embraces it as a religious truth. The moral conflict that engages him is not between socialism and capitalism but between Democratic Socialism and Revolutionary Socialism, which Sinclair translates into a holy war between democracy and tyranny. Thus, explaining his view of the world situation to Truman, Lanny begins with what appears to be a straightforward socialist critique (Truman has asked what the United States has done to alienate the Soviet Union):

> "What we have done. . . . is to be a bourgeois nation, the biggest and richest in the world. Our affairs are run by immensely wealthy capitalists who choose dummy legislators and tell them what to do. The capitalists are automatically driven by the forces of an expanding economy to reach out to every corner of the earth for raw materials and markets. We take these by purchase where possible, but where we encounter resistance we are ready to use force. By this means we reduce all colonial peoples to the status of peons and we keep them there."

Instead of pursuing the logic of this argument, Lanny shifts the grounds of his attack and becomes ironic:

> "But now come the heroic Bolsheviks, the followers of the Marxist-Stalinist-Leninist line, calling upon the awakening proletariat to arise and expropriate the expropriators. I don't know whether you understand that jargon, Mr. Truman, but you have to learn it because that is what we have to face the balance of our lives."
>
> "I have heard it, Mr. Budd, but it is hard to make it real to myself."
>
> "It is just the realest thing going. It is being recited day and night by tens of thousands of inspired fanatics. They are teaching it to millions; they are teaching it to the young, and in one generation more there will be whole countries full of people who have never heard anything else and who take it just as seriously as you take the Gospels according to Matthew, Mark, Luke, and John." (120-21)

After more of this palaver in which Lanny draws a picture of hate-filled hordes using every possible means to bring about the destruction of the United States, Truman concludes that the country will have to rearm, but that having a large army will not be incompatible with social progress. Lanny goes away happy.

That the ideal of social progress per se is uppermost neither in Sinclair's mind nor his hero's at this time becomes all the more obvious when it is expressed by another sympathetic character, Professor Charles T. Alston, New Dealer, foreign policy expert, and general insider. Speaking on the radio program sponsored by Lanny's "Peace Foundation"—now sounding the alert on World Communism—he argues,

> "The only possible chance of defeating Communist dictatorship is by setting up a system of industrial democracy by constitutional methods in which our political freedoms would be retained. That is one way we can gain and keep the support of the masses and bring the Red dictatorships to defeat." (166)

Lanny's half sister, Bessie, always strong in her views, becomes in this volume one of the communist "fanatics" against whom Lanny supposedly scores point after point in bitter debates (though she is too far gone to realize it), whom he sorrowfully denounces to the FBI as an espionage suspect, and whose long-suffering husband he not only sets free but provides with a more suitable mate. In his arguments with Bessie, Lanny seems never really to answer her charges but rather presents countercharges about communist methods that are meant to be unanswerable. He has, in short, ceased being merely a bore and has himself become a zealot whose anticommunist preaching fills several hundred pages. The conclusion of the Lanny Budd series in a grand peroration brings Sinclair's career full circle, a story of the triumph of moral ardor over the art of fiction.

9 Farrell and the Aesthetics of Nostalgia

In "Literature and Morality" James Farrell raised what he took to be a "crucial question of our times," the distinction between social and personal morality. "Social morality," he wrote, "assumes that major evils are derivable from, or at least *decisively* influenced by, the structural character of society itself. Consequently the aim of social morality is to change society by changing and lifting moral practice to a higher level, or to eradicate those conditions and attitudes which sanction . . . practices which result in social harm, in the deformation of human personalities, and in the exploitation of groups, classes, and nations." Such a morality had its basis in Marxism. Personal morality, on the other hand, assumes "that the major moral problem facing man is the regeneration of the individual rather than the change of society." Pointing out the dangers in setting social and personal morality in opposition to one another, Farrell argues for a synoptic view:

> Man . . . lives out his personal drama on the plane of society; man's very self and his personality are socially directed, socially delimited, socially organized. The self is a social product, not a separate, individual entity, superior to, anterior to, separable from, society. Nor can one consider society as outside of man, superior to man, or the sole responsible agent for what is called

immoral action. . . . when a man is exploited he is not exploited by society in general; he is exploited by individual men. (5)

This view, we learn in "Social Themes in American Realism," is apparently realized in "bottom-dog literature, a literature that is sharply realistic and depicts conditions of dirt, physical misery, and inner frustration [but also] introduces the plebeian classes on a more human level" (23). The new realism, of which Farrell's own work can, with some differences, be considered a part, "states social problems, not in terms of generalizations but rather in terms of direct characterization, of the immediacy of life described on the printed page. . . . social causation is translated into individual motivation and into immediacy of action, thought, dream, and word" (23–24).

The same argument appears in *A Note on Literary Criticism* when Farrell takes issue with Granville Hicks for trying to classify novels as "collective," "complex," or "individualistic":

> Prejudices have been created against the "individualistic" novel, and for the "collective" novel. Some seem to feel that an "individualistic" novel has petty bourgeois survivals, whereas the collective novel is free of such taints. And, in addition, the collective novel permits the novelist, in terms of these prejudices, to convey a clearer sense of groups and classes. (113–14)

The truth, however, is that

> human beings, no matter what group or social class they belong to, do not always function *consciously* as members of a group or class. Sometimes to themselves they seem to function alone. . . .
> A novelist in developing his characters is concerned not only with the fact that they belong to a group or a class, and that that group or class is a conditioning factor in their conduct; he is not concerned only with the fact that his characters have many resemblances to other human beings, and are subject, along with the rest, to the working and the necessities of a whole series of natural laws, including the laws that define the working of social processes. He is concerned, as well, with his characters as unique and distinct from other human beings with whom they

have common experiences, and to whom they show certain human resemblances. (116-18)

Farrell has been talking, all along, about technique; the questions of content, however, seem no less important. What makes Farrell's novels "individualistic" (if this term has any validity) is not their assumption that social forces are meaningless abstractions unless realized in the consciousness and behavior or individual persons. Rather, it is Farrell's absorption with the means of personal salvation in an unregenerate society that is, for the most part, accepted as a given. "When I first began to write," he says in "Reflections at Fifty,"

> I was full of indignation because of the sorrows of this world. I was angry because of cruelty, because of the exploitation of some men and women by others, because of the coldness with which some people manipulate others, because of dirt, poverty, ignorance, aggressiveness, and the other things which ruin and sadden human lives. (62-63)

Although in his more politically conscious days he might have vaguely ascribed the cause of these evils to capitalism, he never in his fiction seriously proposed collective action or revolution—"social morality"—as a solution, not even in the Bernard Carr trilogy, in which he depicts his hero's involvement with communist literati.[1] The note that Farrell strikes in the passage just quoted is "philosophic" not social; the "sorrows of this world" are a part of the way of things, just as cruelty, aggressiveness, and ignorance are a part of human nature:

> My feelings are somewhat different today as I write. There is more tranquility. . . . Indignation has turned to a stoical feeling. I have come to see that pain and agony are the way it is in life. (62)

After this Schopenhauerian statement, he concludes,

> There is no final home on a planet where we are homeless children. In different ways, we find a sense of security, of per-

manence, or of home—for a while. To me, impermanence renders everything good and beautiful all the more rare. It stimulates my ambition and it strengthens the stoicism which is at the root of my outlook about experience. (65)

Studs Lonigan, Farrell says in the introduction to his best-known work, is "a normal American Boy,"

> waiting at the threshold of life. His dream of himself is a romantic projection of his future, conceived in the terms and values of his world. In time, this dream of himself turns backward. It is no longer a romantic projection of things to come. More and more it becomes a nostalgic image turned toward the past. Does this not happen to a greater or lesser degree to all of us? (xiv)

Having rejected the values of family, school, and church—that is, the whole philistine ethos of the Irish-Catholic community—Studs cannot transcend the gang values that seem to offer the only alternative. In his endless struggle to realize the "tough guy" image or to make whatever impression the situation calls for, he reveals that he is almost wholly motivated by vanity. "His good impulses," Farrell writes, "go more and more into the stream of his reverie," a reverie that has little bearing on what he says or does. If, as Farrell insists, Studs is not a genuine gangster or hoodlum, he is still incapable of self-knowledge or social awareness. "There but for the grace of God go I," concluded Farrell, and the Bernard Carr trilogy is his most elaborate attempt to define just what that grace meant.

Like that of his creator, Bernard Carr's rebellion against lace-curtain Irish Chicago (traced in the volumes *Bernard Clare* [1946], *The Road Between* [1949], and *Yet Other Waters* [1952]) takes him to the University of Chicago and to New York City, where after a long struggle he realizes his ambition to become a writer. For Carr, who in escaping the orbit of Chicago faces a void, literary success becomes the only way that will give him an identity and place; and since writing fiction involves a dramatization of his experience and, as he puts it, an "objectification" of his problems, his effort will help to free him from the past, give meaning to his present life, and ward off his recurrent fears of change and death. ("I am somebody trying to make a history of myself. In other words, I am a young man in search of a biography" [*Bernard Clare,* 160]). Carr's short story, "Someday," spells out one of Farrell's chief archetypes of the writer's experience (that is, his own, that of his character Bernard Carr, and that of Carr's character, Richard Clarke). In this story, which haunts Carr throughout the trilogy, the middle-aged writer-hero, who has looked forward in vain to an ideal future, retreats to the past, seeking in nostalgia the "someday" he cannot find in life (11). Returning to Chicago, where he attends a Christmas mass that evokes in him a sharp sense of the loss of all his boyhood dreams, hopes, and emotions, he broods over the image of his childhood sweetheart, Elsie Cavanaugh, whom he has transfigured into a holy lady whose loss or unattainability represents his own lost innocence and purity (17). Under this spell, Clarke "even found himself regretting the loss of religion he had rejected, the religion he hated and was determined to fight" (17). Life, Clarke concludes, was a tragedy; "it hurt men, men who hoped in boyhood and were disillusioned in manhood in an ever-recurring cycle" (18). Although it is obvious that Carr is Clarke, there is a crucial difference, and it lies precisely in the fact that Carr is the creator of Clarke and has fashioned his story. In short, the very writing of the story offers a kind of salvation from the flux in which all men are caught:

> [Bernard] pondered on life as a grim march of men and women who lost their faith and their hopes and entered the oblivious grave. Was that not also to be his own destiny? Must not he, too, be saddened, disillusioned? Might not he be nursing hopes as naive, as innocent as those of his boyhood, those he had put into this story? No, no, no, for he was objectifying these. In doing that he was fulfilling himself, hardening and toughening himself in the face of whatever was to be his destiny. (18)

Self-fulfillment as a writer is to be Carr's most consistent ideal throughout his life. It at once expresses and strengthens his sense of personal difference and isolation from the rest of

3. Self-Detotalizing Heroes

the world and establishes the main direction his "rebellion" will take. Its conflict with other values and ideals underlies the central action of the trilogy, as it does Carr's psychological and intellectual development.

Thus Bernard muses that writing is lonely and cruel: "How lonely it was to be by yourself, cut off from the world that was all about you, shut up with yourself, forced to drag feelings out of yourself and to put them into words that were so much paler than those feelings" (*Road Between,* 231). Paradoxically, writing offers what contact with the world the writer can establish:

> Locked out of the world and trying to touch it with his heart and his mind. And he only touched it with words. No real human contacts seemed to bridge this gap of loneliness as did the imaginary sense of contact gained in writing. (245)

If writing is a lonely business, Bernard is himself a loner, partly by temperament, partly by dint of a natural skepticism and perpetual soul-searching that keeps him the unassimilated, detotalized outsider, whatever the group with which he associates, or the semidetached participant, whatever the human relationship in which he engages. He has all the romantic and sentimental inclinations of the "sensitive young writer," but he is capable of seeing them in perspective. He fears that his feelings for Eva Stone, with whom he is having his first affair, are "literary," or inspired by the need to dramatize his life:

> He wanted to seem dramatic in his own eyes, and again he was afraid that that was what he was really doing now. He wanted this relationship with Eva to be dramatic. It made him dramatic in his own eyes. . . . He could see himself as a character in a book. Bernard Clare who had come here to New York to be a writer, to live in free rebellion—he needed to think his life was more than it was. (*Bernard Clare,* 262)

Directed inward, as here, this kind of skepticism keeps Carr intellectually honest; directed outward, it protects him from conformism, either to the conventions and values of the philistine world or to the dogmas of the Communist party. On the other hand, it leaves him no real outlet for an awakening social consciousness that he can only strive to bring into harmony with his vision of personal fulfillment.

A part of the crowd that has gathered on Union Square to protest the executions of Sacco and Vanzetti about to be announced, Bernard experiences a sudden "sense of identification with the mass" and later joins a march of mourners. "He was one with many," Farrell tells us. "His only emotion was this sudden one of solidarity." And still feeling its effects the following morning, he muses, "This great agony. How petty were his own despairs, his own angers, his own irritations, his own complaints!" (93). There is no reason to doubt the sincerity of Bernard's feelings: the problem is that, at least at this time in his life, they can be nothing but inconsequential, as his eventual speculations indicate:

> —Christ, if humanity could only be saved, saved from senselessness.
> —Won't I be lucky if I save myself?
> He should be up and doing. . . .
> —I can try and make things less wrong for myself. I can't do much with life. How could I?
> —But why should I? Why make a hopeless world better?
> —Because people suffer, are frustrated, because it is all stupid and irrational, and there you are.

Socialism? No solution:

> —I think of humanity, poor humanity, and it is forever seeking for the sun, seeking for the sun it cannot reach.
> —What sun?
> —The real sun must be socialism.
> —But it is the sun.
> —Enough of that Plato-Socrates—Clare: be up and doing. (173)

If these are the ruminations of someone scarcely out of adolescence, they still reflect an ambivalence that Carr's mature thought will not resolve. To survive, he must be "up and doing"—during this period he is a successful salesman who shamefacedly admits he enjoys making a kill. Thus his moments of social feeling never get beyond the sentimental stage. Canvassing an old couple who are about to lose their flowershop to a street-widening project, Bernard is conscience-stricken but can do no more than express his sympathy. A competitor himself, he has no time to brood over the situation; without any genuine understanding of the causes of the old couple's victimization (or his own), having received no help from the textbooks of his political science course, he remains a cultural, but neither a social nor political, rebel.

Carr's deepening involvement with the literati and intellectuals of the New York Communist party is accompanied by a deepening ambivalence that inevitably leads to a complete break. Actually, we are not told how Carr became associated with the communists in the first place—a four-year hiatus exists between his return to Chicago (1927) and the opening of the second novel where we find him, back in New York, with a complete circle of communist friends and acquaintances. But that is precisely the point: Farrell is not interested in depicting in his hero a developing political "consciousness" that will end in party membership. On the contrary, it is Carr's resistance that matters—a resistance associated not with "petit-bourgeois" habits of mind but with "universals" like integrity and independent-mindedness.

There isn't, I believe, a single encounter recorded by Farrell in which Carr is not at odds with the group. On the most frequently discussed subject, the function of the writer, he is inherently opposed to the communist belief that art is a weapon and the writer a propagandist for the proletariat. Correspondingly, the communists reject his ideas about artistic freedom with the argument that there is no such thing as artistic freedom in a capitalist society.

As an already established novelist, Carr insists upon being, and is, treated as an equal, though his own work has nothing in common with the "socialist realism" being produced by his cohorts. His first novel, *The Father* (1931), deals with the Chicago background; his second, *Unshapely Things* (1932), with his affair with Eva Stone. By the time *Paddy Stanton* (1935) appears he is on the verge of a total split with the party; the third book, which deals with an "absolutist," first Catholic and then communist, is panned in the radical press. Nothing characterizes Bernard's mind more accurately, however, than his proposal for a series of articles on American culture:

> "I want to analyze *the broken promises of American life.* The grim contrasts between vision and reality—the split in ideals and actions—these constitute the biggest forged check in history. . . . [The early settlers] thought they were building something that in a century or so, in our own time, would be a paradise on earth. Your throat chokes when you read of what they thought life would be like the very day and age in which we live. . . . Our serious literature reveals the costs of American civilization, and is *full of disastrous frustrations, failures, tragedies,* and our popular culture turns the American Dream into a caricature and *a juvenile reverie.* . . . I want to get how it is that capitalism, in a very concrete way, stands behind this." (*Road Between,* 105-6: my italics)

These ideas are rejected as old hat by the radical editor to whom they were presented but they are obviously something more than clichés. Carr has here projected onto a national and cultural plane his own preoccupation with failed dreams. He vaguely blames "capitalism" for the failure, but it is obvious that "class struggle" and "production relations" are not his main interest.

Thus Carr is and remains a fellow traveler. His sense of personal integrity and his desire for intellectual and artistic freedom always take precedence over his urges to become an anticapitalist activist, just as his skepticism prevents him from embracing communism. For the true communist, such skepticism is not strength but a weakness to be overcome; hence these reflections by the party poet, Sam Leventhal:

> Because Communism was so new, it was hard, hard on the individual. He had to make himself harder. If he didn't, he

> would betray the masses, the masses he wanted to address in poems of comradeship. If he gave way to doubts, what life would he have? In the future, there would be neither life nor victory outside the Movement. You would choke, stifle, die in spiritual isolation if you became a renegade. He had to measure up to the demands of the Party. He would try to. Only this urge to write, these moody feelings he was having tonight seemed so out of place when he was with his comrades. (424)

If for Leventhal you "would choke, stifle, die in spiritual isolation if you became a renegade," for Carr you would, if you did not. A break with the party is inevitable and it comes on an issue that sets "personal integrity," "fairness," and "truth" in opposition to party unity, expedience, and "falsity." Carr is present at a socialist meeting intruded upon and broken up by communists in what appears to be a well-planned action. Thoroughly disgusted by this incident, he is outraged when a phony version, wholly exonerating themselves, is offered by the party leadership and he is prevented from revealing the truth. "I don't know why I ever let myself get involved with them," Bernard says, when it is all over. "It's a conspiracy against freedom, free thinking, free writing, against a free life. It's a conspiracy against mankind" (*Yet Other Waters*, 400). Well and good—the only trouble is that Carr's sense of social injustice, left without any means of effective action, becomes, once again, little more than sentiment.

Personal optimism, set in a context of social and philosophic pessimism, inflates itself to soap opera dimensions as Bernard begins to respond to the possibilities of domestic life. Far from being poignant, as Farrell intended, the final episode of the trilogy, with its baby talk and middle-class cliché, is pure bathos:

> "Daddy, airplane," Philip called in a voice of excitement and wonder.
> In Spain, planes were dropping bombs. In the next war, what? When would it come? What lay ahead?

Farrell and the Aesthetics of Nostalgia 201

> It didn't matter what lay ahead. He'd face it. And in the meantime you lived. He was living and using his life well now. What more could he ask for?
> "Philip looks like you, and he's beginning to acquire your habits, Bernard."
> "He's going to be a good kid."
> "Bernard, we've been happy, haven't we?"
> "Honey, we are happy."
> "We always will be, won't we?"
> "We'll meet whatever comes, honey."
> Her features melted into a loving smile, and she had the glow of a pregnant woman in her eyes. Her face was shining, and she seemed beautiful to him. He was shining, and she seemed beautiful to him. He was happy she was his wife.
> The soft, fading autumn sun was warm. He lay down and put his head in her lap and closed his eyes. She stroked his hair.
> "Elizabeth, sing *Kathleen* for me." (411-12)

Since nothing is permanent in this world, we know that this episode will become the material for nostalgia and turn into one of the "glowing moments" by which Bernard marks the high points of his past. But as a possible end in his quest for values, such domesticity, ignoring as it does the very evils of bourgeois life that until now had made Bernard wary of too close an embrace by Elizabeth, is of little worth. Indeed, the conclusion of the novel seems to give Elizabeth, who, though she never ceases to adulate her husband, has never outgrown the influence of her Chicago-Irish parents, a clear if probably temporary victory in the struggle for Bernard's soul. Thus Bernard finds himself reconciled with his sister and brothers and contemplates remaining in Chicago to finish his next book. It will not be a book we look forward to reading.

10 Socialist Realism
The Undetotalizable Totality

When in *The Russian Revolution* Trotsky asked, "Who led the February Insurrection?" the answer he had in mind was, we can believe, factual, but factual in a way that reflected a major principle on the nature of revolution. The point Trotsky wanted to make is that the Insurrection was not, as popular theory had it, spontaneous; rather it was led by "conscious and tempered workers educated for the most part by the party of Lenin." And Trotsky spells out exactly what that consciousness signified:

> In order correctly to appraise the situation and determine the moment for a blow at the enemy, it was necessary that the masses or their guiding layers should *make their examination* of historical events and *have their criteria* for investigating them. . . . It was necessary that throughout this mass there should be scattered workers who had *thought over* the experience in 1905, *criticized* the constitutional *illusions* of the liberals and the Mensheviks, *assimilated the perspectives of the revolution, meditated* hundreds of times about the question of the army, *watched attentively* what was going on in its midst—workers capable of making revolutionary *inferences* from what they *observed* and communicating them to others. (145; my italics)

Socialist Realism

Thus, in the working masses there was "taking place an independent and deep process of growth, not only of hatred for the rulers, but of critical understanding of their impotence, an accumulation of experience and creative consciousness which the revolutionary insurrection and its victory only completed" (146).

A conscious working class—or conscious cadres of the working class—has undergone an epistemological awakening that has made it possible for it to grasp reality, to apprehend things, relationships, events in their totality that the bourgeois man can see only as fragments. This kind of vision pertains to society in general, as well as to revolution; it also pertains to history and historiography. The man who narrates a revolution must have a consciousness no different in kind from the man who makes one; that is, he must be capable of "scientific objectivism," which provides his reader with the only way of seeing beneath the eyes and tones of the historian to the "inner logic of the narrative itself" (247-48).

By "inner logic" Trotsky is referring, I think, to the dialectical process of history; hence he can say that "changes in mass consciousness are not accidental, but are subject to an objective necessity which is capable of theoretic explanation, and thus makes prophecy and leadership possible." The knowledge of "objective necessity" in all its forms is the goal not only of the prophet and leader but of all men who wish to see the world as it is and to understand how its evils can or will be transcended. This is true especially of the socialist realist who, while dialectically retaining the ability of "critical realism" (namely, to criticize the capitalist/bourgeois state and its culture), brings to it a vision of the socialist future.

If "socialist realism" is, then, a part of the history of realism, according to its proponents (Marxist critics), it dialectically transcends that history just as it does the capitalist state in the qualitative change of revolution that ends in the triumph of socialism. Insofar as it is a critique of bourgeois society, its foundations are in "critical realism," which, as described by

3. Self-Detotalizing Heroes

Georg Lukács, represents the highest form of realism to which the bourgeois writer, devoid of any sense of the future, could aspire. Unlike socialist realism, which in its prerevolutionary stage visualizes the ideal society in which the dialectic of historical materialism ends, critical realism points to nothing beyond its own negations.

Hypothetically, critical realism reflects a "totally detotalized" world, one that is determined by the often gratuitous operations of the free market and characterized by the reification, alienation, and dehumanization imposed upon the working class through the institution of private property. Socialist realism posits, as do Hegel and the Marxist historians, a rational universe, a conception of order under which human relations are essentially harmonious, and corrupt and antiquated feelings and practices associated with bourgeois life are purged.

Despite its being geared to the individual person, capitalism makes authentic individual fulfillment impossible. Men are not "whole" persons; they are merely single, though egocentric, particles or monads. Endless motion, inexhaustable but misdirected energy, are characteristic, Tocqueville reminds us, of an egalitarian polity. In the better-organized socialist state, all movement is logical in form and teleological in direction. Bourgeois Man is a particle in perpetual motion, inhabiting a world permeated by superstition, false knowledge, false faith, and absurdity. In naturalism man is a beast because of biology; in Marxism, he is a beast only because of economics and the social institutions that production forces and production relations have created.

Against this background, we encounter socialist realism, an ambiguous conception from the beginning, as a literary phenomenon. As the chief topic of the First Writers' Congress held in Moscow in 1932, it could be understood in its vulgar aspect —socialist realism as propaganda—or it could be understood in its sophisticated or ideologically complex form—as a reflection of the realities of social life and their progress toward amelioration.

Now, can this method, rooted in a theory of social reality, be taken seriously as an art form when it is adopted (or embraced) by a "great" writer? Can a literature that reflects the "undetotalizable totality" that the final stage of the dialectical process brings forth be anything more than the didactic, melodramatic, and sentimental exercise produced by the hack? Or is a novel like Gorki's *Mother,* a story of the transformation of a working-class mother whose son inspires her to become a rebel, something more than a morality play? Moreover, don't we have to take into account the work of Mikhail Sholokhov, to his countrymen a socialist realist and to the rest of the world a writer worthy of the Nobel Prize?

Boris Suchkov has discussed in detail Sholokhov's major work, *And Quiet Flows the Don,* as an example of socialist realism, and there is no reason to go into the whole matter again. There is, however, a problem that bears a closer look, and that is the one with which this chapter began—the question of epistemology and what it tells us about the psychological and ethical situation of the characters.

But first I have a preliminary question: *And Quiet Flows the Don* is about the life of the Cossacks; exactly what is meant here by *about?* Is Sholokhov as a detached observer simply trying to recreate this ethnic group in all its energy and vitality? Or is he, in tracing their lives, making a moral point? In other words does he find them praiseworthy, blameworthy, or simply noteworthy? That we must ask this question in the first place is, I feel, a healthy sign, for it indicates that the novel is not straightforward, not (as the socialist realist novel is commonly thought to be) didactic or propagandistic. In the absence of authorial intervention, we are asked to draw our own conclusions, even though it is sometimes abundantly clear what conclusions the author would like us to draw.

In Sholokhov's depiction of Cossack life during times of peace, no character, man or woman, acquires that totalizing vision that allows him to see anything more than the world in its impressionistic immediacy or to experience anything more

3. Self-Detotalizing Heroes

than direct, primitive relationships with the persons around him. Honor and lust are the mainsprings of male action; wives are maltreated, sometimes brutally beaten; girls are raped or misled and deserted; violence is the favored mode of response to all questions. A vast equalization prevents characters from standing out as heroes; nor does anyone seem great enough to generate a plot or story around his adventures, which do not end in climax or denouement but simply come to a halt. The central character, Gregor Melekhov, follows a tortuous route toward knowledge, emotional stability, and "consciousness," a route the destination of which he can never reach. His romance with Aksinia, the wife of another volatile Cossack, does not, as Suchkov would have us believe, express his rebellion against the constraints of Cossack tradition. It is almost completely a product of lust, intense on both sides, and it neither elicits nor foreshadows any ennobling emotions that would be intrinsic in an ideal love affair or a part of the moral growth of a hero. Gregor's maltreatment of his wife, Natalia, his defiance of his father, his readiness to engage his brother in virtually mortal physical combat only confirm him as a typically headstrong, hot-tempered Cossack.

He does, however, have certain good instincts (expressed, for instance, when he attempts to rescue a woman from gang rape), but these instincts, constantly vying for supremacy, can only underscore the essentially binary nature of his character, in which contradictions move toward, but can never reach, synthesis. Thus, while Gregor is capable of "heroic" conduct on the battlefield, his thoughts and feelings would earn him no medals:

> Strongly had Gregor defended his Cossack honor, seizing every opportunity of displaying immortal prowess, risking his life in madcap adventures. . . . His heart had grown hard, dry like a salt-marsh in drought; as a marsh will not absorb water, Gregor's heart would not absorb compassion. . . . [He] knew that he no longer laughed as in former days, that his eyes were

sunken and his cheekbones stood out sharply. He knew what prices he had paid for his crosses and medals. (309)

This nihilistic despair, the very antithesis of socialist optimism, indicates how far Gregor has yet to go if he is to find authentic salvation in the totalized world.

Lack of consciousness, both self-awareness, whereby we distance ourselves from ourselves, and social awareness, by which we grasp social reality as it is, has a direct bearing on the way things are described and events narrated when seen from the point of view of a character like Gregor. As war novels often make clear, soldiers in the field, having no strategic perspective, see only the action and terrain that engages them. The Cossack cavalry has no geographical overview that would, for instance, give some kind of order or significance to the endless number of Polish villages through which they pass—villages that for the invading Cossacks might as well be nameless. We recall that in Zola's *La Débâcle* the French High Command, wholly confident that the war would be fought on German soil, issued no maps of France to its officers, with devastating consequences. In this novel, too, strategic and tactical blindness was a metaphor for social blindness. Fighting in Alsace or the Ukraine, the mapless soldier experiences only an indeterminate and defamiliarized or grotesque landscape. To the socialist, the rebel, without an adequate ideology (i.e., Bolshevism), failing to comprehend the social significance of human relations, merely founders about in ignorance and frustration, eventually turning to a vain and spontaneous violence that satisfies him but equally ensures the defeat of the rebellion.

This is in many ways the fate of Gregor, who, at odds with himself, is engaged in a personal civil war—a natural consequence of his exposure to conflicting ideologies and the tortuous path to socialism. Zola's hero, Etienne Lantier, knew and was influenced by any number of mid-nineteenth-century ideologues, including Souverin, the classic, bomb-throwing anarchist, who eventually dynamites the coal mine. An equal num-

3. Self-Detotalizing Heroes

ber of morality players surround Gregor, whose indoctrination is never complete.

Garanzha, whom he meets while recuperating from his eye wounds, reveals truths hitherto unknown to him,

> explaining the real causes of war, and jesting bitterly at the autocratic government. Gregor tried to raise objections, but Garanzha silenced him with simple, murderously simple, questions, and he was forced to agree.

The result is a foregone conclusion:

> All the system upon which Gregor's life had been built up was a smoking ruin. It had already been rotten, eaten up with the canker of the monstrous iniquity of the war, and it needed only a jolt. That jolt was given, and Gregor's mind awoke. He tossed about, seeking a way out, a solution to his predicament, and gladly found it in Garanzha's answers. (269)

Many months later, we find him listening to an anti-Bolshevik, the articulate Izvarin, who warns him that even though the Cossacks favor the Bolsheviks, they do so only because both want peace and that once peace is made, each will go his own way (408, 412). This speech leaves him as confused as ever.

In that the focus in the socialist realist novel is upon communality—all achievement and the struggle for it being seen as collective—the personal narrative about Gregor is analogous to a chronicle or epic. Correspondingly, Gregor's inability to decide among the ideological possibilities available reflects the confusion of the Cossacks in general, whom the civil war has broken into irresolute, often squabbling fragments. The internal contradictions of Russian society at the close of the First World War struggle toward synthesis, just as the chronicler seeks the vision and the apprehension of wholeness that will render his subject meaningful.

Now, there is a great urge for the naturalist novelists to mythify experience, to relate ethical and social states to natural phenomena and thus achieve a new kind of "synthesis."

Hence, the famous passage in *Germinal,* in which Lantier imagines an army of workers waiting to rise up spontaneously and violently against the capitalist world. But this was merely a consequence of desperation, for, as we have seen, when Zola wrote *Germinal* (1865), many forms of socialism were in existence, and no single ideology prevailed. Zola was, in any case, putting his faith in the extremest form of anarchism, a vision that would not be repeated after more rational forms of socialism began appearing on the scene. Germinal, say the Marxists, the myth of death and resurrection, winter and spring, could not be rendered into a stable and meaningful vision, and has ended up not in living symbolism but only in a trash heap of ideas.

That other acclaimed classic of socialist realism, Maxim Gorki's *Mother,* also has mythical overtones insofar as Gorki means his heroine to be a symbol (an earth mother, a source of nourishment and strength that unites all the comrades); she is also a "culture hero," a figure who embodies the virtues and weaknesses of the group or nation she represents and whose story is that of her growing class consciousness, self-awareness, and self-confidence. For Pelagea Nilovna Vlassov, it also means eventual transcendence of all the petit-bourgeois feelings and ideas that had marked her attitudes toward her son Pavel, who has been following his own, much more public, path to socialist knowledge and success. Pelagea never finds herself closer to her son, whose natural aloofness is compounded by his status as a revolutionary leader—one who has already spent time in prison—than when her protectiveness and possessiveness are weakened by her political activities and the exposure to new values that goes with them.

In its attention to theme, almost to the exclusion of form, socialist realism often comes perilously close to conflating didactic prose with fictive description (as when in *And Quiet Flows the Don* Sholokhov presents socialist speeches verbatim, and we sense their presence to be only of propaganda value and not a comment on the character who is speaking). No less important is the absence of suspense, an absence encouraged by a style in which, owing to a highly restrictive belief in the reality of discontinuity, the "inner narrative logic is illogical."

And Quiet Flows the Don, The Don Flows Home to the Sea, and *Mother* are actually what can be called transitional novels since they are not coeval with the final postsocialist stage. Were they so, they would be dealing with a different set of problems, ones that most preoccupied society at the time. Being coeval with a prerevolutionary epoch, they raise questions that are still pertinent to class struggle, or to the individual person and his moral choices. And they still share with critical realism the need to criticize bourgeois culture and the capitalist economy.

Thus the socialist realist, typically dialectical, embodies and transcends his bourgeois counterpart; he sees himself historically destined to surpass critical realism—no matter what his present inferiority—just as he believes the socialist state is destined historically to surpass the capitalist world, which though presently entrenched will become increasingly weakened as time goes on.

In a sense the socialist state is historically irreversible. Even if a counterrevolution were possible, it is not a part of the process by which change occurs, contradictions are resolved, and higher stages reached. Thus the postsocialist state is a synthesis that is not destined to be challenged by history—it is an undetotalizable totality, just as is the literature that reflects its conditions.

This is not to say that it couldn't be challenged by an ahistorical force—by rebellion or spontaneous uprising, a purely destructive, gratuitous force that might or might not be successful, depending on a variety of imponderables. *Rebellion* is, simply put, an instrument of detotalization, nothing more, nothing less. *Revolution* is a retotalizing force; it destroys to recreate. It cannot destroy and recreate what it has already destroyed and recreated without being redundant or tautological.

But all this is no more than wordplay. We cannot evaluate socialist realism outside its context. On the one hand, it is a form that lacks even the sophistication of naturalism; still it can be appreciated best by a Russian audience to whom its conventions and devices or, better, its themes, are vital and fraught with meaning, not simply platitudinous and arid. On the other hand, whatever its weaknesses, *And Quiet Flows the Don* is a powerful, expansive novel that we reject at our peril, whether we are Russians or not.

Notes
Works Cited
Index

Notes

Introduction

1. *The Monological Jew* (University of Wisconsin Press: Madison, 1988).

2. For a study of Zola's encounters with socialists and socialism, see Joseph Genuzio's *Jules Guesde et Emile Zola ou le socialisme dans l'oeuvre de Zola*. For the study of naturalism and the Marxist critics that follows I've made use of J. H. Matthews' introduction. The chief texts, for our purposes, are Jean Fréville's *Zola: Semeur d'orages* and Jan Varloot's "Zola vivant," parts 1 and 2. Marxist comment on the individual novels will be cited appropriately.

3. This list comprises merely those figures that I have selected for discussion. Some omissions are Dos Passos's Mac (*USA*), Steinbeck's John Nolan (*In Dubious Battle*), and Richard Wright's Cross Damon (*The Outsider*). No doubt the reader can add others. I must apologize specifically for not including any women, either writers or protagonists, with the exception of Cornelia Thornwell, the socialite socialist of Sinclair's *Boston*. I've also discussed de Beauvoir's *Ethics of Ambiguity*, though I didn't venture into her most ambitious novel, *The Mandarins*, a work that is not precisely naturalist, socialist, or existential in the way I've been using these terms. I might also have dealt with Lessing or Woolf, both of whom were attracted to socialism but whose novels transcended the philosophic, literary, and political categories upon which I have been focusing.

4. "Totalité détotalisée." See Sartre's *L'Etre et le néant*, 712 (*Being and Nothingness*, 623).

5. According to Goldmann, that future is already here. Always a reflection of the stage of capitalism through which society is passing, fiction now expresses a consumer capitalism in which a total reification has occurred. After the fragmentation or atomization suffered under earlier stages of capitalism, in which individualist values completely prevailed over "trans-individual" (communal) values, Western society has entered a period of integration. Unfortunately, it is an integration marked not by the emergence of communal values but rather by that of technological ones that have prevailed over individualism. The fiction produced in this era—Robbe-Grillet and the French New Wave novelists being typical—"describes a perfectly structured . . . universe where . . . the deformed, flattened human is entirely dominated and is obliterated . . . by inert objects, which now take the primary role and become the true active elements of this universe" (*Cultural Creation,* 86).

In this history of the novel, which Goldmann sees as a "homologue" to the history of capitalism, the process began with the "problematic hero," "continued in existentialist philosophy and the novel of the dissolution of character in a decomposed, anguished world and issued in the reappearance of a stable, balanced, but rigorously ahuman universe" (86). As provocative as it might be, I'm not sure that the theory of homologues answers all the important questions about the development of the novel, even if we assume the accuracy of Goldmann's description. I feel that it is too blunt an instrument to record the differences of one writer from another, one novel from another by the same writer, or indeed one section of a novel from another. Most important for us is that it doesn't distinguish between differing conscious political beliefs and intentions, to say nothing of aesthetic ones.

1. The World as Will

1. Thus Huysmans wrote to Zola, "I know that you do not believe in pessimism and that the Bordeaux preface of the *Pensées* of Schopenhauer declares that this prodigious man was afraid of death—but the theory rises above the man who does not apply these ideas to himself . . . . these ideas are surely the most consoling, the most logical, the most evident possible" (*Lettres inédites,* 99, my translation). I am indebted to Hemmings' article on the current state of Zola studies (1956), in which both Baillot and Huysmans are cited.

3. Zola II

1. See *Studies in European Realism,* chapter 4. There is a long tradition of Marxist appreciation of Balzac at Zola's expense. See also "Les marxistes, Balzac, et Zola" by André Wurmser.

2. The three others were *Travail* (*Work*), *Vérité* (*Truth*), and the unwritten *Justice.*

3. "Competing socialist theories of equal weight to Zola": this was the case in 1865 when the novel takes place.

4. The hero as depicted by socialist realism will be discussed in detail in the concluding chapter. The subject is, I feel, too important to be dealt with in a digression.

5. In its essence *Germinal* remains true to its naturalist origins and to Zola's republican politics. Thus, seeking to naturalize and mythify the miners, the mines, and indeed the whole socioeconomic process, Zola betrayed how far he stood from the working class. As Graham Holderness puts it in "Miners and the Novel," Zola perceived the mines both "as a material fact, a part of a particular economic system; and as a mythological monster, a diabolical and bestial creature which devours men and women, feeding on their labour and destroying their lives." What is necessary to turn this bourgeois vision into one that is suitable for a truly working-class writer, Holderness argues, is the removal of all sense of mystery associated with myth. In such demystification, human beings are represented as "human beings, capable both of patient everyday endurance and of disciplined collective struggle." Here social life in a mining community is presented as "knowable," "a model both of the conflict-ridden industrial system and of a potential future society of equality and cooperation." Industry itself is presented as "a material object capable of being politically and economically transformed into a new democratic system of social organization" (22-23). This is, I believe, the central issue not only in our study of Zola, but in that of any realist writer with socialist aspirations.

6. The treatment of the Germans, or lack of it, in *La Débâcle,* is a study in itself. "Where are the Germans?" one reviewer complained. Since Zola's subject is in large part the deserved demise of the Second Empire, full characterization of the Germans, including say the political motives of Bismarck, would have certainly lessened the impact of the argument.

7. For the standard Marxist critique of *L'Argent* see Paul Lafargue in *Critiques litteraires,* 193-211.

4. Sartre I

1. "A brief consideration" of Hegel in all his complexity is, of course, impossible. I am relying heavily on W. T. Stace's presentation in *The Philosophy of Hegel,* which gives the essentials, but should not be taken as a substitute for the much denser original. I am interested only in those aspects of the philosophy that have a bearing on the present discussion. An early, less-detailed version of this argument appears in *The Monological Jew,* chapter 3. Applied as they are to differing subjects, these discussions complement, rather than replace, one another.

2. See Desan, *The Marxism of Jean-Paul Sartre,* 117-18.

5. Sartre II

1. The example of the waiter originally appeared in *Being and Nothingness,* 59. "The waiter in the cafe plays with his condition in order to *realize it,*" says Sartre. "Society demands that he limit himself to his function . . . just as the soldier at attention makes himself into a soldier-thing." He concludes, "There are indeed many precautions to imprison a man in what he is, as if he lived in perpetual fear that he might escape from it, that he might break away and suddenly elude his condition." Clearly, this is a different perspective on the problem from the one Sartre gives us in Mathieu.

2. I am aware that this whole line of reasoning conflicts with Sartre's assertion that "I can be ashamed only as my freedom escapes me in order to become a *given* object. . . . I am in a world that the other has made alien to me" (*Being and Nothingness,* 261). Nonetheless, I shall continue to regard my argument as one of my possibilities in my project of interpreting the novel.

3. For Sartre's discussion of the ontological contradictions in trying to apprehend one's self as evil, see *Being and Nothingness,* 273-74.

7. Orwell's Unrevolutionary Rebels

1. William Steinhoff discusses Jack London's influence on Orwell in his comprehensive and informative study *George Orwell and the Origins of* 1984. His emphasis is different from my own in that I am trying to prove a point and he is not.

2. This distinction between a static and a dynamic society reflects the distinction between "metaphysical" and "dialectical" in Marxist epistemology (see, for example, Norman and Sayers' *Hegel, Marx, and Dialectic: A Debate*). Capitalist society sees itself as fixed, universal,

and eternal; this is the metaphysical view, in which reality is interpreted in terms of abstractions and autonomous self-justifying structures and institutions. In the dialectical standpoint, reality is interpreted in terms of the concrete interaction of things; that is, in terms of relationships that are characterized by struggle and change. Based as it is on the single-minded and indefatigable effort to bring history or time to a stop, to eliminate change and therefore all internal threat to its security, Oceania is trying to become the totally undetotalizable totality, but in its dystopian, not utopian, form. It is the utter antithesis of all things dialectical, even to the point of not recognizing its antithetical nature, since that would be an admission that it were part of a (nonexistent) dialectical process. By *doublethink,* Oceania cannot be an antithesis to anything that does not exist nor, in fact, to anything that does, since antithesis implies dialectic.

3. Steinhoff has a summary of Burnham's books and discusses in detail the ideas in them that appealed to or repelled Orwell. He sees no contradiction in Orwell's attitude toward Burnham, which, he claims, was hostile only until Orwell gained a fuller understanding of Burnham's position. Steinhoff and I draw the same conclusions but for different reasons.

4. For a highly informative discussion of Julia from a feminist viewpoint, see Leslie Tentler's " 'I'm Not Literary, Dear': George Orwell on Women and the Family." Tentler argues that Orwell held strong traditional ideas about the family and believed that motherhood was the social obligation—and the fulfillment—of women. Similarly, Orwell thought that "women are creatures of instinct and emotion rather than intellect" and that they were "constitutionally incapable of dealing with the world on any but the limited terms of their own needs and experiences." Hence, Julia's "inability to grapple with the ideas that obsess Winston." *Vicisti, O Aspidistra!*

5. For an extensive comparison of Orwell and Marcuse, see Alfred G. Mayer's "The Political Theory of Pessimism." Professor Mayer writes as a political scientist and his perspective is considerably different from my own.

8. Sinclair's Socialite Socialists

1. *The Radical Novel in the United States, 1900-1954: Some Interrelations of Literature and Society,* 35-36. For an account of Sinclair's difficulties in completing the novel see Leon Harris's *Upton Sinclair: American Rebel,* 75-77. Harris points out that Sinclair was never satisfied with any of the several conclusions he had written.

2. In his highly sympathetic book, *Upton Sinclair: A Study in Social Protest,* Floyd Dell points out the dubious use of aristocratic heroes in *Metropolis* (1908) and *The Moneychangers* (1908). Although he sees this approach in *King Coal* as a disability, he still finds the novel a "brilliant" success. I should make it clear that I am not saying that after Jurgis Rudkus Sinclair wholly abandoned the proletarian as a central character—Jimmy Higgins, the "typical" socialist worker in the novel bearing his name (1919), being a case in point. There is a difference, however, between a "central character," depicted as a victim or a pawn or an Everyman, and a "hero," depicted as a leader or an especially endowed person.

The opinion that Sinclair was aiming *King Coal* at a bourgeois audience, whom he hoped to waken to the conditions of the miners, should be qualified. Publishing many of his own works and selling them at a low price, Sinclair apparently had a working-class audience as well (see Dell, 181–83).

3. One of the best commentaries on Sinclair's weakness both in the Lanny Budd series and in general can be found in S. Gorley Putts, *Scholars of the Heart,* 87–109. Jon A. Yoder also has a good account of the Lanny Budd novels in *Upton Sinclair,* his useful survey of Sinclair's life and career as a socialist writer. Yoder sees the problems of contemporary liberalism as the central theme of the series, as well as of *Boston.*

9. Farrell and the Aesthetics of Nostalgia

1. A whole book has been devoted to Farrell and socialism, *James T. Farrell: The Revolutionary Socialist Years* by Alan M. Wald. This book is valuable for its historical detail as it traces Farrell's associations with many socialist organizations, figures, and causes and records their influence on his thinking and writing. Wald sees Farrell's relationship with Trotsky, through George Novak, as the central one. Even here, Farrell evades all classification. "What about Trotsky and his importance to you?" asks an interviewer. "I admired Leon Trotsky tremendously," replies Farrell. "He affected my political thinking more than my literary thinking. . . . I still look at him as a great hero. He had an extraordinary mind. But, I mean, history has not turned out the way he or anybody else expected it to be" (Jack Salzman and Dennis Flynn).

Closer to my own approach is Lewis Fried's "Bernard Carr and

His Trials of the Mind," which defines one of the major contradictions of Carr's view of the world:

> [Carr was willing] to explore and (adapt) the major theses of Marxism, the alienated nature of labor under capitalism, the economically self-devouring process of capitalism, and the historically expressed relationship between consciousness and work that mark the phases of dialectical materialism. Yet he is not ready to throw in his lot with the Party. . . . For one, he is not sure that the Party can solve America's economic problems. For another . . . he knows that the complexity of the American experience cannot be reduced to historical generalizations. No less importantly, he does not believe that the artist has to be a politicized creature.

Fried tells us that originally Carr saw himself as an "aggregate of somebodies"—that is, as an almost totally detotalized figure. (Mere aggregate does not establish totality on any meaningful level.) He has recently succeeded, however, in "grasping the essential nature of an integrated life: truthful inquiry about oneself and society binds private and public conduct." In that binding of public and private, self and society, lies the ideal unification and resolution of the inner contradictions that were tearing apart the state and "totaling" the citizenry. The craving for violence and murder leads to the massive destruction out of which emerges the new world. Dialogue now replaces monologue and on the site of the Tower of Babel, crumbled to dust, there rises a new edifice and a new language by which God enters into dialogue with mankind and mankind with itself.

This is a very Hebraic, a very Buberian, interpretation of reality. It is neither the interpretation of socialism nor of naturalism (nihilism); nor is it that of existential individualism, all of which have other voices calling for attention, and other rooms to show.

Works Cited

Baillot, Alexandre. *Influence de la philosophie de Schopenhauer en France (1860-1900)*. Paris: J. Vrin, 1927.

Batalov, Edouard. *The Philosophy of Revolt (Criticism of Left Radical Ideology)*. Trans. Katherine Judelson. Moscow: Progress Publishers, 1975.

Beauvoir, Simone de. *The Ethics of Ambiguity*. Trans. Bernard Frechtman. New York: Citadel, 1961.

———. *The Force of Circumstance*. Trans. Richard Howard. New York: Penguin, 1968.

Brée, Germaine. *Camus and Sartre: Crisis and Commitment*. New York: Dell, 1972.

Camus, Albert. *The Stranger*. Trans. Stuart Gilbert. New York: Vintage, 1946.

———. *The Plague*. Trans. Stuart Gilbert. New York: Knopf, 1960.

———. *The Rebel*. Trans. Anthony Bower. New York: Vintage, 1960.

———. *Resistance, Rebellion, and Death*. Trans. Justin O'Brien. New York: Vintage, 1960.

———. *The Fall*. Trans. Justin O'Brien. London: Hamish and Hamilton, 1962.

———. *Lyrical and Critical Essays*. Ed. Philip Thody. Trans. Ellen Conroy Kennedy. New York: Knopf, 1968.

———. *The Myth of Sisyphus*. Trans. Justin O'Brien. New York: Vintage, 1962.

———. *The Note Books: 1935-1942*. Trans. Philip Thody. New York: Random House, 1965.

———. *The Note Books: 1942-1951.* Trans. Justin O'Brien. New York: Knopf, 1965.
Cauté, David. *Communism and the French Intellectuals, 1914-1960.* New York: Macmillan, 1964.
Contat, Michel, and Michel Rybalka. *Les écrits de Sartre, chronologie, bibliographie commentée.* Paris: Gallimard, 1970.
Dell, Floyd. *Upton Sinclair: A Study in Social Protest.* New York: Boni, 1930.
Desan, Wilfrid. *The Tragic Finale: An Essay on the Philosophy of Jean-Paul Sartre.* Cambridge: Harvard University Press, 1954.
———. *The Marxism of Jean-Paul Sartre.* Toronto: Doubleday, 1965.
Farrell, James T. *A Note on Literary Criticism.* New York: Vanguard, 1936.
———. *Bernard Clare.* New York: Vanguard, 1946.
———. *Literature and Morality.* New York: Vanguard, 1947.
———. *The Road Between.* New York: Vanguard, 1949.
———. *Yet Other Waters.* New York: Vanguard, 1952.
———. *Reflections at Fifty.* New York: Vanguard, 1954.
———. *Studs Lonigan.* New York: Signet, 1965.
Fréville, Jean. *Zola: Semeur d'orages.* Paris: Editions Sociale, 1952.
Fried, Lewis. "Bernard Carr and *His* Trials of the Mind." *Twentieth Century Literature* 22, 1 (Feb. 1976).
Genuzio, Joseph. *Jules Guesde et Emile Zola, ou le socialisme dans l'oeuvre de Zola.* Paris: Bari, 1964.
Goldmann, Lucien. *Cultural Creation in Modern Society.* Trans. Bart Grahl. St. Louis: Telos Press, 1976.
Grisoli, Christian. "Interview with J. P. Sartre." *Paru* 13, Dec. 1945. See also Contat and Rybalka, 115.
Harris, Leon. *Upton Sinclair, American Rebel.* New York: Crowell, 1975.
Hegel, G. W. E. *The Phenomenology of Mind.* Trans. J. P. Baillie. New York: Harper Torchbooks, 1967.
Hemmings, F. W. J. *Emile Zola.* Oxford: Clarendon, 1953.
———. "The Present Position of Zola Studies." *French Studies* 10, 3 (April 1956).
Hicks, Granville. *The Great Tradition: An Interpretation of American Literature since the Civil War.* Chicago: Quadrangle, 1969.
Holderness, Graham. "Miners in the Novel: From Bourgeois to Proletarian Fiction." In *The British Working-Class Novel in the Twenti-*

eth Century, ed. Jeremy Hawthorne. London: Edward Arnold, 1984.
Kateb, George. "The Road to *1984.*" In *Twentieth Century Interpretations of 1984,* ed. Samuel Hynes. Englewood Cliffs, N.J.: Prentice-Hall, 1971.
Lafargue, Paul. *"L'Argent."* In *Critiques littéraires.* Paris: n.p., 1936.
Leites, Nathan. "The Stranger." In *Art and Psychoanalysis,* ed. William Phillips. Cleveland and New York: World/Meridian, 1963.
Lissagary, Prosper. *History of the Commune of 1871.* Trans. Eleanor Marx Aveling. 1898. Reprint. New York: Monthly Review Press, 1967.
London, Jack. *The Iron Heel.* New York: Hill and Wang, 1957.
Lukács, Georg. *Realism in Our Time: Literature and the Class Struggle.* Trans. John and Necke Wander. New York: Harper and Row, 1964.
――――. *Studies in European Realism.* New York: Grosset and Dunlap, 1964.
Marcuse, Herbert. *Studies in Critical Philosophy.* Trans. Joris de Bres. London: NLB, 1971.
――――. *One Dimensional Man: Studies in the Ideology of Advanced Industrial Society.* Boston: Beacon Press, 1964.
Marx, Karl. *The Paris Commune,* 1871. Ed. Christopher Hitchens. London: Sidgwick and Jackson, 1971.
Marx, Karl, and Friedrich Engels. *Selected Works.* Moscow: Foreign Languages Pub. House, 1958.
Mayer, Alfred G. "The Political Theory of Pessimism: George Orwell and Herbert Marcuse." In *The Future of Nineteen Eighty-Four,* ed. Ejner Jensen. Ann Arbor: University of Michigan Press, 1984.
Micaud, Charles. *Communism and the French Left.* New York: Praeger, 1963.
Norman, Richard, and Sean Sayers. *Hegel, Marx, and Dialectics: A Debate.* Brighton: Harvester Press, and Atlantic Highlands, N.J.: Humanities Press, 1980.
Orwell, George. *Animal Farm.* New York: New American Library, 1946.
――――. *Coming Up for Air.* New York: Harcourt, Brace, 1950.
――――. *Keep the Aspidistra Flying.* New York: Harcourt, Brace, 1956.
――――. *A Clergyman's Daughter.* New York: Harcourt, Brace, 1960.

———. *Homage to Catalonia.* New York: Harcourt, Brace, 1962.
———. *Burmese Days.* New York: New American Library, 1963.
———. *The Road to Wigan Pier.* New York: Berkeley, 1967.
———. *The Collected Essays, Journalism, and Letters.* 4 vols. London: Secker and Warburg, 1968. See vl. 1, pp. 235-51, "Shooting an Elephant." See vol. 4, pp. 330-69, "Such, Such Were the Joys."
———. *Nineteen Eighty-Four.* New York: New American Library, Signet, 1981.
Ovcharenko, A. *Socialist Realism and the Modern Literary Process.* Trans. Igor Puchkov. Moscow: Progress Publishers, 1978.
Pascal, Roy. "Georg Lukács, the Concept of Totality." In *Georg Lukács: The Man, His Work, and Ideas,* ed. G. H. L. Parkinson. New York: Vintage, 1970.
Putts, S. Gorely. *Scholars of the Heart.* London: Faber, 1962.
Rideout, Walter. *The Radical Novel in the United States, 1900-1954: Some Interrelations of Literature and Society.* New York: Hill and Wang, 1966.
Salzman, Jack, and Dennis Flynn. "An Interview with James T. Farrell." In *Twentieth Century Literature* 22, 1 (Feb. 1976): 5.
Sartre, Jean-Paul. *The Roads to Liberty.* 4 vols. I: *The Age of Reason.* Trans. Eric Sutton. New York: Knopf, 1947. II: *The Reprieve.* Trans. Eric Sutton. New York: Knopf, 1947. III: *Troubled Sleep* (also called "Iron in the Soul"). Trans. Gerald Hopkins. New York: Knopf, 1950. IV (projected): "The Last Chance." Untranslated and unpublished except for a section called *Drôle d'amitié,* which appeared in *Les Temps modernes* (Nov. and Dec. 1949).
———. *Anti-Semite and Jew.* Trans. George Becker. New York: Schocken, 1948.
———. *Nausea.* Trans. Lloyd Alexander. New York: New Directions, 1949.
———. *What Is Literature?* Trans. Bernard Frechtman. New York: Philosophical Library, 1949.
———. *Baudelaire.* Trans. Martin Turnell. New York: New Directions, 1950.
———. *Being and Nothingness, an Essay on Phenomenological Ontology.* Trans. Hazel Barnes. Philosophical Library, 1952.
———. *Literary and Philosophical Essays.* Trans. Annette Michelson. New York: Collier-Macmillan, 1955.
———. *Literary Essays.* Trans. Annette Michelson. New York: Philosophical Library, 1957.

———. *Sartre on Theater,* Ed. Michel Contat and Michael Rybalka. New York: Pantheon, 1976.
———. *Search for a Method.* Trans. Hazel Barnes. New York: Knopf, 1963.
———. *Situations.* Trans. Benita Eisler. New York: Braziller, 1965.
Schopenhauer, Arthur. *The World as Will and Representation.* Trans. E. F. J. Payne. 2 vols. New York: Dover, 1969.
Sholokhov, Mikhail. *And Quiet Flows the Don.* Trans. Stephen Garry. New York: Knopf, 1967 [1934].
Sinclair, Upton. *The Jungle.* New York: Grosset and Dunlap, 1906.
———. *King Coal.* New York: Macmillan, 1917.
———. *Oil!* New York: Boni, 1927.
———. *Boston.* New York: Boni, 1928.
———. From the Lanny Budd series:
  World's End. New York: Viking, 1940.
  Between Two Worlds. New York: Viking, 1941.
  Dragon's Teeth. New York: Viking, 1942.
  Wide Is the Gate. New York: Viking, 1943.
  Presidential Agent. New York: Viking, 1944.
  O Shepherd Speak! New York: Viking, 1949.
  The Return of Lanny Budd. New York: Viking, 1953.
Stace, W. T. *The Philosophy of Hegel.* New York: Dover, 1955.
Steinhoff, William. *The Origins of George Orwell's 1984.* Ann Arbor: University of Michigan Press, 1976.
Suchkov, Boris. *A History of Realism.* Moscow: Progress Publishers, 1973.
Tentler, Leslie. "'I'm Not Literary, Dear': George Orwell on Women and the Family." In *The Future of Nineteen Eighty-Four,* ed. Ejner Jensen. Ann Arbor: University of Michigan Press, 1984.
Tocqueville, Alexis de. *Democracy in America.* 2 vols. New York: Vintage, 1945.
Trotsky, Leon. *The Russian Revolution.* Selected and edited by F. W. Dupee. New York: Doubleday, 1959.
Varloot, Jan. "Zola vivant," parts I and II. *La Pensée* 44 (Sept.-Oct. 1952) and 46 (Jan.-Feb. 1953).
Wald, Alan M. *James T. Farrell: The Revolutionary Socialist Years.* New York: New York University Press, 1978.
Wurmser, Andre. "Les marxistes, Balzac, et Zola." *Cahiers naturalistes* 28 (1964): 137-48.

Yoder, Jon A. *Upton Sinclair.* New York: Ungar, 1975.
Zola, Emile. *Money.* Trans. Ernest A. Vizetelly. London: Chatto and Windus, 1894.
———. *The Zest for Life.* Trans. Ernest A. Vizetelly. London: Chatto and Windus, 1901.
———. *The Fortune of the Rougons.* Ed. Ernest Z. Vizetelly. New York: Albert and Charles Boni, 1925.
———. *Oeuvres complètes.* Notes et commentaires de Maurice Le Blond. Paris: Fasquelle, 1927-28.
———. *The Human Beast.* Trans. Louis Colman. New York: United Book Guild, 1948.
———. *Germinal.* Trans. Leonard Tancock. Baltimore: Penguin Books, 1954.
———. *The Kill.* Trans. A. Teixeira De Mattos. New York: Farrar, Straus and Young, 1954.
———. *Earth.* Trans. Ann Lindsay. New York: Grove Press, 1955.
———. *Dr. Pascal.* Trans. Vladimir Kean. London: Elek Books, 1957.
———. *His Excellency, Eugene Rougon.* Trans. Alec Brown. London: Elek Books, 1958.
———. "Ebauches" in *Zola: les Rougon-Macquart.* Presentation et notes de Pierre Cogny. Paris: Editions Du Seuill, 1969. Vol. 1: *La Fortune des Rougon.* Vol. 2: *Son Excellence, Eugene Rougon, L'Assommoir.* Vol. 3: *Nana.* Vol. 4: *La Joie de Vivre, Germinal.* Vol. 5: *La Terre, La Bête humaine.* Vol. 6: *L'Argent, La Débâcle, Le Docteur Pascal.*
———. *L'Assommoir.* Trans. Arthur Symons. New York: Citdel, 1970.
———. *The Debacle.* Trans. L. W. Tancock. Baltimore: Penguin Books, 1972.
———. *Nana.* Trans. George Holden. Baltimore: Penguin Books, 1972.
Zwerlding, Alex. "Orwell's Psychopolitics." In *The Future of Nineteen Eighty-Four,* ed. Ejner Jensen, pp. 87-110. Ann Arbor: University of Michigan Press, 1984.

Index

Absurd, the, 79–80, 118, 119–25, 131, 136; philosophy of, 122–25, 128
Allegory, 135–36, 161
Anarchy, 54, 115, 173, 179, 209
Anguish, *angst, angoisse,* 83–84, 87, 92
Aristocracy, 27, 180, 183
Atomism, 6, 78, 96; social atomization, 27, 38, 216*n*

Baillot, Alexandre, 15
Balzac, Honoré de, 39–40, 43
Barbusse, Henri, 55
Barthes, Roland, 135
Batalov, Edward, 168
Baudelaire, Charles-Pierre, 85, 87, 107
Beauvoir, Simon de, 86, 93–94, 96–97, 114
Biology, 9, 23, 204; biologism, 63. *See also* Heredity
Bourgeois society, 4, 5, 45, 173, 198; false stability of, 7; in Sartre, 99–100, 114; in Orwell, 148, 157–58; in Sinclair, 180; in Farrell, 201; and socialist realism, 203–4

Breton, André, 111
Buber, Martin, 3–4, 143
Burnham, James, 164, 166

Camus, Albert, 18, 58, 69–79, 117–44; *L'Homme Révolté,* 69, 72–73, 74, 119; *L'Etranger,* 69, 121, 123–24, 125, 131; rebellion in, 72–73, 75–76, 147–48, 161; the Absurd in, 79–80, 118, 119–25, 131, 136; solidarity in, 89–90; *Le Mythe de Sisyphe,* 118–19; the legal system in, 121, 123; *La Peste,* 126, 134–39, 141–42; *Lettres à un ami allemand,* 126, 127, 131; freedom in, 129; solar thought in, 130–31, 133–34, 161; as a historical novelist, 136; *La Chute,* 139–44; and Orwell, comparison of, 147–48. *See also* specific works
Capitalism, 5, 114, 162, 203–4, 210; social conditions under, 8, 10; naturalist view of, 60; and nausea, 86; in Orwell, 159–60, 164, 165; Marcuse on, 167, 168; in Sinclair, 172, 179, 180, 187; Farrell on, 193, 199

Catholicism, 21-22, 116, 199
Cauté, David, 111
Class consciousness, 114, 136
Class distinctions, 97, 111
Class struggle, 29, 38, 39-40, 210;
 and detotalization, in Marx, 7;
 naturalist perspective on, 8; in
 Orwell, 160, 161; in Sinclair,
 175; in Farrell, 199
Combat (journal), 127
Communism, 114, 148, 190, 199.
 See also Marxism; Socialism
Communist Party, 197, 198
Competition, 21, 22, 44, 46, 54-55;
 and egalitarianism, 23, 29
Connolly, Cyril, 148
Consciousness, 71-79, 101, 136,
 207; reflective, 81-82, 87, 100;
 social, 82-83, 202; and will, in
 Schopenhauer, 117; and the will
 to power, 162; and revolution,
 202-3. *See also* Self-consciousness
Crime: of passion, 64-65; in
 Camus, 129, 131, 140; in
 Sinclair, 171

Darwin, Charles, 23, 181
Death: and rebirth, in Zola,
 24-25; in Sartre, 70; acceptance
 of, 75; in Camus, 127; in
 Farrell, 195; and resurrection,
 myth of, 209
Democracy, 18, 22, 27, 159, 189
Desan, Wilfrid, 7
Despair, 8, 86, 144, 159
Determinism, 10, 27, 28
Detotalization: in Marx, 7-8; in
 Sartre, 7-8, 112; and the
 naturalist text, 9; transcendence
 of, 10; and naturalism, 15-65; in
 Zola, 26-65; self-, 45; in France,
 95-96; and prison camp condi-
 tions, 112; in Camus, 143; in
 Orwell, 154, 166-67; and critical

realism, 204; rebellion as an
 instrument of, 210. *See also*
 Detotalized totalities; Totalities
Detotalized totalities: defined, 6;
 interpretation of, and socialist
 realism, 11; in Zola, 65; and the
 loss of God, 79-80; and freedom,
 94; in Sartre, 94-95; and the
 Absurd, in Camus, 119. *See also*
 Detotalization; Totalities
Dialectical: logic, 29, 78, 79;
 processes, 78, 85, 168, 203
Dialectics, law of, 6

Egalitarianism, 20, 161, 204; and
 universal competition, 23; of the
 Second Empire, 27, 38, 55
Egalitarian society, 21-22, 29,
 36-37, 39, 56
Ego, the, 75
Egocentricity, 6, 92
Egoism, 47
Entropy, Law of, 6-8
Epistemology, 15-19, 53
Eternal justice, 17, 18-19, 81,
 117-18
Ethics, 81, 176; of ambiguity
 (Beauvoir), 96-97, 116. *See also*
 Morality
Evil, 65, 108, 137, 139, 180; good
 and, 17, 60-61, 115, 187; in
 Orwell, 165; in Sinclair, 188
Existentialism: the Other, 80;
 seriality, 80; *Mit-Sein*, 80-81;
 angoisse, 83-84, 87, 92; freedom,
 85, 92; *Néant*, 92; *le regard* (the
 "look"), 97; bad faith, 101, 105.
 See also Nihilism

Factography, 8, 9
Family, the, 26-38, 40-41
Farrell, James, 5, 191-201; "Liter-
 ature and Morality," 191-92; *A
 Note on Literary Criticism*, 192-93;

Index

"Reflections at Fifty," 193;
Bernard Carr trilogy, 193,
194-201
Fascism, 132, 148, 158-60, 163;
in Sinclair, 180, 184, 187
Fatalism, 29
Freedom, 70, 71, 92; in Sartre,
81-83, 92, 96, 105; in Camus,
129, 140; artistic, 198, 199. *See
also* Existentialism
Fréville, Jean, 46

Germany, Nazi, 15, 54, 99,
132-33, 160; occupation of Paris,
93-94; pact with the Soviets
(1939), 111. *See also* Nazism
Germinal (Zola), 5, 38, 46-51, 59,
99; death and rebirth in, 24-25;
class struggle in, 39, 54; coal
mining industry in, 54, 63, 97;
conclusion of, 168, 172; socialism
in, 168, 209; characterization in,
173
God, 18, 73, 76, 129; death of, 8,
130; in Sartre, 78, 79, 109, 112,
115, 116; as *en sui causa,* 79; will
of, 117; in Camus, 118, 130,
137, 138, 140
Goldmann, Lucien, 4
Good, 24, 93; and evil, 17, 60-61,
115, 187; common, in Camus,
125, 127-28. *See also* Ethics; Evil;
Morality
Gorer, Geoffrey, 159
Gorki, Maxim, 205, 209, 210
Gratuity, 85-86, 89, 92
Guilt, 120, 128, 140, 149

Hegel, G. W. F., 23, 71-80, 106,
110, 204
Heidegger, Martin, 80-81
Hemmings, F. W. J., 46
Heredity, 172, 186
Hero, the, 10, 47, 93, 94; Absurd,

in Camus, 124, 125, 126;
detotalized, in Orwell, 156;
"culture," 209
Hicks, Granville, 9-10, 192
Historiography, 203
History, 6, 9, 164, 203; totalizing
forces of, 7; Marxist view of, 29,
162; in Zola, 29-30; in Sartre,
70, 88, 116; in Camus, 76; and
Syndicalism, 130; and the postsocialist state, 210
Humanism, 10, 23, 24, 84, 131;
anti-, in Sartre, 115
Human nature, 64, 161, 193
Huysmans, J.-K., 15, 216n

Idealism, 25
Ideals, 114-15, 167
Identity, 84, 89, 94; in Sartre,
98, 100-101; and rebellion, in
Camus, 128
Immortality, 168
Imperialism, 150, 153
Independent Labour Party, 148
Individual, the: and the collective,
7, 80; in Sartre, 80, 85, 99;
detotalized, in Orwell, 154, 156;
and revolution, in Orwell, 161.
See also Individualism; Self-
consciousness
Individualism, 6-7, 204; and
material self-interest, 27; in Zola,
56; in Sartre, 80, 85, 91-92; in
Camus, 128; in Farrell, 192-93.
See also Individual, the; Self-
consciousness
Individualistic ethic, 4-5
Instinct, 10, 23, 27, 38
Integrity, 198, 200

James, William, 10
Jew, the monological, 4
Justice, 23, 24, 126, 134

Kafka, Franz, 8, 9
Kant, Immanuel, 16, 72, 76
Kateb, George, 165
Kessous, Aziz, 134
Knowledge, 204; and will, in Schopenhauer, 18, 77, 117-18; true, in Zola, 35; in Hegel, 71; in Camus, 131; of limits, 134

Labor, 75
La Débâcle (Zola), 25, 32, 39, 51-59, 207; Jean Macquart in, 45, 51-53, 58; retotalization in, 53; detotalization in, 54
Leadership, 160-61, 203
L'Homme révolté (Camus), 69, 72-73, 74, 119; the Absurd in, 123; nihilism in, attack on, 125; ethical basis of, 126; metaphysical rebellion in, 127-30, 133
Lissagaray, Prosper, 58-59
London, Jack, 162
Lucretius, 129
Lukács, Georg, 8, 9, 45, 135, 204; on Balzac, 39, 40; on modernist writers, 86

Madness, 28, 86, 123, 140
Man: -kind, primitive nature of, 8; as bestial, 24, 27; civilized, 27; Natural, in Zola, 61; bourgeois, 84, 99-100; Cartesian, 109; the Absurd, 119, 120; Mediterranean, 131; the sick, 143-44
Manichaean: imagery, 131; viewpoint, in Sinclair, 187
Mann, Thomas, 8, 9
Marcel, Gabriel, 132
Marcuse, Herbert, 167-68
Marx, Karl, 3-4, 7, 32, 57, 163; and Sartre, 70, 115; and Hegel, 71. *See also* Marxism
Marxism, 6-11, 168, 204; totalizing in, 6; and Sartre, 80. *See also*
Communism; Marx, Karl; Socialism
Master-slave relationship, 71, 74-76, 84-85; in Sartre, 97, 106; and rebellion, in Camus, 127, 144; and social morality, 191
Materialism, 7, 112; historical, 10, 204
Meaning: in Camus, 69, 126; -lessness, in Sartre, 69, 87-88
Mediterranean mind, 130-31
Michelet, Jules, 88, 89
Modernism, 8, 86
Moments, "perfect," 89
Monotheism, 4
Morality, 22, 23, 24, 46; plays, 25, 205; in Sartre, 115; in Camus, 119, 125-26, 131, 139, 140; in Sinclair, 183, 185, 186, 188-89, 190; in Farrell, 191-93; social, 191-92, 193. *See also* Ethics
Murder, 129, 131, 134; "calculated," in Camus, 137-38. *See also* Crime
Myth, 147, 168

Napoleon I, 37
Napoleon III, 18, 26, 27, 32, 36
Narcissism, 35, 36
Naturalism, 5, 8-11, 204, 210, 221n; and detotalization, 15-65 *passim*; in Zola, 24; and civilized man, 27; fatalism of, 29; vs. socialism, in Zola, 39-65; and love of the land, 41; and war, 51; in Sinclair, 169-70. *See also* Naturalist
Naturalist: psychology, 49; myth, and national history, 53; view of financial speculation, 59-60; view of capitalism, 60; definition of totality, 65. *See also* Naturalism
Nature, 44; human, 64, 161, 193

Index

Nazism, 180, 183, 184, 187-88.
  See also Germany, Nazi
Necessity: historical, 29; and
  freedom, in Sartre, 85
Negation, 119, 122, 125, 129, 131.
  See also Sartre
Nemesis, 139, 144
Nietzsche, Friedrich, 129
Nihilism, 4, 207; as a detotalizing force, 6; and socialism, 8, 10-11, 92; and Camus, 70, 125, 126; and Sartre, 70, 92
Nostalgia, 191-201

Objectivity, 72, 177-78
Objects: external, 101; encroachment of, 102-3
Ontology, 15, 97, 102
Optimism, 77, 78, 80, 207
Orwell, George, 5, 147-68, 176; pessimism of, 147, 160, 162, 165, 168; *Homage to Catalonia*, 148; passivity in, 148, 155; *The Lion and the Unicorn*, 148, 160; *The Road to Wigan Pier*, 148, 155-56; *Nineteen Eighty-Four*, 149, 162-68; "Such, Such Were the Joys," 149; *Burmese Days*, 151-53; *A Clergyman's Daughter*, 154; *Keep the Aspidistra Flying*, 155; *Coming Up for Air*, 157; *Animal Farm*, 160-61
Other, the, 72, 74, 76; in Sartre, 77-78, 79, 80, 97, 105-9
Otherness, 72, 75, 188
Ovcharenko, A., 11

Paris Commune of 1848, 57
Paris Commune of 1871, 53, 56-58
Passos, John Dos, 55
Patriotism, 55, 114
Personalities, struggle of, 29-30
Pessimism, 15, 168, 200; Orwell's, 147, 160, 162, 165, 168
Pluralities, 6, 72, 78

Power: in Camus, 140, 141, 161; in Orwell, 161, 162, 163, 164; the will to, 162, 163
Primitivism, 10
Prison camps, 112-13
Production, 96-97; relations, 29, 199, 204
Proletariat, 10, 58, 156, 198; woman, in Orwell, 168
Prometheus, 129
Property, ownership of, 40-41, 204
Psychoanalysis, existential, 84, 85, 115
Psychology, 58, 63, 97, 187; political, in Orwell, 148, 149-50

Rationality, 86, 143, 161, 204.
  See also Reason
Realism: critical, 8, 203-4, 210; socialist, 9-11, 198, 202-211; in Balzac, 39-40; in Camus, 135
Reason, 22, 46, 77, 130; principle of sufficient, 19; in Hegel, 23, 72; in Schopenhauer, 24; in Camus, 130, 132; in Sinclair, 186, 187, 188. *See also* Rationality
Rebellion: metaphysical, 18, 72-73, 127-37; explanation of, in Zola, 56-57; in Camus, 119, 126, 127-39, 147-48; historical, 127; failed, 147-48; in Orwell, 147-50, 153, 154-55, 165-68; in Sinclair, 170; in Farrell, 196, 198; and an instrument of detotalization, 210. *See also* Revolution
Reflection, authentic, 101
Reification, 204
Representation, 15-25
Resistance movement, 69, 93, 94, 126; *Combat*, 127; and Camus, 131, 133, 135-36
Retotalization, 6, 53, 210
Revolution, 4, 10; vs. reform, 9; in

Revolution *(continued)*
  Zola, 47, 51; and the workers, consciousness of, 82-83: Caesarian, 130; in Orwell, 160-61; betrayal of, 161; Trotsky on, 202; as a retotalizing force, 210. *See also* Rebellion
Rideout, Walter, 169

Sacco-Vanzetti case, 176-79, 197
Salvation, 81, 114, 119; and consciousness, 127; in Sinclair, 180; in Farrell, 193, 195
Sartre, Jean-Paul, 3, 6-7, 69-116; *Being and Nothingness*, 6, 101, 105; detotalization in, 7-8; *La Nausée*, 69, 70-71, 86-90, 91, 99; and Camus, 69-70; the Other in, 75; and Hegel, 76; conflict in, 77; freedom in, 81-85, 92-94, 98-101, 104-5, 109-11; nothingness in, 83, 84, 105, 109; anguish in, 83-84, 85-86, 92-93, 100-102; nausea in, 85-90; experiences in a prison camp, 90, 91-92; *Les Chemins de la liberté*, 92-93; *Le Sursis*, 94-98, 108, 114; and the metaphor of coral, 95, 99; *L'Etre et le néant*, 96; the ethics of ambiguity in, 96-97, 116; bad faith in, 101-2; *La Morte dans l'âme*, 109-11, 114; *Le Diable et le bon dieu*, 115; *Les Séquestres d'Altona*, 115-16
Schopenhauer, Arthur, 3-4, 15-25, 119; the will as the essence of life in, 16, 23, 117; suffering in, 16-18, 20-21, 45, 58, 117-18; eternal justice in, 17, 18-19, 81, 117-18; the will-in-itself in, 17, 19; self-consciousness and the master-slave relation in, 76; the will in, negation of, 76-77, 81, 138; conflict in, 81; and Camus, 130-31
Self-consciousness: recognitive, 71-74, 75, 78; reflective, 81-82, 87, 100; and the master-slave relation, 76, 77; universal, 78; in Sartre, 79, 101; in Orwell, 155. *See also* Consciousness
Self-detotalization, 45
Self-interest, 30, 31, 37, 179
Seriality, 80-81
Sexuality, 98, 154, 167; in Zola, 42, 44, 49-50, 63
Shame, 106
Sholokhov, Mikhail, 205-6, 209, 210, 211
Sinclair, Upton, 5, 169-90; *The Jungle*, 169-71, 173; *King Coal*, 172-73, 176; *Oil!*, 175-76; *Boston*, 176-79; Lanny Budd series, 180-90; *World's End*, 180-81; *Between Two Worlds*, 182; *Dragon's Teeth*, 183; *Wide Is the Gate*, 184-85; *O Shepherd Speak!*, 185, 188; *The Presidential Agent*, 186; *The Return of Lanny Budd*, 188-90
Socialism, 4-5, 8, 10, 84; as a totalizing force, 6; Sartre and, 92; English, 148, 160; Orwell and, 148, 155-57, 159-60, 162-63, 166; in Sinclair, 169-72, 179-80, 185-90; in Farrell, 197, 220n. *See also* Communism; Marxism
Socialist realism, 198, 202-11
Solar thought, 130-31, 133-34, 161
Solidarity, 85, 89-90, 91-92; in Camus, 126, 127, 128, 132-37 *passim*, 139; as metaphysical, 128; in Farrell, 197
Solipsism, 142, 143, 144, 162
Solitude, 126, 127, 128, 133
Suchkov, Boris, 9-10, 65, 205, 206

Index

Suffering, 21, 52; in Schopenhauer, 16-18, 20-21, 45, 117; in Sartre, 82, 113-14; in Camus, 127, 138
Suicide, 108, 119, 140, 153
Surrealism, 86, 111
Syndicalism, 130

Taine, Hippolyte, 23, 27
Thody, Philip, 135
Tocqueville, Alexis de, 15-25, 204; democracy in, 18, 27; the family in, 27, 33. *See also* Egalitarianism; Egalitarian society
Totalitarianism, 161-62, 164, 166-67
Totalities: Marxist definition of, 65; naturalist definition of, 65; undetotalizable, 202-11. *See also* Detotalization; Detotalized totalities
Totalization: and the Self, 7; re-, 6, 53, 210
Transcendence, 114, 119, 128, 158, 203
Trotsky, Leon, 202
Truth, 72, 144, 177, 178, 188
Tynan, Kenneth, 94

Understanding, 71, 76
Unions, 48-49, 170
Unity, and plurality, 72, 78
Utopianism, 25, 168

Values, 35, 70, 149; individualistic, 4-5; transcendent, 10; communal, erosion of, 27, 38; family, 167

Varloot, Jan, 8

Will, the, 15-25, 76-77, 81, 117
Will-in-itself, 17, 19
Workers, 48-49. *See also* Working class
Working class: consciousness of, 82-83, 203; in Orwell, 148, 160, 163, 167; in Sinclair, 172. *See also* Workers
World: phenomenal, in Schopenhauer, 16-17, 22, 24; as a disintegrating whole, 80
Wright, Richard, 111

Zola, Emile, 26-65, 207; *Germinal,* 5, 38, 46-51, 59, 99; reliance on biology, 9, 63; Rougon-Macquart novels, 9, 15, 24, 25, 26, 32; and Schopenhauer, comparison of, 15; the world as Will in, 15-16, 23-25; *La Terre,* 25; *Les Quatre Evangiles,* 25, 42, 50, 62; *La Curée,* 27, 32-35; genetic theories of, 28; detotalization in, 29; *The Fortunes of Rougon,* 29-32, 35-38; *La Terre,* 39-45, 59, 178; Marxist criticism of, 45-46; *L'Assommoir,* 46, 178; *Le Docteur Pascal,* 49, 50; *L'Argent,* 59-60; *La Bête humaine,* 63-65, 186; human nature in, 64; evil in, 65; heredity in, 172, 186. *See also* specific works
Zwerdling, Alex, 165